LEAN AND GREEN COOKBOOK

2 Books in 1:

500 Satisfying & Healthy Recipes for Beginners | Improve your Wellness and Regain the Desired Body Shape | Ideal for Quick Weight Loss and Lifelong Success

Evelyn West

Table Of Contents

1 - 250+ Lean and Green Cookbook Optavia

2 - 250+ Optavia Diet Cookbook

1

250+ LEAN AND GREEN COOKBOOK OPTAVIA

Introduction

The Optavia diet focuses on making changes in your diet plan that will actually increase the metabolism of your body, while also allowing the body to obtain the adequate nutrition for building new muscle.

The basic Optavia diet is a very simple. For one month, people on the Optavia diet eat between 1000 and 1500 calorie meals.

Optavia is a diet plan that entails eating a restricted-calorie diet with specific lean protein, fat, fiber, and carbohydrates. It is linked to an app that you have to use for one month for optimum results, and if you choose to renew the app it is USD$57. The app helps you plan your meals and allows you to input your weight, activity level, goals, and food preferences to produce results that match your needs.

The diet that they provide takes into account the fact that you lose weight faster and more consistently when you are on a diet that restricts your calories. It is rare for people to consistently over-eat fat and protein; even though this may happen from time to time. However, most people under-eat healthy fats and healthy protein regularly. They also provide you with a tracker to help you monitor your protein and fat intake. This diet uses a specific calorie limit, which changes daily. I liked that there was a table that showed what the daily calorie intake would be and what it would be for each phase (phase 1, phase 2, phase 3, phase 4, phase 5, and the last phase.) This is extremely helpful in planning your diet. It also gives you 'goal targets' for those days. The goal targets include that you should lose a specific amount of weight per week and that you should burn a specific number of calories each week. I found the idea of a goal target to be very motivating. I was also happy to note that you are not locked into a certain number of pounds per week. I believe that is not a healthy way to go about losing weight.

This diet uses lean protein and good fats as the basis for the diet. I found this to be very interesting because I had not heard of this concept before. I believe it is an excellent idea. I see protein and good fats as essential for a healthy diet. They also provide you with certain food products, like the Optavia Fix. The Optivia Fix is a package of meal bars, baked food items like bread and cookies that work with the app. Their purpose is to make it easier to follow the diet. There are also some prepackaged meals and snacks, such as lunches and dinners, that they provide. This is helpful because it means you do not have to do all the cooking yourself. Overall, this is an excellent diet for those who get bored with their diet and would like something different rather than a menu. The app also allows you to alter your food plan for certain days if you want to switch things up.

One of the common issues with this diet is that it can be hard to follow due to the lack of variety, especially in the early stages. It can also be expensive, especially if you choose to get the full Optavia Diet.

I would recommend this diet to others who are unable to plan meals for themselves or have a difficult time with variety.

CHAPTER 1:

What Is the Optavia Diet?

The Optavia Diet is the brainchild of the man behind the multimillion-dollar company Medifast– Dr. William Vitale. Now carrying the brand Optavia since 2017, the goal of this diet is to encourage healthy and sustainable weight loss among its clientele. While there are many types of diet regimen that are available in the market, the Optavia Diet is ranked in the top 30 Best Diets in the United States.

Basically, this diet regimen is not only for people who want to lose weight but also for people who have diabetes, people suffering from gout, nursing moms, seniors as well as teens.

With the OPTAVIA diet plan, you will enjoy more than 60 Fueling options. However, you will find it difficult to stop going on that diet. Also, you would get to take in more Optavia meal every time without taking stock of what you are consuming. This is because there are no sugars, points, or calories to record.

More studies showed that sticking to the Optavia diet plan is easy compared to other regular eating regimens. According to a 2008 study published in the Diabetes Educator, 16 out of 119 Medifast dietitians completed the eating regimen in 86 weeks. In contrast, only eight out of the 119 participants that tried regular diets were able to continue for 86 weeks.

Recipes are available on different online platforms. Besides, it is possible to have a complete Optavia meal for dinner. It is fast and cheap to order meals and cook them. Adherents can also depend on their OPTAVIA instructors and online forums for knowledge and techniques.

The official Pinterest page of Optavia is an excellent example of where beginners can get some tips on the best lean and green meals. You can use the page as a conversion recipe guide to help you incorporate their ideas into your cooking plans.

Why Optavia Is so Special?

Structured Diet Plan: The Optavia diet has a structured diet plan, making it one of the most nutritious diets available. Everything is formulated for you, so you don't need to understand if you are following the diet correctly. As it is very easy to follow, it is ideal for people who are always busy or who do not have the ability to cook their food.

Ideal for Portion Controllers - One of the hardest parts of the diet is learning to control portions and stick to them. The Optavia diet is accompanied by the reload phase that helps keep your meals in check.

Practice long-term relationship with food: Guiding the community to follow the Optavia diet can help improve a long-term positive relationship with food. Over time, you come to realize the types of foods you are allowed to eat and appreciate the healthy options you have.

No Responsibility Partner Needed: While some diets encourage you to make a friend to the diet, the Optavia diet is ideal for people who have no responsibility partners. The point is that people are connected to a community of dietitians who can provide the necessary support during the phases of this diet.

Better Overall Health - This particular diet is known to help improve overall well-being. In addition to weight loss, several studies have also shown that the Optavia diet can help people maintain blood sugar levels and stable blood pressure due to the limited sodium intake in food. In fact, Optavia provides less than 2,300 milligrams of sodium a day.

CHAPTER 2:

What Is the Effect of The Optavia Diet on Health?

Most "supplies" contain between 100 and 110 calories each, which means you can consume around 1000 calories a day on this diet. As a result of this approach, the US News and World Report ranked it second on its list of the best diets for fast weight loss, but 32nd on its list of the best diets for healthy eating. London recognizes that there are other ways to lasting weight loss: "Eat meals and snacks that incorporate lots of products, seeds, nuts, greens, 100% whole grains, eggs, seafood, poultry, greens, low-fat dairy products. Fat, lean meat plus a little indulgence is the best way to lose weight sustainably in the long run. " So, will the Optavia diet help you lose weight?

The amount of weight you lose after following the OPTAVIA diet programs depends on factors such as your starting weight, as well as your activity and loyalty to following the plan. OPTAVIA, launched in 2017, represents the Medifast lifestyle brand and the coaching community. Previous studies have been done using Medifast products, not the new OPTAVIA products. Although the OPTAVIA products represent a new line, Medifast reported to US News that they have an identical macronutrient profile, making them interchangeable with Medifast products. Consequently, we believe that the following studies are applicable in the evaluation of this diet. Little specific research has been published on the OPTAVIA brand. The studies, like most diets, were small, with numerous dropouts. Research seems to confirm this. On the other hand, the long-term expectation is less promising

Here's a more detailed look at the data:

According to a 2017 Medifast-sponsored study, more than 70% of overweight adults who received individual behavioral support and underwent Medifast have lost more than 5% of their body weight since their last visit, which is four to 24 weeks. then.

According to a 2016 study published in the journal Obesity and with partial support from Medifast, obese adults lost 8.8% of their body weight after 12 weeks with OPTAVIA style training and Medifast products, and also 12, 1% of your body weight if you were taking phentermine at the same time, which is a weight loss drug that can reduce binge eating.

However, the researchers found only one long-term study, which indicated no benefit for these 12-month plans. The researchers found that there is also an increased risk of complications, such as gallstones, on ultra-low-calorie programs.

However, the study found that the effect was reduced beyond six months of reporting the results.

During a small study, designed and funded by Medifast and published in 2010 in the Nutrition Journal, 90 obese adults were randomly assigned to either the low-calorie diet or the 5 & 1 plan according to government guidelines. The Medifast dieters, however, regained more than 4.5 kg 24 weeks later, after the calories gradually increased. The others gained only 2 pounds. Compared to the initial exercise, the Medifast group had more muscle mass and less body fat at week 40, but it did not outperform the control group. Eventually, about half of the Medifast group and more than half of the control group withdrew.

According to a Medifast-funded study of 119 overweight or obese type 2 diabetics published in Diabetes Educator in 2008, dieters were randomly assigned to either a Medifast diabetes plan or a diet based on the recommendations of the American Association of Diabetes. After 34 weeks, the Medifast group had lost an average of 4.5 kilos, but had regained almost 1.5 kilos after 86 weeks. Over 34 weeks, those who followed the ADA-based diet lost an average of 3 pounds; they got everything back plus an extra pound in 86 weeks. By the end of the year, about 80% had given up

According to an analysis funded by Medifast and published in 2008 in the journal Eating and Weight Disorders, researchers analyzed the medical records of 324 people who were on a diet who were overweight or obese and who were also taking a prescription appetite suppressant. In 12 weeks, they lost an average of 21 pounds, in 24 weeks they weighed 26 1/2 pounds, and 27 pounds in 52 weeks.

Furthermore, for approximately 80% of them, at least 5% of the initial weight had been lost in all three evaluations. This is great if you are obese, because losing just 5-10% of your current weight can help prevent some diseases.

However, these numbers are accompanied by some asterisks. First, because they are based on people who completed or completed the 52-week program, they were more likely to lose weight. (Weight loss was still effective, but less pronounced in a cessation analysis.)

Second, a review of patient data is given less importance than a study with a control group. Finally, in a survey in which researchers divided dieters into consumer groups on Medifast, that is, those who recognized that they consume at least two shakes a day at each check-in and those who are inconsistent, it is say, the rest. , weight loss was not significantly different

In a 2013 study in the International Journal of Obesity that looked at 120 men and women ages 19 to 65, half of whom were using Medifast, while the other half were limited to cutting calories, researchers found that those who on the Medifast diet lost an average of 16 1/2 pounds after 26 weeks, compared to the control group, who lost 4 kg.

CHAPTER 3:

The 5&1 Medifast Plan

The Optavia program gives extra instruments to help weight reduction and upkeep, including tips and motivation by means of instant message, network discussions, week-by-week bolster calls, and an application that permits you to set dinner updates and track food admission and movement.

Despite the fact that Optavia offers these particular plans, it's indistinct whether this diet is ok for individuals with certain ailments. Furthermore, young people and breastfeeding moms have exceptional supplement and calorie needs that may not be met by the Optavia diet.

Aside from these 3 plans, the Optavia program enhances weight maintenance and loss with tools like giving inspirational tips via text messages, weekly support calls, community forums, including an app that has been designed such that you set meal reminders and monitor your food intake and activity.

People with gout, diabetes, nursing mothers, teens, and seniors all have specific plans offered by the company that has been designed solely based on their conditions. Even though there are specialized programs for people with special medical conditions, you might need to talk to your doctor if you have an individual medical condition before going forth with the program. Nursing mothers and teenagers also have a specific calorie daily intake that may not be achieved if they follow the Optavia diet plan. Hence, it is best anyone in this category speak with his or her doctor before starting to avoid future health complications.

5&1 Optimal Weight

Consuming 6 small meals a day is the 1st Healthy Habit you will absorb. On the 5&1 Optimal Weight Plan, the body goes in a gentle but well-organized fat burning state at the same time, maintaining and retaining lean muscle mass. You can choose from more than sixty convenient, scientifically designed and nutritionally interchangeable Fuelings including shakes, biscuits, soups, bars, pretzels, brownies, hot beverages, hearty choices, pudding and brownies. Each individual Fueling has an approximately similar nutritional profile curated by our team of skilled food scientists and refined by our registered, expert dietitians and nutrition team.

In addition to consuming 5 Fuelings per day, you will learn an alternative healthy habit, which is to know how to curate a Lean & Green food that is perfect for you and your loved ones. You will start to absorb what optimal nutrition appears to be and soon enough, healthy eating will be considered as second nature.

Our scientifically tested and proven 5&1 Optimal Weight Plan teaches the clients to consume 6 small meals a day, an essential practice that will help the clients sustain a healthy weight. It is easy to follow, fast, no hassle, and is based on the healthy habit of consuming 6 small meals per day, with an interval of one meal every 2-3 hours. With the support of your chosen Optavia Coach and our Community you will start to make progress in an instant.

- **3&3 Optimal Health**

This diet is intended for upkeep, this one incorporates three Optavia fueling and three adjusted Lean and Green dinners every day.

Once you have achieved your healthy weight, it is imperative to sustain the good habits you have learned, including fueling your body once every two to three hours. To help sustain your healthy weight, we have developed 3&3 the Optimal Health Plan, which emphases on nutritionally well-adjusted small meals consumed once every two to three hours (similar to that of the Optimal Weight 4&2&1 Plan), while incorporating additional food choices in the right servings. Your chosen Optavia Coach can give more details regarding the Optimal Health 3&3 Plan developed by our registered and expert dietitians team.

To keep an eye on the 3 & 3 Optimal Health Plan, consume 3 Optimal Health Fuelings per day with 3 balanced meals of your choice.

The Optavia diet program gives additional tools to assist in losing weight and maintenance, including inspiration and tips via text message, community forums, weekly support calls, and an app that consents you to establish meal reminders and keep track of your food intake and activity.

The corporation also offers specialized plans for teens, individuals with diabetes or gout (or any other chronic illnesses), nursing mothers, and older adults.

Even though Optavia offers these specified plans, the notion that this diet is safe for people with certain medical conditions is still unknown. Furthermore, breastfeeding mothers and teenagers have distinctive calorie and nutrient needs that may not be met by the Optavia diet.

CHAPTER 4:

Breakfast and Smoothies Recipes

1. Optavia Pizza Hack

Preparation Time: 5-10 minutes

Cooking Time: 15-20 minutes

Servings: 1

Ingredients:

- 1/4 fueling of garlic mashed potato
- 1/2 egg whites
- 1/4 tablespoon of baking powder
- 3/4 oz. of reduced-fat shredded mozzarella
- 1/8 cup of sliced white mushrooms
- /16 cup of pizza sauce
- 3/4 oz. of ground beef
- 1/4 sliced black olives
- You also need a sauté pan, baking sheets, and parchment paper

Directions:

1. Start by preheating the oven to 400°.
2. Mix your baking powder and garlic potato packet.
3. Add egg whites to your mixture and stir well until it blends.
4. Line the baking sheet with parchment paper and pour the mixed batter onto it.
5. Put another parchment paper on top of the batter and spread out the batter to a 1/8-inch circle.
6. Then place another baking sheet on top; this way, the batter is between two baking sheets.
7. Place into an oven and bake for about 8 minutes until the pizza crust is golden brown.
8. For the toppings, place your ground beef in a sauté pan and fry till it's brown and wash your mushrooms very well.
9. After the crust is baked, remove the top layer of parchment paper carefully to prevent the foam from sticking to the pizza crust.
10. Put your toppings on top of the crust and bake for an extra 8 minutes.
11. Once ready, slide the pizza off the parchment paper and onto a plate.

Nutrition:

Calories: 478 Protein: 30 g

Carbohydrates: 22 g

Fats: 29 g

2. Amaranth Porridge

Preparation Time: 5 minutes

Cooking Time: 30 minutes

Servings: 2.

Ingredients:

- 2 cups coconut milk

- 2 cups alkaline water
- 1 cup amaranth
- 2 tbsps. coconut oil
- 1 tbsp. ground cinnamon

Directions:

1. In a saucepan, mix in the milk with water, then boil the mixture.
2. You stir in the amaranth, then reduce the heat to medium.
3. Cook on the medium heat, then simmer for at least 30 minutes as you stir it occasionally.
4. Turn off the heat.
5. Add in cinnamon and coconut oil then stir.
6. Serve.

Nutrition:

Calories: 434 kcal

Fat: 35g

Carbs: 27g

Protein: 6.7g

3. Pancakes with Berries

Preparation Time: 5 minutes

Cooking Time: 20 minutes

Servings: 2

Ingredients:

- Pancake:
- 1 egg
- 50 g spelled flour
- 50 g almond flour
- 15 g coconut flour
- 150 ml of water
- salt

Filling:

- 40 g mixed berries
- 10 g chocolate
- 5 g powdered sugar
- 4 tbsp yogurt

Directions:

1. Put the flour, egg, and some salt in a blender jar.
2. Add 150 ml of water.
3. Mix everything with a whisk.
4. Mix everything into a batter.
5. Heat a coated pan.
6. Put in half of the batter.
7. Once the pancake is firm, turn it over.
8. Take out the pancake, add the second half of the batter to the pan and repeat.
9. Melt chocolate over a water bath.
10. Let the pancakes cool.
11. Brush the pancakes with the yogurt.
12. Wash the berry and let it drain.
13. Put berries on the yogurt.
14. Roll up the pancakes.
15. Sprinkle them with the powdered sugar.
16. Decorate the whole thing with the melted chocolate.

Nutrition: kcal: 298 Carbohydrates: 26 g Protein: 21 g Fat: 9 g

4. Omelette à la Margherita

Preparation Time: 10 minutes

Cooking Time: 20 minutes

Servings: 2

Ingredients:

- 3 eggs

- 50 g parmesan cheese
- 2 tbsp heavy cream
- 1 tbsp olive oil
- 1 teaspoon oregano
- nutmeg
- salt
- pepper
- For covering:
- 3 - 4 stalks of basil
- 1 tomato
- 100 g grated mozzarella

Directions:
1. Mix the cream and eggs in a medium bowl.
2. Add the grated parmesan, nutmeg, oregano, pepper and salt and stir everything.
3. Heat the oil in a pan.
4. Add 1/2 of the egg and cream to the pan.
5. Let the omelette set over medium heat, turn it, and then remove it.
6. Repeat with the second half of the egg mixture.
7. Cut the tomatoes into slices and place them on top of the omelets.
8. Scatter the mozzarella over the tomatoes.
9. Place the omelets on a baking sheet.
10. Cook at 180 degrees for 5 to 10 minutes.
11. Then take the omelets out and decorate them with the basil leaves.

Nutrition:
kcal: 402 Carbohydrates: 7 g
Protein: 21 g
Fat: 34 g

5. Omelette With Tomatoes and Spring Onions

Preparation Time: 5 minutes
Cooking Time: 20 minutes
Servings:
Ingredients:
- 6 eggs
- 2 tomatoes
- 2 spring onions
- 1 shallot
- 2 tbsp butter
- 1 tbsp olive oil
- 1 pinch of nutmeg
- salt
- pepper

Directions:
1. Whisk the eggs in a bowl.
2. Mix them and season them with salt and pepper.
3. Peel the shallot and chop it up.
4. Clean the onions and cut them into rings.
5. Wash the tomatoes and cut them into pieces.
6. Heat butter and oil in a pan.
7. Braise half of the shallots in it.
8. Add half the egg mixture.
9. Let everything set over medium heat.
10. Scatter a few tomatoes and onion rings on top.
11. Repeat with the second half of the egg mixture.
12. At the end, spread the grated nutmeg over the whole thing.

Nutrition: kcal: 263 Carbohydrates: 8 g
Protein: 20.3 g Fat: 24 g

6. Coconut Chia Pudding with Berries

Preparation Time: 20 minutes

Cooking Time: 45 minutes

Servings: 2

Ingredients:

- 150 g raspberries and blueberries
- 60 g chia seeds
- 500 ml coconut milk
- 1 teaspoon agave syrup
- ½ teaspoon ground bourbon vanilla

Directions:

1. Put the chia seeds, agave syrup, and vanilla in a bowl.
2. Pour in the coconut milk.
3. Mix thoroughly and let it soak for 30 minutes.
4. Meanwhile, wash the berries and let them drain well.
5. Divide the coconut chia pudding between two glasses.
6. Put the berries on top.

Nutrition:

kcal: 662

Carbohydrates: 18 g

Protein: 8 g

Fat: 55 g

7. Eel on Scrambled Eggs and Bread

Preparation Time: 5 minutes

Cooking Time: 10 minutes

Servings: 2

Ingredients:

- 4 eggs
- 1 shallot
- 4 slices of low carb bread
- 2 sticks of dill
- 200 g smoked eel
- 1 tbsp oil
- salt
- White pepper

Directions:

1. Mix the eggs in a bowl and season with salt and pepper.
2. Peel the shallot and cut it into fine cubes.
3. Chop the dill.
4. Remove the skin from the eel and cut it into pieces.
5. Heat the oil in a pan and steam the shallot in it.
6. Add in the eggs in and let them set.
7. Use the spatula to turn the eggs several times.
8. Reduce the heat and add the dill.
9. Stir everything.
10. Spread the scrambled eggs over four slices of bread.
11. Put the eel pieces on top.
12. Add some fresh dill and serve everything.

Nutrition:

kcal: 830 Carbohydrates: 8 g

Protein: 45 g Fat: 64 g

8. Chia Seed Gel with Pomegranate and Nuts

Preparation Time: 5 minutes

Cooking Time: 10 minutes

Servings: 3

Ingredients:

- 20 g hazelnuts

- 20 g walnuts
- 120 ml almond milk
- 4 tbsp chia seeds
- 4 tbsp pomegranate seeds
- 1 teaspoon agave syrup
- Some lime juices

Directions:

1. Finely chop the nuts.
2. Mix the almond milk with the chia seeds.
3. Let everything soak for 10 to 20 minutes.
4. Occasionally stir the mixture with the chia seeds.
5. Stir in the agave syrup.
6. Pour 2 tablespoons of each mixture into a dessert glass.
7. Layer the chopped nuts on top.
8. Cover the nuts with 1 tablespoon each of the chia mass.
9. Sprinkle the pomegranate seeds on top and serve everything.

Nutrition:
kcal: 248
Carbohydrates: 7 g
Protein: 1 g
Fat: 19 g

9. Lavender Blueberry Chia Seed Pudding

Preparation Time: 1 hour 10 minutes
Cooking Time: 0 minutes
Servings: 4
Ingredients:

- 100 g blueberries
- 70 g organic quark
- 50 g soy yogurt

- 30 g hazelnuts
- 200 ml almond milk
- 2 tbsp chia seeds
- 2 teaspoons agave syrup
- 2 teaspoons of lavender

Directions:

1. Bring the almond milk to a boil along with the lavender.
2. Let the mixture simmer for 10 minutes at a reduced temperature.
3. Let them cool down afterwards.
4. If the milk is cold, add the blueberries and puree everything.
5. Mix the whole thing with the chia seeds and agave syrup.
6. Let everything soak in the refrigerator for an hour.
7. Mix the yogurt and curd cheese.
8. Add both to the crowd.
9. Divide the pudding into glasses.
10. Finely chop the hazelnuts and sprinkle them on top.

Nutrition:
kcal: 252
Carbohydrates: 12 g
Protein: 1 g
Fat: 11 g

10. Yogurt with Granola and Persimmon

Preparation Time: 5 minutes
Cooking Time: 5 minutes
Servings: 1
Ingredients:

- 150g Greek style yogurt
- 20g oatmeal
- 60g fresh persimmons

- 30 ml of tap water

Directions:

1. Put the oatmeal in the pan without any fat.
2. Toast them, stirring constantly, until golden brown.
3. Then put them on a plate and let them cool down briefly.
4. Peel the persimmon and put it in a bowl with the water. Mix the whole thing into a fine puree.
5. Put the yogurt, the toasted oatmeal, and the puree in layers in a glass and serve.

Nutrition:

kcal: 286

Carbohydrates: 29 g

Protein: 1 g

Fat: 11 g

11. Smoothie Bowl with Spinach, Mango and Muesli

Preparation Time: 10 minutes

Cooking Time: 0 minutes

Servings: 1

Ingredients:

- 150g yogurt
- 30g apple
- 30g mango
- 30g low carb muesli
- 10g spinach
- 10g chia seeds

Directions:

1. Soak the spinach leaves and let them drain.
2. Peel the mango and cut it into strips.

3. Remove apple core and cut it into pieces.
4. Put everything except the mango together with the yogurt in a blender and make a fine puree out of it.
5. Put the spinach smoothie in a bowl.
6. Add the muesli, chia seeds, and mango.
7. Serve the whole thing

Nutrition:

kcal: 362

Carbohydrates: 21 g

Protein: 12 g Fat: 21 g

12. Fried Egg with Bacon

Preparation Time: 5 minutes

Cooking Time: 10 minutes

Servings: 1

Ingredients:

- 2 eggs
- 30 grams of bacon
- 2 tbsp olive oil
- salt
- pepper

Directions:

1. Heat oil in the pan and fry the bacon.
2. Reduce the heat and beat the eggs in the pan.
3. Cook the eggs and season with salt and pepper.
4. Serve the fried eggs hot with the bacon.

Nutrition:

kcal: 405

Carbohydrates: 1 g

Protein: 19 g

Fat: 38 g

13. Smoothie Bowl with Berries, Poppy Seeds, Nuts and Seeds

Preparation Time: 15 minutes
Cooking Time: 0 minutes
Servings: 2
Ingredients:

- 5 chopped almonds
- 2 chopped walnuts
- 1 apple
- ¼ banana
- 300 g yogurt
- 60 g raspberries
- 20 g blueberries
- 20 g rolled oats, roasted in a pan
- 10 g poppy seeds
- 1 teaspoon pumpkin seeds
- Agave syrup

Directions:

1. Clean the fruit and let it drain.
2. Take some berries and set them aside.
3. Place the remaining berries in a tall mixing vessel.
4. Cut the banana into slices. Put a few aside.
5. Add the rest of the banana to the berries.
6. Remove the core of the apple and cut it into quarters.
7. Cut the quarters into thin wedges and set a few aside.
8. Add the remaining wedges to the berries.
9. Add the yogurt to the fruits and mix everything into a puree.
10. Sweeten the smoothie with the agave syrup.
11. Divide it into two bowls.
12. Serve it with the remaining fruit, poppy seeds, oatmeal, nuts and seeds.

Nutrition: kcal: 284 Carbohydrates: 21 g Protein: 11 g Fat: 19 g

14. Whole Grain Bread and Avocado

Preparation Time: 5 minutes
Cooking Time: 0 minutes
Serving: 1
Ingredients:

- 2 slices of whole meal bread
- 60 g of cottage cheese
- 1 stick of thyme
- ½ avocado
- ½ lime
- Chili flakes
- salt
- pepper

Directions:

1. Cut the avocado in half.
2. Remove the pulp and cut it into slices.
3. Pour the lime juice over it.
4. Wash the thyme and shake it dry.
5. Remove the leaves from the stem.
6. Brush the whole wheat bread with the cottage cheese.
7. Place the avocado slices on top.
8. Top with the chili flakes and thyme.
9. Add salt and pepper and serve.

Nutrition:

kcal: 490 Carbohydrates: 31 g

Protein: 19 g Fat: 21 g

15. Porridge with Walnuts

Preparation Time: 5 minutes

Cooking Time: 10 minutes

Servings: 1

Ingredients:

- 50 g raspberries
- 50 g blueberries
- 25 g of ground walnuts
- 20 g of crushed flaxseed
- 10 g of oatmeal
- 200 ml nut drink
- Agave syrup
- ½ teaspoon cinnamon
- salt

Directions:

1. Warm the nut drink in a small saucepan.
2. Add the walnuts, flaxseed, and oatmeal, stirring constantly.
3. Stir in the cinnamon and salt.
4. Simmer for 8 minutes.
5. Keep stirring everything.
6. Sweet the whole thing.
7. Put the porridge in a bowl.
8. Wash the berries and let them drain.
9. Add them to the porridge and serve everything.

Nutrition:

kcal: 378

Carbohydrates: 11 g

Protein: 18 g

Fat: 27 g

16. Whole-Wheat Blueberry Muffins

Preparation Time: 5 minutes

Cooking Time: 25 minutes

Servings: 8

Ingredients: 1/2 cup plant-based milk

- 1/2 cup unsweetened applesauce
- 1/2 cup maple syrup
- 1 teaspoon vanilla extract
- 2 cups whole-wheat flour
- 1/2 teaspoon baking soda
- 1 cup blueberries

Directions:

1. Preheat the oven to 375°F.
2. In a large bowl, mix the milk, applesauce, maple syrup, and vanilla.
3. Stir in the flour and baking soda until no dry flour is left, and the batter is smooth.
4. Gently fold in the blueberries until they are evenly distributed throughout the batter.
5. In a muffin tin, fill eight muffin cups with three-quarters full of batter. Bake for 25 minutes, or until you can stick a knife into the center of a muffin and it comes out clean. Allow cooling before serving.

Tip: both frozen and fresh blueberries will work great in this recipe. The only difference will be that muffins using fresh blueberries will cook slightly quicker than those using frozen.

Nutrition: Fat: 1 g Carbohydrates: 45 g Fiber: 2 g Protein: 4 g

17. Hemp Seed Porridge

Preparation Time: 5 minutes

Cooking Time: 5 minutes

Servings: 6

Ingredients:

- 3 cups cooked hemp seed
- 1 packet Stevia
- 1 cup coconut milk

Directions:

1. In a saucepan, mix the rice and the coconut milk over moderate heat for about 5 minutes as you stir it constantly.
2. Remove the pan from the burner then add the Stevia. Stir.
3. Serve in 6 bowls.
4. Enjoy.

Nutrition:

Calories: 236 kcal

Fat: 1.8 g

Carbs: 48.3 g

Protein: 7 g

18. Walnut Crunch Banana Bread

Preparation Time: 5 minutes

Cooking Time: 1 hour and 30 minutes

Servings: 1

Ingredients:

- 4 ripe bananas
- 1/4 cup maple syrup
- 1 tablespoon apple cider vinegar
- 1 teaspoon vanilla extract
- 11/2 cups whole-wheat flour
- 1/2 teaspoon ground cinnamon
- 1/2 teaspoon baking soda

- 1/4 cup walnut pieces (optional)

Directions:

1. Preheat the oven to 350°F.
2. In a large bowl, use a fork or mixing spoon to mash the bananas until they reach a puréed consistency (small bits of banana are acceptable). Stir in the maple syrup, apple cider vinegar, and vanilla.
3. Stir in the flour, cinnamon, and baking soda. Fold in the walnut pieces (if using).
4. Gently pour the batter into a loaf pan, filling it no more than three-quarters of the way full. Bake for 1 hour, or until you can stick a knife into the middle and it comes out clean.
5. Remove from the oven and allow cooling on the countertop for a minimum of 30 minutes before serving.

Nutrition:

Fat: 1g Carbohydrates: 40 g

Fiber: 5 g Protein: 4 g

19. Plant-Powered Pancakes

Preparation Time: 5 minutes

Cooking Time: 15 minutes

Servings: 8

Ingredients:

- 1 cup whole-wheat flour
- 1 teaspoon baking powder
- 1/2 teaspoon ground cinnamon
- 1 cup plant-based milk
- 1/2 cup unsweetened applesauce
- 1/4 cup maple syrup

- 1 teaspoon vanilla extract

Directions:

1. In a large bowl, combine the flour, baking powder, and cinnamon.
2. Stir in the milk, applesauce, maple syrup, and vanilla until no dry flour is left, and the batter is smooth.
3. Heat a large, nonstick skillet or griddle over medium heat. For each pancake, pour 1/4 cup of batter onto the hot skillet. Once bubbles form over the top of the pancake and the sides begin to brown, flip and cook for 1 or 2 minutes more.
4. Repeat until all of the batter is used, and serve.

Nutrition:

Fat: 2 g

Carbohydrates: 44 g

Fiber: 5 g

Protein: 5 g

20. Mini Mac in a Bowl

Preparation Time: 5 minutes

Cooking Time: 15 minutes

Servings: 1

Ingredients:

- 5 ounces of lean ground beef
- Two tablespoons of diced white or yellow onion.
- 1/8 teaspoon of onion powder
- 1/8 teaspoon of white vinegar
- 1 ounce of dill pickle slices
- One teaspoon sesame seed
- 3 cups of shredded Romaine lettuce
- Cooking spray
- Two tablespoons reduced-fat shredded cheddar cheese
- Two tablespoons of Wish-Bone light thousand island as dressing

Directions:

1. Place a lightly greased small skillet on fire to heat.
2. Add your onion to cook for about 2-3 minutes.
3. Next, add the beef and allow cooking until it's brown.
4. Next, mix your vinegar and onion powder with the dressing.
5. Finally, top the lettuce with the cooked meat and sprinkle cheese on it, add your pickle slices.
6. Drizzle the mixture with the sauce and sprinkle the sesame seeds.
7. Your mini mac in a bowl is ready for consumption.

Nutrition:

Calories: 150

Protein: 21 g

Carbohydrates: 32 g

Fats: 19 g

21. Shake Cake Fueling

Preparation Time: 5 minutes

Cooking Time: 0 minutes

Servings: 1

Ingredients:

- One packet of Optavia shakes.
- 1/4 teaspoon of baking powder

- Two tablespoons of eggbeaters or egg whites
- Two tablespoons of water
- Other options that are not compulsory include sweetener, reduced-fat cream cheese, etc.

Directions:

1. Begin by preheating the oven.
2. Mix all the ingredients. Begin with the dry ingredients, and then add the wet ingredients.
3. After the mixture/batter is ready, pour gently into muffin cups.
4. Inside the oven, place, and bake for about 16-18 minutes or until it is baked and ready. Allow it to cool completely.
5. Add additional toppings of your choice and ensure your delicious shake cake is refreshing.

Nutrition:

Calories: 896 Fat: 37 g

Carbohydrate: 115 g Protein: 34 g

22. Optavia Biscuit Pizza

Preparation Time: 5 minutes

Cooking Time: 15-20 minutes

Servings: 1

Ingredients:

- 1/4 sachet of Optavia buttermilk cheddar and herb biscuit
- 1/4 tablespoon of tomato sauce
- 1/4 tablespoon of low-fat shredded cheese
- ¼ bottle of water
- Parchment paper

Directions:

1. Begin by preheating the oven to about 350°F
2. Mix the biscuit and water and stir properly.
3. In the parchment paper, pour the mixture and spread it into a thin circle. Allow cooking for 10 minutes.
4. Take it out and add the tomato sauce and shredded cheese.
5. Bake it for a few more minutes.

Nutrition:

Calories: 478 Protein: 30 g

Carbohydrates: 22 g Fats: 29 g

23. Lean and Green Smoothie 1

Preparation Time: 5 minutes

Cooking Time: 0 minutes

Servings: 1

Ingredients:

- 2 1/2 cups of kale leaves
- 3/4 cup of chilled apple juice
- 1 cup of cubed pineapple
- 1/2 cup of frozen green grapes
- 1/2 cup of chopped apple

Directions:

1. Place the pineapple, apple juice, apple, frozen seedless grapes, and kale leaves in a blender.
2. Cover and blend until it's smooth.
3. Smoothie is ready and can be garnished with halved grapes if you wish.

Nutrition:

Calories: 81 Protein: 2 g

Carbohydrates: 19 g Fats: 1 g

24. Lean and Green Smoothie 2

Preparation Time: 5 minutes

Cooking Time: 0 minutes

Servings: 1

Ingredients:

- Six kale leaves
- Two peeled oranges
- 2 cups of mango kombucha
- 2 cups of chopped pineapple
- 2 cups of water

Directions:

1. Break up the oranges, place in the blender.
2. Add the mango kombucha, chopped pineapple, and kale leaves into the blender.
3. Blend everything until it is smooth.
4. Smoothie is ready to be taken.

Nutrition:

Calories: 81

Protein: 2 g

Carbohydrates: 19 g

Fats: 1 g

25. Lean and Green Chicken Pesto Pasta

Preparation Time: 5 minutes

Cooking Time: 15 minutes

Servings: 1

Ingredients:

- 3 cups of raw kale leaves
- 2 tbsp. of olive oil
- 2 cups of fresh basil
- 1/4 teaspoon salt
- 3 tbsp. lemon juice
- Three garlic cloves
- 2 cups of cooked chicken breast
- 1 cup of baby spinach
- 6 ounces of uncooked chicken pasta
- 3 ounces of diced fresh mozzarella
- Basil leaves or red pepper flakes to garnish

Directions:

1. Start by making the pesto; add the kale, lemon juice, basil, garlic cloves, olive oil, and salt to a blender and blend until it's smooth.
2. Add salt and pepper to taste.
3. Cook the pasta and strain off the water. Reserve 1/4 cup of the liquid.
4. Get a bowl and mix everything, the cooked pasta, pesto, diced chicken, spinach, mozzarella, and the reserved pasta liquid.
5. Sprinkle the mixture with additional chopped basil or red paper flakes (optional).
6. Now your salad is ready. You may serve it warm or chilled. Also, it can be taken as a salad mix-ins or as a side dish. Leftovers should be stored in the refrigerator inside an air-tight container for 3-5 days.

Nutrition:

Calories: 244

Protein: 20.5 g

Carbohydrates: 22.5 g

Fats: 10 g

26. Open-Face Egg Sandwiches with Cilantro-Jalapeño Spread

Preparation Time: 20 minutes

Cooking Time: 10 minutes

Servings: 2

Ingredients:

For the cilantro and jalapeño spread

- 1 cup filled up fresh cilantro leaves and stems (about a bunch)
- 1 jalapeño pepper, seeded and roughly chopped
- ½ cup extra-virgin olive oil
- ¼ cup pepitas (hulled pumpkin seeds), raw or roasted
- 2 garlic cloves, thinly sliced
- 1 tablespoon freshly squeezed lime juice
- 1 teaspoon kosher salt

For the eggs

- 4 large eggs
- ¼ cup milk
- ¼ to ½ teaspoon kosher salt
- 2 tablespoons butter

For the sandwich

- 2 slices bread
- 1 tablespoon butter
- 1 avocado, halved, pitted, and divided into slices
- Microgreens or sprouts, for garnish

Directions:

To make the cilantro and jalapeño spread

1. In a food processor, combine the cilantro, jalapeño, oil, pepitas, garlic, lime juice, and salt. Whirl until smooth. Refrigerate if making in advance; otherwise set aside.

To make the eggs

2. In a medium bowl, whisk the eggs, milk, and salt.
3. Dissolve the butter in a skillet over low heat, swirling to coat the bottom of the pan. Pour in the whisked eggs.
4. Cook until they begin to set then, using a heatproof spatula, push them to the sides, allowing the uncooked portions to run into the bottom of the skillet.
5. Continue until the eggs are set.

To assemble the sandwiches

1. Toast the bed and spread with butter.
2. Spread a spoonful of the cilantro-jalapeño spread on each piece of toast. Top each with scrambled eggs.
3. Arrange avocado over each sandwich and garnish with microgreens.

Nutrition:

Calories: 711 Total fat: 4 g

Cholesterol: 54 mg Fiber: 12 g

Protein: 12 g Sodium: 327 mg

27. Tasty Breakfast Donuts

Preparation Time: 5 minutes

Cooking Time: 5 minutes

Servings: 4

Ingredients: 43 grams cream cheese

- 2 eggs
- 2 tablespoons almond flour

- 2 tablespoons erythritol
- 1 ½ tablespoons coconut flour
- ½ teaspoon baking powder
- ½ teaspoon vanilla extract
- 5 drops Stevia (liquid form)
- 2 strips bacon, fried until crispy

Directions:

1. Rub coconut oil over donut maker and turn on.
2. Mix all ingredients except bacon in a blender or food processor until smooth (should take around 1 minute).
3. Pour batter into donut maker, leaving 1/10 in each round for rising.
4. Leave for 3 minutes before flipping each donut. Leave for another 2 minutes or until a fork comes out clean when piercing them.
5. Take donuts out and let cool.
6. Repeat steps 1-5 until all batter is used.
7. Crumble bacon into bits and use to top donuts.

Nutrition:
Calories: 60 Fat: 5 g Carbs: 1 g
Fiber: 0 g Protein: 3 g

28. Cheesy Spicy Bacon Bowls

Preparation Time: 10 minutes
Cooking Time: 22 minutes
Servings: 12
Ingredients:

- 6 strips Bacon, pan-fried until cooked but still malleable
- 4 eggs
- 60 grams' cheddar cheese
- 40 grams' cream cheese, grated
- 2 Jalapenos, sliced and seeds removed
- 2 tablespoons coconut oil
- ¼ teaspoon onion powder
- ¼ teaspoon garlic powder
- Dash of salt and pepper

Directions:

1. Preheat oven to 375 degrees Fahrenheit
2. In a bowl, beat together eggs, cream cheese, jalapenos (minus 6 slices), coconut oil, onion powder, garlic powder, and salt and pepper.
3. Using leftover bacon grease on a muffin tray, rubbing it into each insert. Place bacon-wrapped inside the parameters of each insert.
4. Pour beaten mixture halfway up each bacon bowl.
5. Garnish each bacon bowl with cheese and leftover jalapeno slices (placing one on top of each).
6. Leave in the oven for about 22 minutes, or until the egg is thoroughly cooked and cheese is bubbly.
7. Remove from oven and let cool until edible.
8. Enjoy!

Nutrition:
Calories: 259 Fat: 24g Carbs: 1g
Fiber: 0g Protein: 10g

29. Apple Kale Cucumber Smoothie

Preparation Time: 5 minutes

Cooking Time: 5 minutes

Servings: 1

Ingredients:

- ¾ cup water
- ½ green apple, diced
- ¾ cup kale
- ½ cucumber

Directions:

1. Toss all your ingredients into your blender then process till smooth and creamy.
2. Serve immediately and enjoy.

Nutrition: Calories: 86 Fat: 0.5g Carbs: 21.7g Protein: 1.9g Fiber: 0g

30. Refreshing Cucumber Smoothie

Preparation Time: 5 minutes

Cooking Time: 5 minutes

Servings: 2

Ingredients:

- 1 cup ice cubes
- 20 drops liquid stevia
- 2 fresh lime, peeled and halved
- 1 tsp lime zest, grated
- 1 cucumber, chopped
- 1 avocado, pitted and peeled
- 2 cups kale
- 1 tbsp creamed coconut
- ¾ cup coconut water

Directions:

1. Toss all your ingredients into your blender then process till smooth and creamy.
2. Serve immediately and enjoy.

Nutrition: Calories: 313 Fat: 25.1g Carbs: 24.7g Protein: 4.9g Fiber: 0g

31. Cauliflower Veggie Smoothie

Preparation Time: 5 minutes

Cooking Time: 5 minutes

Servings: 4

Ingredients:

- 1 zucchini, peeled and chopped
- 1 Seville orange, peeled
- 1 apple, diced
- 1 banana
- 1 cup kale
- ½ cup cauliflower

Directions:

1. Toss all your ingredients into your blender then process till smooth and creamy.
2. Serve immediately and enjoy.

Nutrition: Calories: 71 Fat: 0.3g Carbs: 18.3g Protein: 1.3g Fiber: 0g

32. Soursop Smoothie

Preparation Time: 5 minutes

Cooking Time: 5 Minutes

Servings: 2

Ingredients:

- 3 quartered frozen Burro Bananas

- 1-1/2 cups of Homemade Coconut Milk
- 1/4 cup of Walnuts
- 1 teaspoon of Sea Moss Gel
- 1 teaspoon of Ground Ginger
- 1 teaspoon of Soursop Leaf Powder
- 1 handful of Kale

Directions:

1. Prepare and put all ingredients in a blender or a food processor.
2. Blend it well until you reach a smooth consistency.
3. Serve and enjoy your Soursop Smoothie!
4. Useful Tips:
5. If you don't have frozen Bananas, you can use fresh ones.

Nutrition: Calories: 213 Fat: 3.1g Carbs: 6g Protein: 8g Fiber: 4.3g

33. Cucumber-Ginger Water

Preparation Time: 5 minutes

Cooking Time: 5 Minutes

Servings: 2

Ingredients:

- 1 sliced Cucumber
- 1 smashed thumb of Ginger Root
- 2 cups of Spring Water

Directions:

1. Prepare and put all ingredients in a jar with a lid.
2. Let the water infuse overnight. Store it in the refrigerator.

3. Serve and enjoy your Cucumber-Ginger Water throughout the day!

Nutrition: Calories: 117 Fat: 2g Carbs: 6g Protein: 9.7g Fiber: 2g

34. Strawberry Milkshake

Preparation Time: 5 minutes

Cooking Time: 5 Minutes

Servings: 2

Ingredients:

- 2 cups of Homemade Hempseed Milk
- 1 cup of frozen Strawberries
- Agave Syrup, to taste

Directions:

1. Prepare and put all ingredients in a blender or a food processor.
2. Blend it well until you reach a smooth consistency.
3. Serve and enjoy your Strawberry Milkshake!
4. Useful Tips:
5. If you don't have Homemade Hempseed Milk, you can add Homemade Walnut Milk instead.
6. If you don't have frozen Strawberries, you can use fresh ones.

Nutrition: Calories: 222 Fat: 4g Carbs: 3g Protein: 6g Fiber: 1g

35. Cactus Smoothie

Preparation Time: 5 minutes

Cooking Time: 10 Minutes

Servings: 2

Ingredients:

- 1 medium Cactus
- 2 cups of Homemade Coconut Milk
- 2 frozen Baby Bananas
- 1/2 cup of Walnuts
- 1 Date
- 2 teaspoons of Hemp Seeds

Directions:

1. Take the Cactus, remove all pricks, wash it, and cut into medium pieces.
2. Put all the listed ingredients in a blender or a food processor.
3. Blend it well until you reach a smooth consistency.
4. Serve and enjoy your Cactus Smoothie!
5. Useful Tips
6. If you don't have Homemade Coconut Milk, you can add Homemade Walnut Milk or Homemade Hempseed Milk instead.
7. If you don't have frozen Bananas, you can use fresh ones.
8. If you don't have Baby Bananas, add 1 Burro Banana instead.

Nutrition: Calories: 123 Fat: 3g Carbs: 6g Protein: 2.5g Fiber: 0g

36. Prickly Pear Juice

Preparation Time: 5 minutes

Cooking Time: 10 Minutes

Servings: 2

Ingredients:

- 6 Prickly Pears
- 1/3 cup of Lime Juice
- 1/3 cup of Agave
- 1-1/2 cups of Spring Water*

Directions:

1. Take Prickly Pear, cut off the ends, slice off the skin, and put in a blender. Do the same with the other pears.
2. Add Lime Juice with Agave to the blender and blend well for 30–40 seconds.
3. Strain the prepared mixture through a nut milk bag or cheesecloth and pour it back into the blender.
4. Pour Spring Water in and blend it repeatedly.
5. Serve and enjoy your Prickly Pear Juice!
6. Useful Tips:
7. If you want a cold drink, add a tray of ice cubes instead.
8. like and serve it on top of the braised greens.

Nutrition: Calories: 312 Fat: 6g Carbs: 11g Protein: 8g Fiber: 2g

CHAPTER 5:

Lunch Recipes

37. Bacon Wrapped Asparagus
Preparation Time: 10 minutes
Cooking Time: 20 minutes
Servings: 2
Ingredients:

- 1/3 cup heavy whipping cream
- 2 bacon slices, precooked
- 4 small spears asparagus
- Salt, to taste
- 1 tablespoon butter

Directions:

1. Preheat the oven to 360 degrees and grease a baking sheet with butter.
2. Meanwhile, mix cream, asparagus and salt in a bowl.
3. Wrap the asparagus in bacon slices and arrange them in the baking dish.
4. Transfer the baking dish to the oven and bake for about 20 minutes.
5. Remove from the oven and serve hot.
6. Place the bacon wrapped asparagus in a dish and set aside to cool for meal prepping. Divide it in 2 containers and cover the lid. Refrigerate for

about 2 days and reheat in the microwave before serving.

Nutrition:
Calories: 204
Carbs: 1.4g
Protein: 5.9g
Fat: 19.3g
Sugar: 0.5g

38. Spinach Chicken
Preparation Time: 10 minutes
Cooking Time: 10 minutes
Servings: 2
Ingredients:

- 2 garlic cloves, minced
- 2 tablespoons unsalted butter, divided
- ¼ cup parmesan cheese, shredded
- ¾ pound chicken tenders
- ¼ cup heavy cream
- 10 ounces frozen spinach, chopped
- Salt and black pepper, to taste

Directions:

1. Heat 1 tablespoon of butter in a large skillet and add chicken, salt and black pepper.
2. Cook for about 3 minutes on both sides and remove the chicken to a bowl.

3. Melt remaining butter in the skillet and add garlic, cheese, heavy cream and spinach.

4. Cook for about 2 minutes and add the chicken.

5. Cook for about 5 minutes on low heat and dish out to immediately serve.

6. Place chicken in a dish and set aside to cool for meal prepping. Divide it in 2 containers and cover them. Refrigerate for about 3 days and reheat in microwave before serving.

Nutrition:
Calories: 288
Carbs: 3.6g
Protein: 27.7g
Fat: 18.3g
Sugar: 0.3g

39. Lemongrass Prawns
Preparation Time: 10 minutes
Cooking Time: 15 minutes
Servings: 2
Ingredients:

- ½ red chili pepper, seeded and chopped
- 2 lemongrass stalks
- ½ pound prawns, deveined and peeled
- 6 tablespoons butter
- ¼ teaspoon smoked paprika

Directions:

1. Preheat the oven to 390 degrees and grease a baking dish.
2. Mix red chili pepper, butter, smoked paprika and prawns in a bowl.

3. Marinate for about 2 hours and then thread the prawns on the lemongrass stalks.

4. Arrange the threaded prawns on the baking dish and transfer it in the oven.

5. Bake for about 15 minutes and dish out to serve immediately.

6. Place the prawns in a dish and set aside to cool for meal prepping. Divide it in 2 containers and close the lid. Refrigerate for about 4 days and reheat in microwave before serving.

Nutrition:
Calories: 322 Carbs: 3.8g
Protein: 34.8g Fat: 18g
Sugar: 0.1g
Sodium: 478mg

40. Stuffed Mushrooms
Preparation Time: 20 minutes
Cooking Time: 25 minutes
Ingredients:

- 2 ounces bacon, crumbled
- ½ tablespoon butter
- ¼ teaspoon paprika powder
- 2 portobello mushrooms
- 1 oz cream cheese
- ¾ tablespoon fresh chives, chopped
- Salt and black pepper, to taste

Directions:

1. Preheat the oven to 400 degrees and grease a baking dish.
2. Heat butter in a skillet and add mushrooms.
3. Sauté for about 4 minutes and set aside.

4. Mix cream cheese, chives, paprika powder, salt and black pepper in a bowl.
5. Stuff the mushrooms with this mixture and transfer on the baking dish.
6. Place in the oven and bake for about 20 minutes.
7. These mushrooms can be refrigerated for about 3 days for meal prepping and can be served with scrambled eggs.

Nutrition:
Calories: 570
Carbs: 4.6g
Protein: 19.9g
Fat: 52.8g
Sugar: 0.8g
Sodium: 1041mg

41. Honey Glazed Chicken Drumsticks

Preparation Time: 10 minutes
Cooking Time: 20 minutes
Servings: 2
Ingredients:

- ½ tablespoon fresh thyme, minced
- 1/8 cup Dijon mustard
- ½ tablespoon fresh rosemary, minced
- ½ tablespoon honey
- 2 chicken drumsticks
- 1 tablespoon olive oil
- Salt and black pepper, to taste

Directions:

1. Preheat the oven at 325 degrees and grease a baking dish.
2. Combine all the ingredients in a bowl except the drumsticks and mix well.
3. Add drumsticks and coat generously with the mixture.
4. Cover and refrigerate to marinate overnight.
5. Place the drumsticks in in the baking dish and transfer it in the oven.
6. Cook for about 20 minutes and dish out to immediately serve.
7. Place chicken drumsticks in a dish and set aside to cool for meal prepping. Divide it in 2 containers and cover them. Refrigerate for about 3 days and reheat in microwave before serving.

Nutrition:
Calories: 301
Carbs: 6g
Fats: 19.7g
Proteins: 4.5g
Sugar: 4.5g
Sodium: 316mg

42. Zucchini Pizza

Preparation Time: 10 minutes
Cooking Time: 15 minutes
Servings: 2
Ingredients:

- 1/8 cup spaghetti sauce
- ½ zucchini, cut in circular slices
- ½ cup cream cheese
- Pepperoni slices, for topping
- ½ cup mozzarella cheese, shredded

Directions:

1. Preheat the oven to 350 degrees and grease a baking dish.
2. Arrange the zucchini on the baking dish and layer with spaghetti sauce.
3. Top with pepperoni slices and mozzarella cheese.
4. Transfer the baking dish to the oven and bake for about 15 minutes.
5. Remove from the oven and serve immediately.

Nutrition:

Calories: 445 Carbs: 3.6g

Protein: 12.8g

Fat: 42g

Sugar: 0.3g

Sodium: 429mg

43. Omega-3 Salad

Preparation Time: 10 minutes

Cooking Time: 5 minutes

Servings: 2

Ingredients:

- ½ pound skinless salmon fillet, cut into 4 steaks
- ¼ tablespoon fresh lime juice
- 1 tablespoon olive oil, divided
- 4 tablespoons sour cream
- ¼ zucchini, cut into small cubes
- ¼ teaspoon jalapeño pepper, seeded and chopped finely
- Salt and black pepper, to taste
- ¼ tablespoon fresh dill, chopped

Directions:

1. Put olive oil and salmon in a skillet and cook for about 5 minutes on both sides.
2. Season with salt and black pepper, stirring well and dish out.
3. Mix remaining ingredients in a bowl and add cooked salmon to serve.

Nutrition:

Calories: 291

Fat: 21.1g

Carbs: 2.5g

Protein: 23.1g

Sugar: 0.6g

Sodium: 112mg

44. Crab Cakes

Preparation Time: 20 minutes

Cooking Time: 10 minutes

Servings: 2

Ingredients:

- ½ pound lump crabmeat, drained
- 2 tablespoons coconut flour
- 1 tablespoon mayonnaise
- ¼ teaspoon green Tabasco sauce
- 3 tablespoons butter
- 1 small egg, beaten
- ¾ tablespoon fresh parsley, chopped
- ½ teaspoon yellow mustard
- Salt and black pepper, to taste

Directions:

1. Mix all the ingredients in a bowl except butter.
2. Make patties from this mixture and set aside.

3. Heat butter in a skillet over medium heat and add patties.

4. Cook for about 10 minutes on each side and dish out to serve hot.

5. You can store the raw patties in the freezer for about 3 weeks for meal prepping. Place patties in a container and place parchment paper in between the patties to avoid stickiness.

Nutrition:
Calories: 153 Fat: 10.8g
Carbs: 6.7g
Protein: 6.4g
Sugar: 2.4
Sodium: 46mg

45. Salmon Burgers
Preparation Time: 17 minutes
Cooking Time: 3 minutes
Servings: 2
Ingredients:
- 1 tablespoon sugar-free ranch dressing
- ½-ounce smoked salmon, chopped roughly
- ½ tablespoon fresh parsley, chopped
- ½ tablespoon avocado oil
- 1 small egg
- 4-ounce pink salmon, drained and bones removed
- 1/8 cup almond flour
- ¼ teaspoon Cajun seasoning

Directions:
1. Mix all the ingredients in a bowl and stir well.

2. Make patties from this mixture and set aside.

3. Heat a skillet over medium heat and add patties.

4. Cook for about 3 minutes per side and dish out to serve.

5. You can store the raw patties in the freezer for about 3 weeks for meal prepping. Place patties in a container and place parchment paper in between the patties to avoid stickiness.

Nutrition:
Calories: 59
Fat: 12.7g
Carbs: 2.4g
Protein: 6.3g
Sugar: 0.7g
Sodium: 25mg

46. Low Carb Black Beans Chili Chicken
Preparation Time: 10 minutes
Cooking Time: 25 minutes
Servings: 10
Ingredients:
- 1-3/4 pounds of chicken breasts, cubed (boneless skinless)
- 2 sweet red peppers, chopped
- 1 onion, chopped
- 3 tablespoons of olive oil
- 1 can of chopped green chiles
- 4 cloves of garlic, minced
- 2 tablespoons of chili powder
- 2 teaspoons of ground cumin
- 1 teaspoon of ground coriander

- 2 cans of black beans, rinsed and drained
- 1 can of Italian stewed tomatoes, cut up
- 1 cup of chicken broth or beer
- 1/2 to 1 cup of water

Directions:

1. Put oil into a skillet and place over medium heat. Add in the red pepper, chicken, and onion and cook until the chicken is brown, about five minutes.
2. Add in the garlic, chiles, chili powder, coriander, and cumin and cook for an additional minute.
3. Next, add in the tomatoes, beans, half cup of water, and broth and cook until it boils. Decrease the heat, uncover the skillet and cook while stirring for fifteen minutes.
4. Serve.

Nutrition:

Calories: 236 Fat: 6g

Protein: 22g

Carbohydrates: 21g

47. Flavorful Taco Soup

Preparation Time: 5 minutes

Cooking Time: 15

Servings: 8

Ingredients:

- 1 lb of Ground beef
- 3 tablespoons of Taco seasoning, divided
- 4 cup of Beef bone broth
- 2 14.5-oz cans of Diced tomatoes
- 3/4 cup of Ranch dressing

Directions:

1. Put the ground beef into a pot and place over medium high heat and cook until brown, about ten minutes.
2. Add in ¾ cup of broth and two tablespoons of taco seasoning. Cook until part of the liquid has evaporated.
3. Add in the diced tomatoes, rest of the broth, and rest of the taco seasoning. Stir to mix, then simmer for ten minutes.
4. Remove the pot from heat, and add in the ranch dressing. Garnish with cilantro and cheddar cheese. Serve.

Nutrition:

Calories: 309

Fat: 24g

Protein: 13g

48. Delicious Instant Pot Buffalo Chicken Soup

Preparation Time: 10 minutes

Cooking Time: 20 minutes

Servings: 6

Ingredients:

- 1 tablespoon of Olive oil
- 1/2 Onion, diced)
- 1/2 cup of Celery, diced
- 4 cloves of Garlic, minced
- 1 lb of Shredded chicken, cooked
- 4 cup of Chicken bone broth, or any chicken broth
- 3 tablespoons of Buffalo sauce
- 6 oz of Cream cheese
- 1/2 cup of Half & half

Directions:

1. Switch the instant pot to the saute function. Add in the chopped onion, oil, and celery. Cook until the onions are brown and translucent, about ten minutes.
2. Add in the garlic and cook until fragrant, about one minute. Switch off the instant pot.
3. Add in the broth, shredded chicken, and buffalo sauce. Cover the instant pot and seal. Switch the soup feature on and set time to five minutes.
4. When cooked, release pressure naturally for five minutes and then quickly.
5. Scoop out one cup of the soup liquid into a blender bowl, then add in the cheese and blend until smooth. Pour the puree into the instant pot, then add in the calf and half and stir to mix.
6. Serve.

Nutrition:

Servings: 1 cup
Calories: 270
Protein: 27g
Fat: 16g
Carbohydrates: 4g

49. Creamy Low Carb Cream of Mushroom Soup

Preparation Time: 15 minutes
Cooking Time: 15 minutes
Servings: 5
Ingredients:

- 1 tablespoons of Olive oil
- 1/2 Onion, diced

- 20 oz of Mushrooms, sliced
- 6 cloves of Garlic, minced
- 2 cup of Chicken broth
- 1 cup of Heavy cream
- 1 cup of Unsweetened almond milk
- 3/4 teaspoon of Sea salt
- 1/4 teaspoon of Black pepper

Directions:

1. Place a pot over medium heat and add in olive oil. Add in the mushrooms and onions and cook until browned, about fifteen minutes. Next, add in the garlic and cook for another one minute.
2. Add in the cream, chicken broth, sea salt, almond milk, and black pepper. Cook until boil, then simmer for fifteen minutes.
3. Puree the soup using an immersion blender until smooth. Serve.

Nutrition:

Servings: 1 cup
Calories: 229
Fat: 21g
Protein: 5g
Carbohydrates: 8g

50. Tropical Greens Smoothie

Preparation Time: 5 Minutes
Cooking Time: 0 Minutes
Servings: 1
Ingredients:

- One banana
- 1/2 large navel orange, peeled and segmented
- 1/2 cup frozen mango chunks

- 1 cup frozen spinach
- One celery stalk, broken into pieces
- One tablespoon cashew butter or almond butter
- 1/2 tablespoon spiraling
- 1/2 tablespoon ground flaxseed
- 1/2 cup unsweetened nondairy milk
- Water, for thinning (optional)

Directions:

1. In a high-speed blender or food processor, combine the bananas, orange, mango, spinach, celery, cashew butter, spiraling (if using), flaxseed, and milk.

    2. Blend until creamy, adding more milk or water to thin the smoothie if too thick. Serve immediately—it is best served fresh.

Nutrition:
Calories: 391 Fat: 12g
Protein: 13g
Carbohydrates: 68g
Fiber: 13g

51. Vitamin C Smoothie Cubes

Preparation Time: 5 minutes
Cooking Time: 8 hours to chill
Servings: 1
Ingredients:

- 1/8 large papaya
- 1/8 mango
- 1/4 cups chopped pineapple, fresh or frozen
- 1/8 cup raw cauliflower florets, fresh or frozen
- 1/4 large navel oranges, peeled and halved
- 1/4 large orange bell pepper stemmed, seeded, and coarsely chopped

Directions:

1. Halve the papaya and mango, remove the pits, and scoop their soft flesh into a high-speed blender.

    2. Add the pineapple, cauliflower, oranges, and bell pepper. Blend until smooth.

    3. Evenly divide the puree between 2 (16-compartment) ice cube trays and place them on a level surface in your freezer. Freeze for at least 8 hours.

    4. The cubes can be left in the ice cube trays until use or transferred to a freezer bag. The frozen cubes are good for about three weeks in a standard freezer, or up to 6 months in a chest freezer.

Nutrition:
Calories: 96
Fat: 1 g
Protein: 2 g
Carbohydrates: 24 g
Fiber: 4 g

52. Overnight Chocolate Chia Pudding

Preparation Time: 2 minutes

Cooking Time: overnight to chill

Servings: 1

Ingredients:

- 1/8 cup chia seeds
- 1/2 cup unsweetened nondairy milk
- One tablespoon raw cocoa powder
- 1/2 teaspoon vanilla extract
- 1/2 teaspoon pure maple syrup

Directions:

1. Stir together the chia seeds, milk, cacao powder, vanilla, and maple syrup in a large bowl.

2. Divide between two (1/2-pint) covered glass jars or containers.

3. Refrigerate overnight.

4. Stir before serving.

Nutrition:

Calories: 213

Fat: 10 g

Protein: 9 g

Carbohydrates: 20 g

Fiber: 15 g

53. Slow Cooker Savory Butternut Squash Oatmeal

Preparation Time: 15 minutes

Cooking Time: 6 to 8 hours

Servings: 1

Ingredients:

- 1/4 cup steel-cut oats
- 1/2 cups cubed (1/2-inch pieces), peeled butternut squash (freeze any leftovers after preparing a whole squash for future meals)
- 3/4 cups of water
- 1/16 cup unsweetened nondairy milk
- 1/4 tablespoon chia seeds
- 1/2 teaspoons yellow miso paste
- 3/4 teaspoons ground ginger
- 1/4 tablespoon sesame seeds, toasted
- 1/4 tablespoon chopped scallion, green parts only
- Shredded carrot, for serving (optional)

Directions:

1. In a slow cooker, combine the oats, butternut squash, and water.

2. Cover the slow cooker and cook on low for 6 to 8 hours, or until the squash is fork-tender.

3. Using a potato masher or heavy spoon, roughly mash the cooked butternut squash.

4. Stir to combine with the oats.

5. Whisk together the milk, chia seeds, miso paste, and ginger in a large bowl. Stir the mixture into the oats.

6. Top your oatmeal bowl with sesame seeds and scallion for more plant-based fiber, top with shredded carrot (if using).

Nutrition:

Calories: 230

Fat: 5 g

Protein: 7 g

Carbohydrates: 40 g

Fiber: 9 g

54. Carrot Cake Oatmeal

Preparation Time: 10 minutes

Cooking Time: 15 minutes

Servings: 1

Ingredients:

- 1/8 cup pecans
- 1/2 cup finely shredded carrot
- 1/4 cup old-fashioned oats
- 5/8 cups unsweetened nondairy milk
- 1/2 tablespoon pure maple syrup
- 1/2 teaspoon ground cinnamon
- 1/2 teaspoon ground ginger
- 1/8 teaspoon ground nutmeg
- One tablespoon chia seed

Directions:

1. Over medium-high heat in a skillet, toast the pecans for 3 to 4 minutes, often stirring, until browned and fragrant (watch closely, as they can burn quickly).

2. Pour the pecans onto a cutting board and coarsely chop them. Set aside.

3. In an 8-quart pot over medium-high heat, combine the carrot, oats, milk, maple syrup, cinnamon, ginger, and nutmeg.

4. When it is already boiling, reduce the heat to medium-low.

5. Cook, uncovered, for 10 minutes, stirring occasionally.

6. Stir in the chopped pecans and chia seeds. Serve immediately.

Nutrition:

Calories: 307

Fat: 17 g

Protein: 7 g

Carbohydrates: 35 g

Fiber: 11 g

55. Bacon Spaghetti Squash Carbonara

Preparation Time: 20 minutes

Cooking Time: 40 minutes

Servings: 4

Ingredients:

- 1 small spaghetti squash
- 6 ounces' bacon (roughly chopped)
- 1 large tomato (sliced)
- 2 chives (chopped)
- 1 garlic clove (minced)

- 6 ounces low-fat cottage cheese
- 1 cup Gouda cheese (grated)
- 2 tablespoons olive oil
- Salt and pepper, to taste

Directions:

1. Preheat the oven to 350°F.

2. Cut the squash spaghetti in half, brush with some olive oil and bake for 20–30 minutes, skin side up. Remove from the oven and remove the core with a fork, creating the spaghetti.

3. Heat one tablespoon of olive oil in a skillet. Cook the bacon for about 1 minute until crispy.

4. Quickly wipe out the pan with paper towels.

5. Heat another tablespoon of oil and sauté the garlic, tomato, and chives for 2–3 minutes. Add the spaghetti and sauté for another 5 minutes, occasionally stirring to keep from burning.

6. Begin to add the cottage cheese, about two tablespoons at a time. If the sauce becomes thick, add about a cup of water. The sauce should be creamy but not too runny or thick. Allow cooking for another 3 minutes.

7. Serve immediately.

Nutrition:
Calories: 305 Total Fat: 21 g
Net Carbs: 8 g Protein: 18 g

56. Spiced Sorghum and Berries

Preparation Time: 5 minutes
Cooking Time: 1 hour
Servings: 1
Ingredients:

- 1/4 cup whole-grain sorghum
- 1/4 teaspoon ground cinnamon
- 1/4 teaspoon Chinese five-spice powder
- 3/4 cups water
- 1/4 cup unsweetened nondairy milk
- 1/4 teaspoon vanilla extract
- 1/2 tablespoons pure maple syrup
- 1/2 tablespoon chia seed
- 1/8 cup sliced almonds
- 1/2 cups fresh raspberries, divided

Directions:

1. Using a large pot over medium-high heat, stir together the sorghum, cinnamon, five-spice powder, and water.

2. Wait for the water to a boil, cover it, and reduce the heat to medium-low.

3. Cook for one hour, or until the sorghum is soft and chewy. If the sorghum grains are still hard, add

another water cup and cook for 15 minutes more.

4. Using a glass measuring cup, whisk together the milk, vanilla, and maple syrup to blend.

5. Add the mixture to the sorghum and the chia seeds, almonds, and one cup of raspberries. Gently stir to combine.

6. When serving, top with the remaining one cup of fresh raspberries.

Nutrition: Calories: 289 Fat: 8 g Protein: 9 g Carbohydrates: 52 g Fiber: 10 g

57. Raw-Cinnamon-Apple Nut Bowl

Preparation Time: 15 minutes
Cooking Time: 1 hour to chill
Servings: 1
Ingredients:

- One green apple halved, seeded, and cored
- 3/4 Honeycrisp apples, halved, seeded, and cored
- 1/4 teaspoon freshly squeezed lemon juice
- One pitted Medrol dates
- 1/8 teaspoon ground cinnamon
- Pinch ground nutmeg
- 1/2 tablespoons chia seeds, plus more for serving (optional)
- 1/4 tablespoon hemp seed
- 1/8 cup chopped walnuts
- Nut butter, for serving (optional)

Directions:

1. Finely dice half the green apple and one Honey crisp apple. With the lemon juice, store it in an airtight container while you work on the next steps.

2. Coarsely chop the remaining apples and the dates. Transfer to a food processor and add the cinnamon and nutmeg.

3. Check it several times to see if it's mixing, then processes for 2 to 3 minutes to puree. Stir the puree into the reserved diced apples.

4. Stir in the chia seeds (if using), hemp seeds, and walnuts.

5. Chill for at least one hour.

6. Enjoy!

7. Serve as it is or top with additional chia seeds and nut butter (if using).

Nutrition: Calories: 274 Fat: 8 g Protein: 4 g Carbohydrates: 52 g Fiber: 9 g

58. Peanut Butter and Cacao Breakfast Quinoa

Preparation Time: 5 Minutes
Cooking Time: 10 Minutes
Servings: 1
Ingredients:

- 1/3 cup quinoa flakes

- 1/2 cup unsweetened nondairy milk,
- 1/2 cup of water
- 1/8 cup raw cacao powder
- One tablespoon natural creamy peanut butter
- 1/8 teaspoon ground cinnamon
- One banana, mashed
- Fresh berries of choice, for serving
- Chopped nuts of choice, for serving

Directions:

1. Using an 8-quart pot over medium-high heat, stir together the quinoa flakes, milk, water, cacao powder, peanut butter, and cinnamon.
2. Cook and stir it until the mixture begins to simmer. Turn the heat to medium-low and cook for 3 to 5 minutes, stirring frequently.
3. Stir in the bananas and cook until hot.
4. Serve topped with fresh berries, nuts, and a splash of milk.

Nutrition: Calories: 471 Fat: 16g Protein: 18g Carbohydrates: 69g Fiber: 16g

59. Vanilla Buckwheat Porridge

Preparation Time: 5 minutes
Cooking Time: 25 minutes
Servings: 1

Ingredients:

- One cup of water
- 1/4 cup raw buckwheat grouts
- 1/4 teaspoon ground cinnamon
- 1/4 banana, sliced
- 1/16 cup golden raisins
- 1/16 cup dried currants
- 1/16 cup sunflower seeds
- 1/2 tablespoons chia seeds
- 1/4 tablespoon hemp seeds
- 1/4 tablespoon sesame seeds, toasted
- 1/8 cup unsweetened nondairy milk
- 1/4 tablespoon pure maple syrup
- 1/4 teaspoon vanilla extract

Directions:

1. Boil the water in a pot. Stir in the buckwheat, cinnamon, and banana.
2. Cook the mixture. Mix it and wait for it to boil, then reduce the heat to medium-low.
3. Cover the pot and cook for 15 minutes, or until the buckwheat is tender.
4. Remove from the heat.
5. Stir in the raisins, currants, sunflower seeds, chia seeds, hemp seeds, sesame seeds, milk, maple syrup, and vanilla. Cover the

pot. Wait for 10 minutes before serving.

6. Serve as it is or top as desired.

Nutrition:

Calories: 353

Fat: 11 g

Protein: 10 g

Carbohydrates: 61 g

Fiber: 10 g

60. Polenta with Seared Pears

Preparation Time: 10 minutes

Cooking Time: 50 minutes

Servings: 1

Ingredients:

- One cup water, divided, plus more as needed
- 1/2 cups coarse cornmeal
- One tablespoon pure maple syrup
- 1/4 tablespoon molasses
- 1/4 teaspoon ground cinnamon
- 1/2 ripe pears, cored and diced
- 1/4 cup fresh cranberries
- 1/4 teaspoon chopped fresh rosemary leaves

Directions:

1. In a pan, cook 5 cups of water to a simmer.

2. While whisking continuously to avoid clumping, slowly pour in the cornmeal. Cook, often stirring with a heavy spoon,

for 30 minutes. The polenta should be thick and creamy.

3. While the polenta cooks, in a saucepan over medium heat, stir together the maple syrup, molasses, the remaining 1/4 cup of water, and the cinnamon until combined.

4. Bring it to a simmer. Add the pears and cranberries. Cook for 10 minutes, occasionally stirring, until the pears are tender and start to brown.

5. Remove from the heat. Stir in the rosemary and let the mixture sit for 5 minutes. If it is too thick, add another 1/4 cup of water and return to the heat.

6. Top with the cranberry-pear mixture.

Nutrition:

Calories: 282

Fat: 2 g

Protein: 4 g

Carbohydrates: 65 g

Fiber: 12 g

61. Best Whole Wheat Pancakes

Preparation Time: 10 minutes

Cooking Time: 20 minutes

Servings: 1

Ingredients:

- 3/4 tablespoons ground flaxseed
- Two tablespoons warm water

- 1/2 cups whole wheat pastry flour
- 1/8 cup rye flour
- 1/2 tablespoons double-acting baking powder
- 1/4 teaspoon ground cinnamon
- 1/8 teaspoon ground ginger
- One cup unsweetened nondairy milk
- 3/4 tablespoons pure maple syrup
- 1/4 teaspoon vanilla extract

Directions:

1. Mix the warm water and flaxseed in a large bowl. Set aside for at least 5 minutes.

2. Whisk together the pastry and rye flours, baking powder, cinnamon, and ginger.

3. Whisk together the milk, maple syrup, and vanilla in a large bowl. Make use of a spatula, fold the wet ingredients into the dry ingredients. Fold in the soaked flaxseed until fully incorporated.

4. Heat a large skillet or nonstick griddle over medium-high heat.

5. Working in batches, three to four pancakes at a time, add 1/4-cup portions of batter to the hot skillet.

6. Until golden brown, cook for 3 to 4 minutes each

side or no liquid batter is visible.

Nutrition:
Calories: 301
Fat: 4 g
Protein: 10 g
Carbohydrates: 57 g
Fiber: 10 g

62. Spiced Pumpkin Muffins

Preparation Time: 15 minutes
Cooking Time: 20 minutes
Servings: 1
Ingredients:

- 1/6 tablespoons ground flaxseed
- 1/24 cup of water
- 1/8 cups whole wheat flour
- 1/6 teaspoons baking powder
- 5/6 teaspoons ground cinnamon
- 1/12 teaspoon baking soda
- 1/12 teaspoon ground ginger
- 1/16 teaspoon ground nutmeg
- 1/32 teaspoon ground cloves
- 1/6 cup pumpkin puree
- 1/12 cup pure maple syrup
- 1/24 cup unsweetened applesauce
- 1/24 cup unsweetened nondairy milk
- 1/2 teaspoons vanilla extract

Directions:

1. Preheat the oven to 350°F. Line a 12-cup metal muffin pan with parchment paper liners or use a silicone muffin pan.

2. First, mix the flaxseed and water in a large bowl then keep it aside.

3. In a medium bowl, stir together the flour, baking powder, cinnamon, baking soda, ginger, nutmeg, and cloves.

4. In a medium bowl, stir up the maple syrup, pumpkin puree, applesauce, milk, and vanilla. Crease the wet ingredients into the dry ingredients making use of a spatula.

5. Fold the soaked flaxseed into the batter until evenly combined, but do not over mix the batter, or your muffins will become dense. Spoon about 1/4 cup of batter per muffin into your prepared muffin pan.

6. Bake for 18 to 20 minutes, or until a toothpick inserted into the center of a muffin comes out clean. Remove the muffins from the pan.

7. Transfer to a wire rack for cooling.

8. Store in an airtight container that is at room temperature.

Nutrition:

Calories: 115

Fat: 1 g

Protein: 3 g

Carbohydrates: 25 g

Fiber: 3 g

63. Pesto Zucchini Noodles

Preparation Time: 10 minutes

Cooking Time: 30 minutes

Servings: 4

Ingredients:

- 4 zucchinis, spiralized
- 1 tbsp. avocado oil
- 2 garlic cloves, chopped
- 2/3 cup olive oil
- 1/3 cup parmesan cheese, grated
- 2 cups fresh basil
- 1/3 cup almonds
- 1/8 tsp. black pepper
- 3/4 tsp. sea salt

Directions:

1. Add zucchini noodles into a colander and sprinkle with 1/4 teaspoon of salt.

2. Cover and let sit for 30 minutes.

3. Drain zucchini noodles well and pat dry.

4. Preheat the oven to 400 F.

5. Place almonds on a parchment-lined baking sheet and bake for 6-8 minutes.

6. Transfer toasted almonds into the food processor and process until coarse.

7. Add olive oil, cheese, basil, garlic, pepper, and remaining salt in a food processor with almonds and process until pesto texture.

8. Heat avocado oil in a large pan over medium-high heat.

9. Add zucchini noodles and cook for 4-5 minutes.

10. Pour pesto over zucchini noodles, mix well and cook for 1 minute.

11. Serve immediately with baked salmon.

Nutrition:
Calories: 525 Cal
Fat: 47.4 g
Carbohydrates: 9.3 g
Sugar: 3.8 g
Protein: 16.6 g
Cholesterol: 30 mg

64. Stewed Herbed Fruit

Preparation Time: 15 minutes
Cooking Time: 6 to 8 hours
Servings: 12
Ingredients:

- 2 cups dried apricots
- 2 cups prunes
- 2 cups dried unsulphured pears
- 2 cups dried apples
- 1 cup dried cranberries
- 1/4 cup honey
- 6 cups water
- 1 teaspoon dried thyme leaves
- 1 teaspoon dried basil leaves

Directions:

1. In a 6-quart slow cooker, mix all of the ingredients.

2. Cover and cook on low for 6 to 8 hours, or until the fruits have absorbed the liquid and are tender.

3. Store in the refrigerator for up to 1 week.

4. You can freeze the fruit in 1-cup portions for more extended storage.

Nutrition:
Calories: 242 Cal Carbohydrates: 61 g
Sugar: 43 g Fiber: 9 g
Fat: 0 g Saturated Fat: 0 g
Protein: 2 g Sodium: 11 mg

65. African Sweet Potato Stew

Preparation Time: 15 minutes
Cooking Time: 7 to 8 hours
Servings: 4
Ingredients:

- 4 cups peeled diced sweet potatoes
- 1 (15-ounce) can red kidney beans, drained and rinsed

- 1 (14.5-ounce) can diced tomatoes, drained
- 1 cup diced red bell pepper
- 2 cups Very Easy Vegetable Broth (here) or store bought
- 1 medium yellow onion, chopped
- 1 (4.5-ounce) can chopped green chiles, drained
- 1 teaspoon minced garlic (2 cloves)
- 1½ teaspoons ground ginger
- 1 teaspoon ground cumin
- 4 tablespoons creamy peanut butter
- Pinch salt
- Freshly ground black pepper

Directions:

1. Combine the sweet potatoes, kidney beans, diced tomatoes, bell pepper, vegetable broth, onion, green chiles, garlic, ginger, and cumin in a slow cooker. Mix well

2. Cover and cook on low for 7 to 8 hours.

3. Ladle a little of the soup into a small bowl and mix in the peanut butter, then pour the mixture back into the stew

4. Season with salt and pepper. Mix well and serve.

Nutrition:

Calories: 514

Total fat: 10g

Protein: 22g

Sodium: 649mg

Fiber: 17g

66. Sweet-And-Sour Tempeh

Preparation Time: 15 Minutes

Cooking Time: 7 To 8 Hours

Servings: 4

Ingredients:

For the Sauce:

- ¾ cup fresh or canned pineapple chunks
- ½ cup crushed tomatoes
- ½ cup water
- ¼ cup chopped onion
- ¼ cup soy sauce
- 2 tablespoons rice vinegar
- ¼ teaspoon red pepper flakes
- 1 (½-inch) piece fresh ginger, peeled

For the Tempeh:

- 2 (8-ounce) packages tempeh, cut into cubes
- 2 cups diced bell pepper
- 1½ cups diced pineapple
- ½ cup diced onion
- Cooked rice, for serving

Directions:

1. Put the pineapple chunks, crushed tomatoes, water, onion, soy sauce, rice vinegar, red pepper flakes, and ginger in a blender; blend until smooth.

2. Combine the sauce, tempeh, bell pepper, diced pineapple, and onion in a slow cooker; stir well.

3. Cover and cook on low for 7 to 8 hours.

4. Serve over cooked rice.

Nutrition:

Calories: 324

Total fat: 13g

Protein: 24g

Sodium: 974mg

Fiber: 4g

67. Jackfruit Cochinita Pibil

Preparation Time: 15 Minutes

Cooking Time: 8 Hours

Servings: 4

Ingredients:

- 2 (20-ounce) cans jackfruit, drained, hard pieces discarded
- 2/3 cup freshly squeezed lemon juice
- 1/3 cup orange juice
- 2 habanero peppers, seeded and chopped
- 2 tablespoons achiote paste
- 2 teaspoons ground cumin
- 2 teaspoons smoked paprika
- 2 teaspoons chili powder
- 2 teaspoons ground coriander
- Pinch salt
- Freshly ground black pepper
- Warmed corn tortillas, for serving

Directions:

1. Combine the jackfruit, lemon juice, orange juice, habanero peppers, achiote paste, cumin, smoked paprika, chili powder, and coriander in a slow cooker; mix well.
2. Cover and cook on low for 8 hours or on high for 4 hours.
3. Use two forks to pull the jackfruit apart into shreds. Season with salt and pepper.
4. Heat tortillas directly over a gas fire, or in a skillet over medium heat for about 1 minute per side. Spoon the jackfruit into the tortillas and serve.

Nutrition:

Calories: 297

Total fat: 2g

Protein: 5g

Sodium: 71mg

Fiber: 6g

68. Delightful Dal

Preparation Time: 15 Minutes

Cooking Time: 7 To 9 Hours

Servings: 4

Ingredients:

- 3 cups red lentils, rinsed
- 6 cups water
- 1 (28-ounce) can diced tomatoes, with juice
- 1 small yellow onion, diced
- 2½ teaspoons minced garlic (5 cloves)
- 1 (1-inch) piece fresh ginger, peeled and minced
- 1 tablespoon ground turmeric
- 2 teaspoons ground cumin
- 1½ teaspoons ground cardamom
- 1½ teaspoons whole mustard seeds
- 1 teaspoon fennel seeds
- 1 bay leaf
- 1 teaspoon salt

- ¼ teaspoon freshly ground black pepper

Directions:

1. Combine the lentils, water, diced tomatoes, onion, garlic, ginger, turmeric, cumin, cardamom, mustard seeds, fennel seeds, bay leaf, salt, and pepper in a slow cooker; mix well.
2. Cover and cook on low for 7 to 9 hours or on high for 4 to 6 hours.
3. Remove the bay leaf, and serve.

Nutrition:

Calories: 585 Total fat: 4g

Protein: 40g Sodium: 616mg

Fiber: 48g

69. Moroccan Chickpea Stew

Preparation Time: 15 Minutes

Cooking Time: 6 To 8 Hours

Servings: 4

Ingredients:

- 1 small butternut squash, peeled and chopped into bite-size pieces
- 3 cups Very Easy Vegetable Broth (here) or store bought
- 1 medium yellow onion, diced
- 1 bell pepper, diced
- 1 (15-ounce) can chickpeas, drained and rinsed
- 1 (14.5-ounce) can tomato sauce
- ¾ cup brown lentils, rinsed
- 1½ teaspoons minced garlic (3 cloves)
- 1½ teaspoons ground ginger
- 1½ teaspoons ground turmeric

- 1½ teaspoons ground cumin
- 1 teaspoon ground cinnamon
- ¾ teaspoon smoked paprika
- ½ teaspoon salt
- 1 (8-ounce) package fresh udon noodles
- Freshly ground black pepper

Directions:

1. Combine the butternut squash, vegetable broth, onion, bell pepper, chickpeas, tomato sauce, brown lentils, garlic, ginger, turmeric, cumin, cinnamon, smoked paprika, and salt in a slow cooker. Mix well.
2. Cover and cook 6 to 8 hours on low or 3 to 4 hours on high. In the last 10 minutes of cooking, add the noodles.
3. Season with pepper, and serve.

Nutrition:

Calories: 427 Total fat: 4g

Protein: 26g Sodium: 1,423mg

Fiber: 24g

70. Broccoli Quinoa Casserole

Preparation Time: 15 minutes

Cooking Time: 30 minutes

Servings: 5

Ingredients:

- Four and a half cups of vegetable stock
- Two and a half cups of quinoa (uncooked)
- Half a tsp. of salt
- Two tablespoons of pesto sauce
- Two teaspoons of cornstarch

- Twelve ounces of mozzarella cheese (skimmed)
- Two cups of spinach (fresh and organic)
- One-third cup of parmesan cheese
- Three medium-sized green onions (chopped)
- Twelve ounces of broccoli florets (fresh)

Directions:

1. Set the temperature of the oven to 400 degrees Fahrenheit and preheat. Take a rectangular baking dish and add the quinoa to it along with the green onions. In the meantime, take a large-sized bowl and add the broccoli florets to it. Microwave the florets at high for about five minutes. Once done, set them aside.

2. Take a large-sized mixing bowl and in it, add the pesto, vegetable sauce, cornstarch, and salt. Use a wire whisk to mix all of them properly. Now, heat this mixture until it starts to boil. You can either do this in the microwave, or you can use your stovetop as well.

3. Now, take the vegetable stock and the spinach and add them to the quinoa. Add the three-quarter of the mozzarella cheese and the parmesan as well. Bake the mixture for thirty to thirty-five minutes. Once done, take the casserole of quinoa out and then mix the broccoli into it. Take the rest of the cheese and

sprinkle on top. Place the preparation back in the oven for another five minutes. By this time, all the cheese will melt.

Nutrition:

Calories: 49

Protein: 27.6g

Fat: 16g

Carbs: 61.3g

Fiber: 9g

71. Chicken and Broccoli Gratin

Preparation Time: 10 minutes,

Cooking Time: 10 minutes

Servings: 2

Ingredients:

- 1pound of chicken breasts
- 1/4 cup almond butter
- 100 cl of fresh cream
- 1 cup goat cheese
- 2 organic eggs
- 2 Crushed garlic cloves
- 1 pinch of salt
- 1 Pinch of pepper

Directions:

1. Cook the broccoli in a pot of water for 10 minutes. It must remain firm.

2. Melt the butter in a skillet; add the crushed garlic clove and the salted and peppered chicken. Let it get a brown color.

3. Drain the broccoli and mix with the chicken.

4. Beat the eggs with the cream, salt, and pepper. Place broccoli and chicken in a baking dish, cover with cream mixture and sprinkle with grated cheese.

5. Put in the oven at 390°F for 20 minutes.

6. When the gratin is ready; set it aside to cool for 3 minutes

7. Cut the gratin into two halves or in four portions

8. Place every two portions of gratin in a container so that you have two containers.

Nutrition:

Calories: 612

Fat: 48 g

Carbs: 11 g

Protein 34 g

Sugar: 1 g

72. Chicken Curry

Preparation Time: 10 minutes

Cooking Time: 30 minutes

Servings: 2

Ingredients:

- 2 chicken breasts
- 1 garlic clove
- 1 small onion
- 1 zucchini
- 2 carrots
- 1 box of bamboo shoots or sprouts
- 1 cup coconut milk
- 1 Tablespoon. tomato paste
- 2 tablespoons. yellow curry paste

Directions:

1. Mince the onion and sauté in a pan with a little oil for a few minutes.

2. Add chicken cut in large cubes and crushed garlic, salt, pepper and sauté quickly over high heat until meat begins to color.

3. Pour zucchini and carrots in thick slices into the pan.

4. Sear over high heat for a few minutes, then add the coconut milk, tomato sauce, bamboo shoots and one to two tablespoons curry paste, depending on your taste.

5. Cook over low heat and cover for 30 to 45 minutes, stirring occasionally

6. Once cooked, divide the chicken curry between 2 containers

7. Store the containers in the refrigerator

Nutrition:

Calories: 626

Fat: 53.2 g

Carbs: 9 g

Protein 27.8 g

Sugar: 3 g;

CHAPTER 6:

Salad Recipes

73. Barb's Asian Slaw

Preparation Time: 5 minutes

Cooking Time: 5 minutes

Servings: 2

Ingredients:

- 1 cabbage head, shredded
- 4 chopped green onions
- ½ cup slivered or sliced almonds

Dressing: ½ cup olive oil

- ¼ cup tamari or soy sauce
- 1 tablespoon honey or maple syrup
- 1 tablespoon baking stevia

Directions:

1. Heat up dressing ingredients in a saucepan on the stove until thoroughly mixed.
2. Mix all ingredients when you are ready to serve.

Nutrition: Calories: 205 Protein: 27g

Carbohydrate: 12g Fat: 10 g

74. Blueberry Cantaloupe Avocado Salad

Preparation Time: 5 minutes

Cooking Time: 0 minutes

Servings: 2

Ingredients:

- 1 diced cantaloupe
- 2–3 chopped avocados

- 1 package of blueberries
- ¼ cup olive oil
- 1/8 cup balsamic vinegar

Directions:

1. Mix all ingredients.

Nutrition:

Calories: 406

Protein: 9g

Carbohydrate: 32g

Fat: 5 g

75. Beet Salad (from Israel)

Preparation Time: 5 minutes

Cooking Time: 0 minutes

Servings: 2

Ingredients:

- 2–3 fresh, raw beets grated or shredded in food processor
- 3 tablespoons olive oil
- 2 tablespoons balsamic vinegar
- ¼ teaspoon salt
- 1/3 teaspoon cumin
- Dash stevia powder or liquid
- Dash pepper

Directions:

1. Mix all ingredients together for the best raw beet salad.

Nutrition:

Calories: 156

Protein: 8g

Carbohydrate: 40g

Fat: 5 g

76. Broccoli Salad

Preparation Time: 5 minutes

Cooking Time: 0 minutes

Servings: 2

Ingredients:

- 1 head broccoli, chopped
- 2–3 slices of fried bacon, crumbled
- 1 diced green onion
- ½ cup raisins or craisins
- ½–1 cup of chopped pecans
- ¾ cup sunflower seeds
- ½ cup of pomegranate

Dressing:

- 1 cup organic mayonnaise
- ¼ cup baking stevia
- 2 teaspoons white vinegar

Directions:

1. Mix all ingredients together. Mix dressing and fold into salad.

Nutrition:

Calories: 239

Protein: 10g

Carbohydrate: 33g

Fat: 2 g

77. Rosemary Garlic Potatoes

Preparation Time: 5 minutes

Cooking Time: 30 minutes

Servings: 2

Ingredients:

- 5 red new potatoes, chopped
- ¼ cup olive oil
- 2–3 cloves of minced garlic
- 1 tablespoon rosemary

Directions:

1. Preheat oven to 425 degrees.
2. Stir all ingredients together in a bowl. Pour onto a baking sheet and bake for 30 minutes.

Nutrition:

Calories: 176

Protein: 5g

Carbohydrate: 30g

Fat: 2 g

78. Sweet and Sour Cabbage

Preparation Time: 5 minutes

Cooking Time: 15 minutes

Servings: 2

Ingredients:

- 1 tablespoon honey or maple syrup
- 1 teaspoon baking stevia
- 2 tablespoons water
- 1 tablespoon olive oil
- ¼ teaspoon caraway seeds
- ¼ teaspoon salt
- 1/8 teaspoon pepper
- 2 cups chopped red cabbage
- 1 diced apple

Directions:

1. Cook all ingredients in a covered saucepan on the stove for 15 minutes.

Nutrition:

Calories: 170 Protein: 17g
Carbohydrate: 20g Fat: 8 g

79. Barley and Lentil Salad

Preparation Time: 5 minutes
Cooking Time: 0 minutes
Servings: 2
Ingredients:

- 1 head romaine lettuce
- ¾ cup cooked barley
- 2 cups cooked lentils
- 1 diced carrot
- ¼ chopped red onion
- ¼ cup olives
- ½ chopped cucumber
- 3 tablespoons olive oil
- 2 tablespoons fresh lemon juice

Directions:

1. Mix all ingredients together. Add kosher salt and black pepper to taste.

Nutrition:

Calories: 213 Protein: 21g
Carbohydrate: 6g Fat: 9 g

80. Taste of Normandy Salad

Preparation Time: 25 minutes
Cooking Time: 5 minutes
Servings: 4 to 6
Ingredients:

For the walnuts:

- 2 tablespoons butter

- ¼ cup sugar or honey
- 1 cup walnut pieces
- ½ teaspoon kosher salt
- For the dressing
- 3 tablespoons extra-virgin olive oil
- 1½ tablespoons champagne vinegar
- 1½ tablespoons Dijon mustard
- ¼ teaspoon kosher salt

For the salad:

- 1 head red leaf lettuce, torn into pieces
- 3 heads endive, ends trimmed and leaves separated
- 2 apples, cored and cut into thin wedges
- 1 (8-ounce) Camembert wheel, cut into thin wedges

Directions:

2. To make the walnuts
3. In a skillet over medium-high heat, melt the butter. Stir in the sugar and cook until it dissolves. Add the walnuts and cook for about 5 minutes, stirring, until toasty. Season with salt and transfer to a plate to cool.
4. To make the dressing
5. In a large bowl, whisk the oil, vinegar, mustard, and salt until combined.
6. To make the salad
7. Add the lettuce and endive to the bowl with the dressing and toss to coat. Transfer to a serving platter.

8. Decoratively arrange the apple and Camembert wedges over the lettuce and scatter the walnuts on top. Serve immediately.

Nutrition:

Calories: 699;

Total fat: 52g;

Total carbs: 44g;

Cholesterol: 60mg;

Fiber: 17g; Protein: 23g;

Sodium: 1170mg

81. Norwegian Niçoise Salad: Smoked Salmon, Cucumber, Egg, and Asparagus

Preparation Time: 20 minutes

Cooking Time: 5 minutes

Servings: 4

Ingredients:

- For the vinaigrette
- 3 tablespoons walnut oil
- 2 tablespoons champagne vinegar
- 1 tablespoon chopped fresh dill
- ½ teaspoon kosher salt
- ¼ teaspoon ground mustard
- Freshly ground black pepper

For the salad:

- Handful green beans, trimmed
- 1 (3- to 4-ounce) package spring greens
- 12 spears pickled asparagus
- 4 large soft-boiled eggs, halved
- 8 ounces smoked salmon, thinly sliced
- 1 cucumber, thinly sliced
- 1 lemon, quartered

Directions:

1. To make the dressing
2. In a small bowl, whisk the oil, vinegar, dill, salt, ground mustard, and a few grinds of pepper until emulsified. Set aside.
3. To make the salad
4. Start by blanching the green beans: Bring a pot of salted water to a boil. Drop in the beans. Cook or 1 to 2 minutes until they turn bright green, then immediately drain and rinse under cold water. Set aside.
5. Divide the spring greens among 4 plates. Toss each serving with dressing to taste. Arrange 3 asparagus spears, 1 egg, 2 ounces of salmon, one-fourth of the cucumber slices, and a lemon wedge on each plate. Serve immediately.

Nutrition:

Calories: 257;

Total fat: 18g;

Total carbs: 6g;

Cholesterol: 199mg;

Fiber: 2g; Protein: 19g;

Sodium: 603mg

82. Taste of Normandy Salad

Preparation Time: 25 minutes

Cooking Time: 5 minutes

Servings: 4 to 6

Ingredients:

For the walnuts

- 2 tablespoons butter
- 1/4 cup sugar or honey
- 1 cup walnut pieces
- 1/2 teaspoon kosher salt

For the dressing

- 3 tablespoons extra-virgin olive oil
- 1 1/2 tablespoons champagne vinegar
- 1 1/2 tablespoons Dijon mustard
- 1/4 teaspoon kosher salt

For the salad

- 1 head red leaf lettuce, shredded into pieces
- 3 heads endive, ends trimmed and leaves separated
- 2 apples, cored and divided into thin wedges
- 1 (8-ounce) Camembert wheel, cut into thin wedges

Directions:

1. To make the walnuts
2. Dissolve the butter in a skillet over medium high heat. Stir in the sugar and cook until it dissolves. Add the walnuts and cook for about 5 minutes, stirring, until toasty. Season with salt and transfer to a plate to cool.
3. To make the dressing
4. Whip the oil, vinegar, mustard, and salt in a large bowl until combined.
5. To make the salad
6. Add the lettuce and endive to the bowl with the dressing and toss to coat. Transfer to a serving platter.
7. Decoratively arrange the apple and Camembert wedges over the lettuce and scatter the walnuts on top. Serve immediately.
8. Meal Prep Tip: Prepare the walnuts in advance—in fact, double the quantities and use them throughout the week to add a healthy crunch to

salads, oats, or simply to enjoy as a snack.

Nutrition: Calories: 699 Fat: 52g Carbs: 44g Protein: 23g

83. Broccoli with Herbs and Cheese

Preparation Time: 8 minutes

Cooking Time: 17 minutes

Servings: 4

Ingredients:

- 1/3 cup grated yellow cheese
- 1 large-sized head broccoli, stemmed and cut small florets
- 2 1/2 tablespoons canola oil
- 2 teaspoons dried rosemary
- 2 teaspoons dried basil
- Salt and ground black pepper, to taste

Directions:

1. Bring a medium pan filled with a lightly salted water to a boil. Then, boil the broccoli florets for about 3 minutes.
2. Then, drain the broccoli florets well; toss them with the canola oil, rosemary, basil, salt and black pepper.
3. Set your oven to 390 degrees F; arrange the seasoned broccoli in the cooking basket; set the timer for 17 minutes. Toss the broccoli halfway through the cooking process.
4. Serve warm topped with grated cheese and enjoy!

Nutrition:

Calories: 111 Fat: 2.1g Carbs: 3.9g Protein: 8.9g

84. Potato Carrot Salad

Preparation Time: 15 Minutes

Cooking Time: 10 Minutes

Servings: 1

Ingredients:

Water

- One potato, sliced into cubes
- 1/2 carrots, cut into cubes
- 1/6 tablespoon milk
- 1/6 tablespoon Dijon mustard
- 1/24 cup mayonnaise
- Pepper to taste
- 1/3 teaspoons fresh thyme, chopped
- 1/6 stalk celery, chopped
- 1/6 scallions, chopped
- 1/6 slice turkey bacon, cooked crispy and crumbled

Directions:

1. Fill your pot with water.
2. Place it over medium-high heat.
3. Boil the potatoes and carrots for 10 to 12 minutes or until tender.
4. Drain and let cool.
5. In a bowl, mix the milk mustard, mayo, pepper, and thyme.
6. Stir in the potatoes, carrots, and celery.
7. Coat evenly with the sauce.
8. Cover and refrigerate for 4 hours.
9. Top with the scallions and turkey bacon bits before serving.

Nutrition:

Calories 106

Fat 5.3 g

Carbohydrates 12.6 g

Protein 2 g

85. Marinated Veggie Salad

Preparation Time: 4 Hours and 30 Minutes

Cooking Time: 3 Minutes

Servings: 1

Ingredients:

- One zucchini, sliced
- Four tomatoes, sliced into wedges
- 1/4 cup red onion, sliced thinly
- One green bell pepper, sliced
- 2 tablespoons fresh parsley, chopped
- 2 tablespoons red-wine vinegar
- 2 tablespoons olive oil
- 1 clove garlic, minced
- 1 teaspoon dried basil
- 2 tablespoons water
- Pine nuts, toasted and chopped

Directions:

1. In a bowl, combine the zucchini, tomatoes, red onion, green bell pepper, and parsley.
2. Pour the vinegar and oil into a glass jar with a lid.
3. Add the garlic, basil, and water.
4. Seal the jar and stir well to combine.
5. Pour the dressing into the vegetable mixture.
6. Cover the bowl.
7. Marinate in the refrigerator for 4 hours.
8. Garnish with the pine nuts before serving.

Nutrition:

Calories 65

Fat 4.7 g

Carbohydrates 5.3 g

Protein 0.9 g

86. Mediterranean Salad

Preparation Time: 20 Minutes

Cooking Time: 5 Minutes

Servings: 1

Ingredients:

- 1 teaspoon balsamic vinegar
- 1/2 tablespoon basil pesto
- 1/2 cup lettuce
- 1/8 cup broccoli florets, chopped
- 1/8 cup zucchini, chopped
- 1/8 cup tomato, chopped
- 1/8 cup yellow bell pepper, chopped
- 1/2 tablespoons feta cheese, crumbled

Directions:

1. Arrange the lettuce on a serving platter.
2. Top with the broccoli, zucchini, tomato, and bell pepper.
3. In a bowl, mix the vinegar and pesto.
4. Drizzle the dressing on top.
5. Sprinkle the feta cheese and serve.

Nutrition:

Calories 100

Fat 6 g

Carbohydrates 7 g

Protein 4 g

87. Potato Tuna Salad

Preparation Time: 4 Hours and 20 Minutes

Cooking Time: 10 Minutes

Servings: 1

Ingredients:

- 1 potato, peeled and sliced into cubes
- 1/12 cup plain yogurt
- 1/12 cup mayonnaise
- 1/6 clove garlic, crushed and minced
- 1/6 tablespoon almond milk
- 1/6 tablespoon fresh dill, chopped
- 1/2 teaspoon lemon zest
- Salt to taste
- 1 cup cucumber, chopped
- 1/4 cup scallions, chopped
- 1/4 cup radishes, chopped
- 9 oz. canned tuna flakes
- 1/2 hard-boiled eggs, chopped
- One cups lettuce, chopped

Directions:

1. Fill your pot with water.
2. Add the potatoes and boil.
3. Cook for 15 minutes or till slightly tender.
4. Drain and let cool.
5. In a bowl, mix the yogurt, mayo, garlic, almond milk, fresh dill, lemon zest, and salt.
6. Stir in the potatoes, tuna flakes, and eggs. Mix well.
7. Chill in the refrigerator for 4 hours.
8. Stir in the shredded lettuce before serving.

Nutrition:

Calories 243

Fat 9.9 g

Carbohydrates 22.2 g

Protein 17.5 g

88. Jicama and Spinach Salad

Preparation Time: 10 Minutes

Cooking Time: 20 Minutes

Servings: 1

Ingredients:

- 2 oz baby spinach, washed and dried
- Grape or cherry tomatoes, cut in half
- 1/2 jicama, washed, peeled, and cut in strips

- Green or Kalamata olives, chopped
- 2 tbsp walnuts, chopped
- 1/2 tsp raw or roasted sunflower seeds
- Maple Mustard Dressing
- 1/2 heaping tbsp Dijon mustard
- Dash cayenne pepper
- 1 tbsp maple syrup
- 1 garlic clove, minced
- 1 to 2 tbsp water
- 1/4 tsp sea salt

Directions:

1. Divide the baby spinach onto four salad plates.
2. Top each serving with 1/4 of the jicama, 1/4 of the chopped olives, and four tomatoes.
3. Sprinkle 1 tsp of the sunflower seeds and 2 tsp of the walnuts.
4. In a small mixing bowl, whisk all the ingredients together until emulsified.
5. Check the taste and add more maple syrup for sweetness.
6. Drizzle 1 1/2 tbsp of the dressing over each salad and serve.

Nutrition:
Calories: 196 Fat: 2 g
Protein: 7 g Carbs: 28 g

89. High Protein Salad

Preparation Time: 5 Minutes
Cooking Time: 5 Minutes
Servings: 1
Ingredients:

- Salad:
- 1 15-oz can green kidney beans
- 1 4 tbsp capers
- 1 4 handfuls arugula
- 1 15-oz can lentils
- Dressing:
- 1 tbsp. caper brine
- 1 tbsp. tamari
- 1 tbsp. balsamic vinegar
- 2 tbsps. peanut butter
- 2 tbsps. hot sauce
- 1 tbsp. tahini

Directions:

1. In a bowl, stir all the ingredients until they come together to form a smooth dressing.
2. Mix the beans, arugula, capers, and lentils.
3. Top with the dressing and serve.

Nutrition:
Calories: 205
Fat: 2 g
Protein: 13 g
Carbs: 31 g

90. Rice and Veggie Bowl

Preparation Time: 5 Minutes
Cooking Time: 15 Minutes
Servings: 1
Ingredients:

- 1/3 tbsp. coconut oil
- 1/2 tsp. ground cumin
- 1/2 tsp. ground turmeric
- 1/3 tsp. chili powder
- 1 red bell pepper, chopped
- 1/2 tbsp. tomato paste
- 1 bunch of broccolis, cut into bite-sized florets with short stems
- 1/2 tsp. salt, to taste
- 1 large red onion, sliced
- 1/2 garlic cloves, minced

- 1/2 head of cauliflower, sliced into bite-sized florets
- 1/2 cups cooked rice
- Newly ground black pepper to taste

Directions:

1. Start with warming up the coconut oil over medium-high heat.
2. Stir in the turmeric, cumin, chili powder, salt, and tomato paste.
3. Cook the content for 1 minute. Stir repeatedly until the spices are fragrant.
4. Add the garlic and onion. Fry for 2 to 3 minutes until the onions are softened.
5. Add the broccoli, cauliflower, and bell pepper. Cover then cook for 3 to 4 minutes and stir occasionally.
6. Add the cooked rice. Stir so it will combine well with the vegetables— Cook for 2 to 3 minutes. Stir until the rice is warm.
7. Check the seasoning and change to taste if desired.
8. Lessen the heat and cook on low for 2 to 3 more minutes so the flavors will meld.
9. Serve with freshly ground black pepper.

Nutrition:

Calories: 260 Fat: 9 g

Protein: 9 g Carbs: 36 g

91. Squash Black Bean Bowl

Preparation Time: 5 Minutes

Cooking Time: 30 Minutes

Servings: 1

Ingredients:

- One large spaghetti squash, halved,

- 1/3 cup water (or 2 tbsp. olive oil, rubbed on the inside of squash)
- Black bean filling
- 1/2 15-oz can of black beans, emptied and rinsed
- 1/2 cup fire-roasted corn (or frozen sweet corn)
- 1/2 cup thinly sliced red cabbage
- 1/2 tbsp. chopped green onion, green and white parts
- 1/4 cup chopped fresh cilantro
- 1/2 lime, juiced or to taste
- Pepper and salt, to taste
- Avocado mash:
- One ripe avocado, mashed
- 1/2 lime, juiced or to taste
- 1/4 tsp. cumin

Pepper and pinch of sea salt

Directions:

1. Preheat the oven to 400°F.
2. Chop the squash in part and scoop out the seeds with a spoon, like a pumpkin.
3. Fill the roasting pan with 1/3 cup of water. Lay the squash, cut side down, in the pan. Bake for 30 minutes until soft and tender.
4. While this is baking, mix all the ingredients for the black bean filling in a medium-sized bowl.
5. In a small dish, crush the avocado and blend in the ingredients for the avocado mash.
6. Eliminate the squash from the oven and let it cool for 5 minutes. Scrape the squash with a fork so that it looks like spaghetti noodles. Then, fill it with black bean filling and top with avocado mash.

7. Serve and enjoy.

Nutrition:

Calories: 85

Fat: 0.5 g

Protein: 4 g

Carbs: 6 g

92. Pea Salad

Preparation Time: 10 Minutes

Cooking Time: 15 Minutes

Servings: 1

Ingredients:

- 1/2 cup chickpeas, rinsed and drained
- 1/2 cups peas, divided
- Salt to taste
- One tablespoon olive oil
- 1/2 cup buttermilk
- Pepper to taste
- 2 cups pea greens
- 1/2 carrots shaved
- 1/4 cup snow peas, trimmed

Directions:

1. Add the chickpeas and half of the peas to your food processor.
2. Season with the salt.
3. Pulse until smooth. Set aside.
4. In a bowl, toss the remaining peas in oil, milk, salt, and pepper.
5. Transfer the mixture to your food processor.
6. Process until pureed.
7. Transfer this mixture to a bowl.
8. Arrange the pea greens on a serving plate.
9. Top with the shaved carrots and snow peas.
10. Stir in the pea and milk dressing.

11. Serve with the reserved chickpea hummus.

Nutrition:

Calories 214

Fat 8.6 g

Carbohydrates 27.3 g

Protein 8 g

93. Snap Pea Salad

Preparation Time: 15 minutes

Cooking Time: 3. minutes

Servings: 1

Ingredients:

- 1/2 tablespoons mayonnaise
- 3/4 teaspoon celery seed
- 1/4 cup cider vinegar
- 1/2 teaspoon yellow mustard
- 1/2 tablespoon sugar
- Salt and pepper to taste
- 1 oz. radishes, sliced thinly
- 2 oz. sugar snap peas, sliced thinly

Directions:

1. In a bowl, combine the mayonnaise, celery seeds, vinegar, mustard, sugar, salt, and pepper.
2. Stir in the radishes and snap peas.
3. Refrigerate for 30 minutes.

Nutrition:

Calories 69 Fat 3.7 g

Carbohydrates 7.1 g Protein 2 g

94. Cucumber Tomato Chopped Salad

Preparation Time: 10 Minutes

Cooking Time: 5 Minutes

Servings: 1

Ingredients:

- 1/4 cup light mayonnaise
- 1/2 tablespoon lemon juice
- 1/2 tablespoon fresh dill, chopped
- 1/2 tablespoon chive, chopped
- 1/4 cup feta cheese, crumbled
- Salt and pepper to taste
- 1/2 red onion, chopped
- 1/2 cucumber, diced
- 1/2 radish, diced
- One tomato, diced
- Chives, chopped

Directions:

1. Combine the mayo, lemon juice, fresh dill, chives, feta cheese, salt, and pepper in a bowl.
2. Mix well.
3. Stir in the onion, cucumber, radish, and tomatoes.
4. Coat evenly.
5. Garnish with the chopped chives.

Nutrition:

Calories 187

Fat 16.7 g

Carbohydrates 6.7 g

Protein 3.3 g

95. Zucchini Pasta Salad

Preparation Time: 4 Minutes

Cooking Time: 5 Minutes

Servings: 1

Ingredients:

- 1 tablespoon olive oil
- 1/2 teaspoons Dijon mustard
- 1/3 tablespoons red-wine vinegar
- 1/2 clove garlic, grated
- 2 tablespoons fresh oregano, chopped
- 1/2 shallot, chopped

- 1/4 teaspoon red pepper flakes
- 4 oz. zucchini noodles
- 1/4 cup Kalamata olives pitted
- 1 cups cherry tomato, sliced in half
- 3/4 cup Parmesan cheese shaved

Directions:

1. Mix the olive oil, Dijon mustard, red wine vinegar, garlic, oregano, shallot, and red pepper flakes in a bowl.
2. Stir in the zucchini noodles.
3. Sprinkle on top the olives, tomatoes, and Parmesan cheese.

Nutrition:

Calories 299

Fat 24.7 g

Carbohydrates 11.6 g

Protein 7 g

96. Egg Avocado Salad

Preparation Time: 10 Minutes

Cooking Time: 30 Minutes

Servings: 1

Ingredients:

- 1/2 avocado
- One hard-boiled egg, peeled and chopped
- 1/4 tablespoon mayonnaise
- 1/4 tablespoons freshly squeezed lemon juice
- 1/4 cup celery, chopped
- 1/2 tablespoons chives, chopped
- Salt and pepper to taste

Directions:

1. Add the avocado to a large bowl.
2. Mash the avocado using a fork.
3. Stir in the egg and mash the eggs.
4. Add the mayo, lemon juice, celery, chives, salt, and pepper.

5. Chill in the refrigerator for at least 20 to 30 minutes before serving.

Nutrition:

Calories 224

Fat 18 g

Carbohydrates 6.1 g

Protein 10.6 g

97. Buttered Carrot-Zucchini with Mayo

Preparation Time: 15 minutes

Cooking Time: 25 minutes

Servings: 4

Ingredients:

- 1 tablespoon grated onion
- 2 tablespoons butter, melted
- 1/2-pound carrots, sliced
- 1-1/2 zucchinis, sliced
- 1/4 cup water
- 1/4 cup mayonnaise
- 1/4 teaspoon prepared horseradish
- 1/4 teaspoon salt
- 1/4 teaspoon ground black pepper
- 1/4 cup Italian breadcrumbs

Directions:

1. Lighten skillet with cooking spray. Add the carrots. Cook for 360 minutes at 360F. Add the zucchini and continue cooking for another 5 minutes.
2. Meanwhile, in a bowl, whisk together the pepper, salt, horseradish, onion, mayonnaise, and water. Pour into a vegetable skillet. Pull well over the coat.
3. In a small bowl, combine the melted butter and breadcrumbs. Sprinkle over the vegetables.

4. Cook for 10 minutes at 390F until tops are lightly browned.
5. Serve and enjoy.

Nutrition:

Calories: 223

Carbs: 13.8g

Protein: 2.7g

Fat: 17.4g

98. Smoked Salmon, Cucumber, Egg, and Asparagus

Preparation Time: 20 minutes

Cooking Time: 5 minutes

Servings: 4

Ingredients:

- For the vinaigrette
- 3 tablespoons walnut oil
- 2 tablespoons champagne vinegar
- 1 tablespoon chopped fresh dill
- 1/2 teaspoon kosher salt
- 1/4 teaspoon ground mustard
- Freshly ground black pepper
- For the salad:
- Handful green beans, trimmed
- 1 (3- to 4-ounce) package spring greens
- 12 spears pickled asparagus
- 4 large soft-boiled eggs, halved
- 8 ounces smoked salmon, thinly sliced
- 1 cucumber, thinly sliced
- 1 lemon, quartered

Directions:

1. To make the dressing
2. In a small bowl, whisk the oil, vinegar, dill, salt, ground mustard, and a few pepper grinds until emulsified. Set aside.

3. To make the salad
4. Start by blanching the green beans: Bring a pot of salted water to a boil. Drop in the beans. Cook or 1 to 2 minutes until they turn bright green, then immediately drain and rinse under cold water. Set aside.
5. Divide the spring greens among 4 plates. Toss each serving with dressing to taste. Arrange 3 asparagus spears, 1 egg, 2 ounces of salmon, one-fourth of the cucumber slices, and a lemon wedge on each plate. Serve immediately.

Nutrition:
Calories: 257;
Fat: 18g;
Carbs: 6g;
Protein: 19g;

99. Almond Flour Battered 'n Crisped Onion Rings

Preparation Time: 10 minutes
Cooking Time: 15 minutes
Servings: 3
Ingredients:

- ½ cup almond flour
- ¾ cup coconut milk
- 1 big white onion, sliced into rings
- 1 egg, beaten
- 1 tablespoon baking powder
- 1 tablespoon smoked paprika
- Salt and pepper to taste

Directions:

1. Preheat the air fryer for 5 minutes.
2. In a mixing bowl, mix the almond flour, baking powder, smoked paprika, salt and pepper.

3. In another bowl, combine the eggs and coconut milk.
4. Soak the onion slices into the egg mixture.
5. Dredge the onion slices in the almond flour mixture.
6. Place in the air fryer basket.
7. Close and cook for 15 minutes at 3250F.
8. Halfway through the cooking time, shake the fryer basket for even cooking.

Nutrition:
Calories: 217
Carbohydrates: 8.6g
Protein:5.3g
Fat: 17.9g

100. Tomato Bites with Creamy Parmesan Sauce

Preparation Time:7 minutes
Cooking Time: 13 minutes
Servings: 4
Ingredients:

- For the Sauce:
- 1/2 cup Parmigiano-Reggiano cheese, grated
- 4 tablespoons pecans, chopped
- 1 teaspoon garlic puree
- 1/2 teaspoon fine sea salt
- 1/3 cup extra-virgin olive oil
- For the Tomato Bites:
- 2 large-sized Roma tomatoes, cut into thin slices and pat them dry
- 8 ounces Halloumi cheese, cut into thin slices
- 1/3 cup onions, sliced
- 1 teaspoon dried basil

- 1/4 teaspoon red pepper flakes, crushed
- 1/8 teaspoon sea salt

Directions:

1. Start by preheating your Air Fryer to 385 degrees F.
2. Make the sauce by mixing all ingredients, except the extra-virgin olive oil, in your food processor.
3. While the machine is running, slowly and gradually pour in the olive oil; puree until everything is well - blended.
4. Now, spread 1 teaspoon of the sauce over the top of each tomato slice. Place a slice of Halloumi cheese on each tomato slice.
5. Add onion slices on top. Put some basil, red pepper, and sea salt.
6. Transfer the assembled bites to the Air Fryer. Add non-stick cooking spray and cook for about 13 minutes.
7. Arrange these bites on a nice serving platter, garnish with the remaining sauce and serve at room temperature. Bon appétit!

Nutrition:

Calories: 428

Fat: 38.4g

Carbs: 4.5g

Protein: 18.8g

101. Simple Green Beans with Butter

Preparation Time: 2 minutes

Cooking Time: 10 minutes

Servings: 4

Ingredients:

- 3/4-pound green beans, cleaned

- 1 tablespoon balsamic vinegar
- 1/4 teaspoon kosher salt
- 1/2 teaspoon mixed peppercorns, freshly cracked
- 1 tablespoon butter
- 2 tablespoons toasted sesame seeds, to serve

Directions:

1. Set your Air Fryer to cook at 390 degrees F.
2. Mix the green beans with all the above ingredients, apart from the sesame seeds. Set the timer for 10 minutes.
3. Meanwhile, toast the sesame seeds in a small-sized nonstick skillet; make sure to stir continuously.
4. Serve sautéed green beans on a nice serving platter sprinkled with toasted sesame seeds. Bon appétit!

Nutrition:

Calories: 73

Fat: 3.0g

Carbs: 6.1g

Protein: 1.6g

102. Mediterranean-Style Eggs with Spinach

Preparation Time: 3 minutes

Cooking Time: 12 minutes

Servings: 2

Ingredients:

- 2 tablespoons olive oil, melted
- 4 eggs, whisked
- 5 ounces' fresh spinach, chopped
- 1 medium-sized tomato, chopped
- 1 teaspoon fresh lemon juice
- 1/2 teaspoon coarse salt

- 1/2 teaspoon ground black pepper
- 1/2 cup of fresh basil, roughly chopped

Directions:

1. Add the olive oil to an Air Fryer baking pan. Make sure to tilt the pan to spread the oil evenly.
2. Simply combine the remaining ingredients, except for the basil leaves; whisk well until everything is well incorporated.
3. Cook in the preheated oven for 8 to 12 minutes at 280 degrees F. Garnish with fresh basil leaves. Serve.

Nutrition:

Calories: 274 Fat: 23.2g

Carbs: 5.7g

Protein: 13.7g

103. Baked Cod & Vegetables

Preparation Time: 15 minutes

Cooking Time: 15 minutes

Servings: 4

Ingredients:

- 1 lb cod fillets
- 8 oz asparagus, chopped
- 3 cups broccoli, chopped
- ¼ cup parsley, minced
- ½ tsp lemon pepper seasoning
- ½ tsp paprika
- ¼ cup olive oil
- ¼ cup lemon juice
- 1 tsp salt

Directions:

1. Preheat oven to 400 F. Line a baking sheet with parchment paper and set aside.

2. In a small bowl, combine the lemon juice, paprika, olive oil, pepper spices, and salt.
3. Place the fish fillets in the center of the greaseproof paper. Arrange the broccoli and asparagus around the fish fillets.
4. Pour lemon juice mixture over the fish fillets and top with parsley.
5. Bake in preheated oven for 13-15 minutes.
6. Serve and enjoy.

Nutrition:

Calories 240

Fat 11 g

Carbs 6 g

Sugar 6 g

Protein 27 g

Cholesterol 56 mg

104. Parmesan Zucchini

Preparation Time: 15 minutes

Cooking Time: 15 minutes

Servings: 4

Ingredients:

- 4 zucchini, quartered lengthwise
- 2 tbsp fresh parsley, chopped
- 2 tbsp olive oil
- ¼ tsp garlic powder
- ½ tsp dried basil
- ½ tsp dried oregano
- ½ tsp dried thyme
- ½ cup parmesan cheese, grated
- Pepper
- Salt

Directions:

1. Preheat the oven to 350 F. Line baking sheet with parchment paper and set aside.
2. In a small bowl, mix together parmesan cheese, garlic powder, basil, oregano, thyme, pepper, and salt.
3. Arrange zucchini onto the prepared baking sheet and drizzle with oil and sprinkle with parmesan cheese mixture.
4. Bake in preheated oven for 15 minutes then broil for 2 minutes or until lightly golden brown.
5. Garnish with parsley and serve immediately.

Nutrition:

Calories 244 Fat 14 g

Carbs 7 g Sugar 5 g Protein 15 g

Cholesterol 30 mg

105. Chicken Zucchini Noodles

Preparation Time: 20 minutes

Cooking Time: 5 minutes

Servings: 2

Ingredients:

- 1 large zucchini, spiralized
- 1 chicken breast, skinless & boneless
- ½ tbsp jalapeno, minced
- 2 garlic cloves, minced
- ½ tsp ginger, minced
- ½ tbsp fish sauce
- 2 tbsp coconut cream
- ½ tbsp honey
- ½ lime juice
- 1 tbsp peanut butter
- 1 carrot, chopped
- 2 tbsp cashews, chopped
- ¼ cup fresh cilantro, chopped
- 1 tbsp olive oil
- Pepper
- Salt

Directions:

1. Heat olive oil in a pan over medium-high heat.
2. Season chicken breast with pepper and salt. Once the oil is hot then add chicken breast into the pan and cook for 3-4 minutes per side or until cooked.
3. Remove chicken breast from pan. Shred chicken breast with a fork and set aside.
4. In a small bowl, mix together peanut butter, jalapeno, garlic, ginger, fish sauce, coconut cream, honey, and lime juice. Set aside.
5. In a large mixing bowl, combine together spiralized zucchini, carrots, cashews, cilantro, and shredded chicken.
6. Pour peanut butter mixture over zucchini noodles and toss to combine.
7. Serve immediately and enjoy.

Nutrition:

Calories 353

Fat 21 g

Carbs 20.5 g

Sugar 8 g

Protein 25 g

Cholesterol 54 mg

106. Tuscan Cauliflower Salad

Preparation Time: 10 minutes;

Cooking time: 10 minutes

Servings: 8

Ingredients

- Cauliflower florets - 4 cups
- Tuscan seasoning - 1 tablespoon
- Apple cider vinegar - 1/4 cup

Directions:

1. Add the Ingredients to a bowl and toss together.
2. Allow the mixture to settle for about 30 minutes. It can stay overnight.
3. Serve.
4. You can store it in your fridge for up to a week.

Nutrition:

Calories: 117

Fat: 9g

Carbs: 4g

Protein: 5g

107. Brussels Sprouts with Balsamic Oil

Preparation Time: 5 minutes

Cooking Time: 15 minutes

Servings: 4

Ingredients:

- 1/4 teaspoon salt
- 1 tablespoon balsamic vinegar
- 2 cups Brussels sprouts, halved
- 2 tablespoons olive oil

Directions:

1. Preheat the air fryer for 5 minutes.
2. Mix all ingredients in a bowl. Coat well zucchini fries.
3. Place in the air fryer basket.
4. Close and cook for 15 minutes for 350F.

Nutrition:

Calories: 82

Carbohydrates: 4.6g

Protein: 1.5g

Fat: 6.8g

108. Kale-Baby Bok Salad and Ranch Dressing

Preparation Time: 10 minutes

Cooking Time: 10 minutes

Servings: 2

Ingredients:

For the Salad:

- Baby bok (shredded) - 3-4 cups
- Kale greens (shredded) - 3-4 cups

For the dressing:

- Light sour cream (or use low-fat yogurt) - 4 tablespoon
- Almond milk (unsweetened) - 1/2 cup
- Rockin' ranch seasoning - 1 tablespoon

Directions:

1. Add the greens to a bowl.
2. Put all Ingredients for the dressing in another bowl and whisk to combine.
3. Allow the dressing to sit for about 10 minutes.
4. Spread the dressing on the salad and toss.
5. Serve.

Nutrition:

Calories: 100 Fat: 4g

Carbs: 13g

Protein: 2g

CHAPTER 7:

Snack recipes

109. Spicy Korean Cauliflower Bites

Preparation Time: 15 minutes

Cooking Time: 30 minutes

Servings: 4

Ingredients:

- 2 eggs
- 1 lb. cauliflower
- 2/3 cups of corn starch
- 2 teaspoon smoked paprika
- 1 teaspoon garlic grated
- 1 teaspoon ginger grated
- 1 lb. panko
- 1 teaspoon sea salt

For the Korean barbecue sauce:

- 1 cup ketchup
- ½ cup Korea chili flakes
- ½ cup minced garlic
- ½ cup red pepper

Directions:

1. Cut the cauliflower into small sizes based on your taste and preference.
2. In a small bowl add cornstarch and eggs and mix them until they are smooth.
3. Add onions, garlic, ginger, smoked paprika and coat them with panko.

4. Apply some pressure so that the panko can stick and repeat this with all the cauliflower.

Nutrition:

Calories: 141 Fat: 12 g

Carbs: 23 g Protein: 27 g

110. Grilled Salmon Burger

Preparation Time: 15 minutes

Cooking Time: 10 minutes

Servings: 4

Ingredients:

- 16 ounces (450 g) pink salmon fillet, minced
- 1 cup (250 g) prepared mashed potatoes
- 1 shallot (about 40 g), chopped
- 1 large egg (about 60 g), lightly beaten
- 2 tablespoons (7 g) fresh coriander, chopped
- 4 Hamburger buns (about 60 g each), split
- 1 large tomato (about 150 g), sliced
- 8 (15 g) Romaine lettuce leaves
- 1/4 cup (60 g) mayonnaise
- Salt and freshly ground black pepper
- Cooking oil spray

Directions:

1. Combine the salmon, mashed potatoes, shallot, egg, and coriander in a mixing bowl. Season with salt and pepper.

2. Spoon about 2 tablespoons of mixture and form into patties.

3. Preheat your grill or griddle on high. Grease with cooking oil spray.

4. Grill the salmon patties for 4-5 minutes on each side or until cooked through. Transfer to a clean plate and cover to keep warm.

5. Spread some mayonnaise on the bottom half of buns. Top with lettuce, salmon patty, and tomato. Cover with bun tops.

6. Serve and enjoy.

Nutrition:

Calories: 395

Fat - 18.0 g

Carbohydrates - 38.8 g

Protein - 21.8 g

Sodium - 383 mg

111. Easy Salmon Burger

Preparation Time: 15 minutes

Cooking Time: 15 minutes

Servings: 6

Ingredients:

- 16 ounces (450 g) pink salmon, minced
- 1 cup (250 g) prepared mashed potatoes
- 1 medium (110 g) onion, chopped
- 1 stalk celery (about 60 g), finely chopped
- 1 large egg (about 60 g), lightly beaten
- 2 tablespoons (7 g) fresh cilantro, chopped
- 1 cup (100 g) breadcrumbs
- Vegetable oil, for deep frying
- Salt and freshly ground black pepper

Directions:

1. Combine the salmon, mashed potatoes, onion, celery, egg, and cilantro in a mixing bowl. Season to taste and mix thoroughly.

Spoon about 2 Tablespoon mixture, roll in breadcrumbs, and then form into small patties.

2. Heat oil in non-stick frying pan. Cook your salmon patties for 5 minutes on each side or until golden brown and crispy.

3. Serve in burger buns and with coleslaw on the side if desired.

4. Enjoy.

Nutrition:

Calories 230

Fat 7.9 g

Carbs 20.9 g

Protein 18.9 g

Sodium 298 mg

112. Salmon Sandwich with Avocado and Egg

Preparation Time: 15 minutes

Cooking Time: 10 minutes

Servings: 4

Ingredients:

- 8 ounces (250 g) smoked salmon, thinly sliced
- 1 medium (200 g) ripe avocado, thinly sliced
- 4 large poached eggs (about 60 g each)
- 4 slices whole wheat bread (about 30 g each)
- 2 cups (60 g) arugula or baby rocket
- Salt and freshly ground black pepper

Directions:

1. Place 1 bread slice on a plate top with arugula, avocado, salmon, and poached egg. Season with salt and pepper. Repeat procedure for the remaining ingredients.

2. Serve and enjoy.

Nutrition:

Calories: 310

Fat: 18.2 g

Carbohydrates: 16.4 g

Protein: 21.3 g

Sodium: 383 mg

113. Salmon Spinach and Cottage Cheese Sandwich

Preparation Time: 15 minutes

Cooking Time: 10 minutes

Servings: 4

Ingredients:

- 4 ounces (125 g) cottage cheese
- 1/4 cup (15 g) chives, chopped
- 1 teaspoon (5 g) capers
- 1/2 teaspoon (2.5 g) grated lemon rind
- 4 (2 oz. or 60 g) smoked salmon
- 2 cups (60 g) loose baby spinach
- 1 medium (110 g) red onion, sliced thinly
- 8 slices rye bread (about 30 g each)
- Kosher salt and freshly ground black pepper

Directions:

1. Preheat your griddle or Panini press.
2. Mix together cottage cheese, chives, capers, and lemon rind in a small bowl.
3. Spread and divide the cheese mixture on 4 bread slices. Top with spinach, onion slices, and smoked salmon.
4. Cover with remaining bread slices.
5. Grill the sandwiches until golden and grill marks form on both sides.
6. Transfer to a serving dish.
7. Serve and enjoy.

Nutrition:

Calories: 261 Fat 9.9 g

Carbohydrates 22.9 g Protein 19.9 g

Sodium - 1226 mg

114. Salmon Feta and Pesto Wrap

Preparation Time: 15 minutes

Cooking Time: 10 minutes

Servings: 4

Ingredients:

- 8 ounces (250 g) smoked salmon fillet, thinly sliced
- 1 cup (150 g) feta cheese
- 8 (15 g) Romaine lettuce leaves
- 4 (6-inch) pita bread
- 1/4 cup (60 g) basil pesto sauce

Directions:

1. Place 1 pita bread on a plate. Top with lettuce, salmon, feta cheese, and pesto sauce. Fold or roll to enclose filling. Repeat procedure for the remaining ingredients.
2. Serve and enjoy.

Nutrition:

Calories: 379 Fat 17.7 g

Carbohydrates: 36.6 g Protein: 18.4 g

Sodium: 554 mg

115. Salmon Cream Cheese and Onion on Bagel

Preparation Time: 15 minutes

Cooking Time: 10 minutes

Servings: 4

Ingredients:

- 8 ounces (250 g) smoked salmon fillet, thinly sliced

- 1/2 cup (125 g) cream cheese
- 1 medium (110 g) onion, thinly sliced
- 4 bagels (about 80g each), split
- 2 tablespoons (7 g) fresh parsley, chopped
- Freshly ground black pepper, to taste

Directions:

1. Spread the cream cheese on each bottom's half of bagels. Top with salmon and onion, season with pepper, sprinkle with parsley and then cover with bagel tops.
2. Serve and enjoy.

Nutrition:

Calories: 309

Fat 14.1 g

Carbohydrates 32.0 g

Protein 14.7 g

Sodium 571 mg

116. Greek Baklava

Preparation Time: 20 minutes

Cooking Time: 20 minutes

Servings: 18

Ingredients:

- 1 (16 oz.) package phyllo dough
- 1 lb. chopped nuts
- 1 cup butter
- 1 teaspoon ground cinnamon
- 1 cup water
- 1 cup white sugar
- 1 teaspoon. vanilla extract
- 1/2 cup honey

Directions:

1. Preheat the oven to 175°C or 350°Fahrenheit. Spread butter on the sides and bottom of a 9-in by 13-in pan.

2. Chop the nuts then mix with cinnamon; set it aside. Unfurl the phyllo dough then halve the whole stack to fit the pan. Use a damp cloth to cover the phyllo to prevent drying as you proceed. Put two phyllo sheets in the pan then butter well. Repeat to make eight layered phyllo sheets. Scatter 2-3 tablespoons nut mixture over the sheets then place two more phyllo sheets on top, butter then sprinkle with nuts. Layer as you go. The final layer should be six to eight phyllo sheets deep.

3. Make square or diamond shapes with a sharp knife up to the bottom of pan. You can slice into four long rows for diagonal shapes. Bake until crisp and golden for 50 minutes.

4. Meanwhile, boil water and sugar until the sugar melts to make the sauce; mix in honey and vanilla. Let it simmer for 20 minutes.

5. Take the baklava out of the oven then drizzle with sauce right away; cool. Serve the baklava in cupcake papers. You can also freeze them without cover. The baklava will turn soggy when wrapped.

Nutrition:

Calories: 393 Total Carbohydrate: 37.5 g

Cholesterol: 27 mg Total Fat: 25.9 g

Protein: 6.1 g Sodium: 196 mg

117. Glazed Bananas in Phyllo Nut Cups

Preparation Time: 30 minutes

Cooking Time: 45 minutes

Servings: 6 servings.

Ingredients:

- 3/4 cup shelled pistachios
- 1/2 cup sugar

- 1 teaspoon. ground cinnamon
- 4 sheets phyllo dough, (14 inches x 9 inches)
- 1/4 cup butter, melted

Sauce:
- 3/4 cup butter, cubed
- 3/4 cup packed brown sugar
- 3 medium firm bananas, sliced
- 1/4 teaspoon. ground cinnamon
- 3 to 4 cups vanilla ice cream

Directions:

1. Finely chop sugar and pistachios in a food processor; move to a bowl then mix in cinnamon. Slice each phyllo sheet to 6 four-inch squares, get rid of the trimmings. Pile the squares then use plastic wrap to cover.

2. Slather melted butter on each square one at a time then scatter a heaping tablespoonful of pistachio mixture. Pile 3 squares, flip each at an angle to misalign the corners. Force each stack on the sides and bottom of an oiled eight-oz. custard cup. Bake for 15-20 minutes in a 350 degrees F oven until golden; cool for 5 minutes. Move to a wire rack to completely cool.

3. Melt and boil brown sugar and butter in a saucepan to make the sauce; lower heat. Mix in cinnamon and bananas gently; heat completely. Put ice cream in the phyllo cups until full then put banana sauce on top. Serve right away.

Nutrition:

Calories: 735 Total Carbohydrate: 82 g

Cholesterol: 111 mg Total Fat: 45 g

Fiber: 3 g Protein: 7 g

Sodium: 468 mg

118. Salmon Apple Salad Sandwich

Preparation Time: 15 minutes

Cooking Time: 10 minutes

Servings: 4

Ingredients: 4 ounces (125 g) canned pink salmon, drained and flaked

- 1 medium (180 g) red apple, cored and diced
- 1 celery stalk (about 60 g), chopped
- 1 shallot (about 40 g), finely chopped
- 1/3 cup (85 g) light mayonnaise
- 8 slices whole grain bread (about 30 g each), toasted
- 8 (15 g) Romaine lettuce leaves
- Salt and freshly ground black pepper

Directions:

1. Combine the salmon, apple, celery, shallot, and mayonnaise in a mixing bowl. Season with salt and pepper.

2. Place 1 slices bread on a plate, top with lettuce and salmon salad, and then covers with another slice of bread. Repeat procedure for the remaining ingredients.

3. Serve and enjoy.

Nutrition: Calories: 315 Fat - 11.3 g

Carbohydrates - 40.4 g Protein - 15.1 g

Sodium - 469 mg

119. Smoked Salmon and Cheese on Rye Bread

Preparation Time: 15 minutes

Cooking Time: 10 minutes

Servings: 4

Ingredients:

- 8 ounces (250 g) smoked salmon, thinly sliced

- 1/3 cup (85 g) mayonnaise
- 2 tablespoons (30 ml) lemon juice
- 1 tablespoon (15 g) Dijon mustard
- 1 teaspoon (3 g) garlic, minced
- 4 slices cheddar cheese (about 2 oz. or 30 g each)
- 8 slices rye bread (about 2 oz. or 30 g each)
- 8 (15 g) Romaine lettuce leaves
- Salt and freshly ground black pepper

Directions:

1. Mix together the mayonnaise, lemon juice, mustard, and garlic in a small bowl. Flavor with salt and pepper and set aside.
2. Spread dressing on 4 bread slices. Top with lettuce, salmon, and cheese. Cover with remaining rye bread slices.
3. Serve and enjoy.

Nutrition:

Calories: 365 Fat: 16.6 g

Carbohydrates: 31.6 g

Protein: 18.8 g

Sodium: 951 mg

120. Pan-Fried Trout

Preparation Time: 15 minutes

Cooking Time: 10 minutes

Servings: 4

Ingredients:

- 1 ¼ pounds trout fillets
- 1/3 cup white, or yellow, cornmeal
- ¼ teaspoon anise seeds
- ¼ teaspoon black pepper
- ½ cup minced cilantro, or parsley
- Vegetable cooking spray
- Lemon wedges

Directions:

1. Coat fish with combined cornmeal, spices, and cilantro, pressing it gently into fish. Spray large skillet with cooking spray; heat over medium heat until hot.
2. Add fish and cook until fish is tender and flakes with fork, about 5 minutes on each side. Serve with lemon wedges.

Nutrition:

Calories: 207

Total Carbohydrate: 19 g

Cholesterol: 27 mg

Total Fat: 16 g

Fiber: 4 g

Protein: 18g

121. Greek Tuna Salad Bites

Preparation Time: 5 Minutes

Cooking Time: 10 Minutes

Servings: 6

Ingredients:

- Cucumbers (2 medium)
- White tuna (2 - 6 oz. cans.)
- Lemon juice (half of 1 lemon)
- Red bell pepper (.5 cup)
- Sweet/red onion (.25 cup)
- Black olives (.25 cup)
- Garlic (2 tablespoon.)
- Olive oil (2 tablespoon.)
- Fresh parsley (2 tablespoon.)
- Dried oregano - salt & pepper (as desired)

Directions:

1. Drain and flake the tuna. Juice the lemon. Dice/chop the onions, olives, pepper, parsley, and garlic up Slice each of the

cucumbers into thick rounds (skin off or on).

2. In a mixing container, combine the rest of the fixings.

3. Place a heaping spoonful of salad onto the rounds and enjoy for your next party or just a snack.

Nutrition:

Calories: 400

Fats: 22 g

Carbs: 26 g

Fiber Content: 8 g

Protein: 30 g

122. Spinach Artichoke-stuffed Chicken Breasts

Preparation Time: 15 Minutes

Cooking Time: 15 Minutes

Servings: 6

Ingredients:

- ¼ cup Greek yogurt
- ¼ cup spinach, thawed & drained
- ½ cup artichoke hearts, thinly sliced
- ½ cup mozzarella cheese, shredded
- 1 ½ lb. chicken breasts
- 2 tablespoons. olive oil
- 4 ozs. cream cheese
- Sea salt & pepper, to taste

Directions:

1. Pound the chicken breasts to a thickness of about one inch. Using a sharp knife, slice a "pocket" into the side of each. This is where you will put the filling.

2. Sprinkle the breasts with salt and pepper and set aside.

3. In a medium bowl, combine cream cheese, yogurt, mozzarella, spinach, artichoke, salt,

and pepper and mix thoroughly. A hand mixer may be the easiest way to combine all the ingredients thoroughly.

4. Spoon the mixture into the pockets of each breast and set aside while you heat a large skillet over medium heat and warm the oil in it. If you have an extra filling you can't fit into the breasts, set it aside until just before your chicken is done cooking.

5. Cook each breast for about eight minutes per side, then pull off the heat when it reaches an internal temperature of about 165° Fahrenheit.

6. Just before you pull the chicken out of the pan, heat the remaining filling to warm it through and to rid it of any cross-contamination from the chicken. Once hot, top the chicken breasts with it.

7. Serve!

Nutrition:

- Calories: 238 Cal
- Fat: 22 g Carbs: 5 g
- Protein: 17 g Fiber: 4 g

123. Chicken Parmesan

Preparation Time: 20 Minutes

Cooking Time: 15 Minutes

Servings: 4

Ingredients:

- ¼ cup of avocado oil
- ¼ cup of almond flour
- ¼ cup parmesan cheese, grated
- ¾ cup of marinara sauce, sugar-free
- ¾ cup mozzarella cheese, shredded
- 2 eggs, beaten
- 2 teaspoons. Italian seasoning
- 3 oz. pork rinds, pulverized

- 4 lbs. chicken breasts, boneless & skinless
- Sea salt & pepper, to taste

Directions:

1. Preheat the oven to 450° Fahrenheit and grease a baking dish.
2. Place the beaten egg into one shallow dish. Place the almond flour in another. In a third dish, combine the pork rinds, parmesan, and Italian seasoning and mix well.
3. Pat the chicken breasts dry and pound them down to about ½" thick.
4. Dredge the chicken in the almond flour, then coat in egg, then coat in crumb.
5. Heat a large sauté pan over medium-high heat and warm oil until shimmering.
6. Once the oil is hot, lay the breasts into the pan and do not move them until they've had a chance to cook. Cook for about two minutes, then flip as gently as possible (a fish spatula is perfect) then cook for two more. Remove the pan from the heat.
7. Place the breasts in the greased baking dish and top with marinara sauce and mozzarella cheese.
8. Bake for about 10 minutes.
9. Serve!

Nutrition:

- Calories: 621 Cal Fat: 24 g
- Carbs: 6 g Protein: 14 g Fiber: 6 g

124. Sheet Pan Jalapeño Burgers

Preparation Time: 10 Minutes
Cooking Time: 20 Minutes
Servings: 4
Ingredients:

Burgers:

- 24 ozs. ground beef

- Sea salt & pepper, to taste
- ½ teaspoon. garlic powder
- 6 slices bacon, halved
- 1 med. onion, sliced into ¼ rounds
- 2 jalapeños, seeded & sliced
- 4 slices pepper jack cheese
- ¼ cup of mayonnaise
- 1 tablespoon. chili sauce
- ½ teaspoon. Worcestershire sauce
- 8 lbs. leaves of Boston or butter lettuce
- 8 dill pickle chips

Directions:

1. Preheat the oven to 425° Fahrenheit and line a baking sheet with non-stick foil.
2. Mix the salt, pepper, and garlic into the ground beef and form 4 patties out of it.
3. Line the burgers, bacon slices, jalapeño slices, and onion rounds onto the baking sheet and bake for about 18 minutes.
4. Top each patty with a piece of cheese and set the oven to boil.
5. Broil for 2 minutes, then remove the pan from the oven.
6. Serve one patty with 3 pieces of bacon, jalapeño slices, onion rounds, and desired amount of sauce with 2 pickle chips and 2 parts of lettuce.
7. Enjoy!

Nutrition:

- Calories: 608 Cal
- Fat: 29 g
- Carbs: 5 g
- Protein: 16 g
- Fiber: 4 g

125. Grilled Herb Garlic Chicken

Preparation Time: 5 Minutes

Cooking Time: 10 Minutes

Servings: 2

Ingredients:

- 1 ¼ lb. chicken breasts, boneless & skinless - 1 tablespoon. garlic & herb seasoning mix
- 2 teaspoons. extra virgin olive oil - Sea salt & pepper, to taste

Directions:

Heat a grill pan or your grill. Coat the chicken breasts in a little bit of olive oil and then sprinkle the seasoning mixture onto them, rubbing it in. Cook the chicken for about eight minutes per side and make sure the chicken has reached an internal temperature of 165°. Serve hot with your favorite sides!

Nutrition:

- Calories: 187 Cal
- Fat: 24 g
- Carbs: 5 g
- Protein: 12 g
- Fiber: 4 g

126. Blackened Salmon with Avocado Salsa

Preparation Time: 30 Minutes

Cooking Time: 21 Minutes

Servings: 6

Ingredients:

- 1 tablespoon. extra virgin olive oil
- 4 filets of salmon (about 6 ozs. each)
- 4 teaspoons. Cajun seasoning
- 2 med. avocados, diced

- 1 cup cucumber, diced
- ¼ cup red onion, diced
- 1 tablespoon. parsley, chopped
- 1 tablespoon. lime juice
- Sea salt & pepper, to taste

Directions:

1. Heat a skillet over medium-high heat and warm the oil in it.
2. Rub the Cajun seasoning into the fillets, then lay them into the bottom of the skillet once it's hot enough.
3. Cook until a dark crust forms, then flip and repeat.
4. In a medium mixing bowl, combine all the ingredients for the salsa and set aside.
5. Plate the fillets and top with ¼ of the salsa yielded.
6. Enjoy!

Nutrition:

- Calories: 445 Cal
- Fat: 31 g
- Carbs: 6 g
- Protein: 10 g
- Fiber: 5 g

127. Delectable Tomato Slices

Preparation Time: 15 Minutes

Cooking Time: 15 Minutes

Servings: 10

Ingredients:

- ½ cup of. mayonnaise
- ½ cup of. ricotta cheese, shredded
- ½ cup part-skim mozzarella cheese, shredded
- ½ cup of parmesan and Romano cheese blend, grated

- 1 teaspoon. garlic, minced
- 1 tablespoon. dried oregano, crushed
- Salt, to taste
- 4 large tomatoes, cut each one in 5 slices

Directions:

1. Preheat the oven to broiler on high. Arrange a rack about 3-inch from the heating element.
2. In a bowl, add the mayonnaise, cheeses, garlic, oregano, and salt and mix until well combined and smooth.
3. Spread the cheese mixture over each tomato slice evenly.
4. Arrange the tomato slices onto a broiler pan in a single layer.
5. Broil for about 3-5 minutes or until the top becomes golden brown.
6. Remove from the oven and transfer the tomato slices onto a platter.
7. Set aside to cool slightly.
8. Serve warm.

Nutrition:

- Calories: 110 Cal Fat: 29 g
- Carbs: 2 g Protein: 16 g
- Fiber: 5 g

128. Grain-free Tortilla Chips

Preparation Time: 15 Minutes

Cooking Time: 16 Minutes

Servings: 6

Ingredients:

- 1½ cup mozzarella cheese, shredded
- ½ cup of almond flour
- 1 tablespoon. golden flaxseed meal
- Salt and freshly ground black pepper, to taste

Directions:

1. Preheat the oven to 375o F. Line 2 large baking sheets with parchment paper.
2. In a microwave-safe bowl, add the cheese and microwave for about 1 minute, stirring after every 15 seconds.
3. In the bowl of melted cheese, add the almond flour, flaxseed meal, salt, and black pepper and with a fork, mix well.
4. With your hands, knead until a dough form.
5. Make 2 equal sized balls from the dough.
6. Place 1 dough ball onto each prepared baking sheet and roll into an 8x10-inch rectangle.
7. Cut each dough rectangle into triangle-shaped chips.
8. Arrange the chips in a single layer.
9. Bake for about 10-15 minutes, flipping once halfway through.
10. Remove from oven and set aside to cool before serving.

Nutrition:

Calories: 80 Cal Fat: 14 g

Carbs: 6 g

Protein: 13 g

Fiber: 4 g

129. Cheeses Chips

Preparation Time: 15 Minutes

Cooking Time: 15 Minutes

Servings: 8

Ingredients:

- 3 tablespoons. coconut flour
- ½ cup strong cheddar cheese, grated and divided
- ¼ cup Parmesan cheese, grated
- 2 tablespoons. butter, melted

- 1 organic egg
- 1 teaspoon. fresh thyme leaves, minced

Directions:

1. Preheat the oven to 350o F. Line a large baking sheet with parchment paper.
2. In a bowl, place the coconut flour, ¼ cup of grated cheddar, Parmesan, butter, and egg and mix until well combined.
3. Set the mixture aside for about 3-5 minutes.
4. Make 8 equal-sized balls from the mixture.
5. Arrange the balls onto the prepared baking sheet in a single layer about 2-inch apart.
6. With your hands, press each ball into a little flat disc.
7. Sprinkle each disc with the remaining cheddar, followed by thyme.
8. Bake for about 13-15 minutes or until the edges become golden brown.
9. Remove from the oven and let them cool completely before serving.

Nutrition:

- Calories: 189 Cal
- Fat: 28 g Carbs: 4 g
- Protein: 14 g
- Fiber: 5 g

130. Snack Parties Treat

Preparation Time: 10 Minutes

Cooking Time: 6 Minutes

Servings: 4

Ingredients:

- 8 bacon slices
- 8 mozzarella cheese sticks, frozen overnight
- 1 cup of. olive oil

Directions:

1. Wrap a bacon slice around each cheese stick and secure it with a toothpick.
2. In a cast-iron skillet, heat the oil over medium heat and fry the mozzarella sticks in 2 batches for about 2-3 minutes or until golden brown from all sides.
3. With a slotted spoon, transfer the mozzarella sticks onto a paper towel-lined plate to drain.
4. Set aside to cool slightly.
5. Serve warm.

Nutrition:

- Calories: 119 Cal
- Fat: 22g
- Carbs: 3 g
- Protein: 11 g
- Fiber: 5 g

131. Sweet Tooth Carving Pana Cotta

Preparation Time: 15 Minutes

Cooking Time: 5 Minutes

Servings: 4

Ingredients:

- 1½ cup of. unsweetened almond milk, divided
- 1 tablespoon. unflavored powdered gelatin
- 1 cup of. unsweetened coconut milk
- 1/3 cup of swerve
- 3 tablespoons. cacao powder
- 2 teaspoons. instant coffee granules
- 6 drops liquid stevia

Directions:

1. In a large bowl, add ½ C. of almond milk and sprinkle evenly with gelatin.

2. Set aside until soaked.

3. In a pan, add the remaining almond milk, coconut milk, Swerve, cacao powder, coffee granules, and stevia and bring to a gentle boil, stirring continuously.

4. Remove from the heat.

5. In a blender, add the gelatin mixture, and hot milk mixture and pulse until smooth.

6. Transfer the mixture into serving glasses and set aside to cool completely.

7. With plastic wrap, cover each glass and refrigerate for about 3-4 hours before serving.

Nutrition:

- Calories: 293 Cal
- Fat: 17 g
- Carbs: 5 g
- Protein: 16 g
- Fiber: 7 g

132. Halloween special Fat Bombs

Preparation Time: 15 Minutes

Cooking Time: 3 Minutes

Servings: 24

Ingredients:

- 4 oz. cream cheese softened
- ½ cup of coconut oil
- ½ cup of homemade pumpkin puree
- ¼ cup of. monk fruit sweetener
- 2 teaspoons. pumpkin pie spice
- ½ cup of. pecans, toasted
- ¼ teaspoon. ground cinnamon

Directions:

1. In a medium pan, add the cream cheese and coconut oil over medium-low heat

and cook for about 2-3 minutes or until smooth, stirring continuously.

2. Remove from the heat and transfer the cream cheese mixture into a bowl.

3. Add the pumpkin puree, monk fruit sweetener, and pumpkin pie spice and with an electric mixer, beat until well combined.

4. Place the mixture into 24 silicone molds evenly.

5. Top each mold with the pecans, and sprinkle with cinnamon.

6. Freeze the molds for about 4 hours before serving.

Nutrition:

- Calories: 76 Cal
- Fat: 10 g
- Carbs: 2 g
- Protein: 2 g
- Fiber: 3 g

133. Breakfast Toast in a Bowl

Preparation Time: 15 Minutes

Cooking Time: 30 Minutes

Servings: 4

Ingredients:

- 4 tablespoons. butter + greasing
- 1 tablespoon. chopped fresh basil
- 12 salami slices
- 8 tomato slices
- 4 low-carb bread slices
- 4 eggs
- Salt and black pepper to taste

Directions:

1. Preheat the oven to 300°F/150°C.

2. Heat 1 tablespoon of butter in a skillet over medium heat and sauté the basil until

fragrant. Stir in the salami and cook for 3 minutes per side or until golden brown. Remove the salami and basil to a plate and set aside.

3. Put the tomatoes in the pan and cook for 3 to 5 minutes per side or until brown around the edges.

4. Brush 4 medium ramekins with some butter and press a bread slice into each bowl to line the walls of the ramekins. If the bread tears in the middle, that's okay.

5. Place one salami each in the center of each bread and then two salamis each against the walls of the ramekin that doesn't have complete bread covering. The goal is to create a cup of food in the ramekins either with bread or salami.

6. Divide the tomatoes into the bread cup and crack an egg into the center of the food cup. Bake in the oven until the egg whites set but the yolks still running.

7. Take out the ramekins, season with salt, black pepper, and serve immediately.

Nutrition:

- Calories: 310 Cal
- Fat: 28 g
- Carbs: 4 g
- Protein: 14 g
- Fiber: 5 g

134. Cocoa and Berry Breakfast Bowl

Preparation Time: 10 Minutes

Cooking Time: 0 Minutes

Servings: 2

Ingredients:

- ½ cup (113.5 g) strawberries, fresh or frozen

- ½ cup (113.5 g) blueberries, fresh or frozen
- 1 cup (240 ml) unsweetened almond milk
- Sugar-free maple syrup to taste
- 2 tablespoons. unsweetened cocoa powder
- 1 tablespoon. cashew nuts for topping

Directions:

1. Divide the berries into 4 serving bowls and pour on the almond milk.

2. Drizzle with the maple syrup and sprinkle the cocoa powder on top, a tablespoon per bowl.

3. Top with the cashew nuts and enjoy immediately.

Nutrition:

- Calories: 298 Cal
- Fat: 23 g
- Carbs: 4 g
- Protein: 12 g
- Fiber: 3 g

135. Turmeric Nut Loaf with Zesty Cream Cheese

Preparation Time: 25 Minutes

Cooking Time: 45 Minutes

Servings: 6

Ingredients:

- 4 eggs, separated
- 1 cup (160 g) swerve sugar, divided
- 1 stick (100 g) butter, room temperature
- ½ teaspoon salt, divided
- ½ cup (113.5g) almond flour
- ½ cup (113.5g) ground almonds
- 1 teaspoon turmeric powder + extra for garnish
- A pinch cinnamon powders

- 1 teaspoon baking powders
- 1 teaspoon fresh lemon zest
- 1 tablespoon. plain vinegar
- 3 tablespoons. sugar-free maple syrup
- 7 oz. (200 g) cream cheese

Directions:

1. Preheat the oven to 350°F/175°C and line a loaf pan with grease-proof paper. Set aside.
2. Using electric beaters, whisk the egg whites and half of the swerve sugar until stiff.
3. Add the remaining swerve sugar, butter, salt, and whisk until smooth.
4. Pour in the egg yolks, almond flour, ground almonds, turmeric powder, cinnamon powder, baking powder, lemon zest, and two-thirds of the vinegar. Mix until smooth batter forms.
5. Pour the batter into the loaf pan and level the top with a spatula. Bake for 45 minutes or until a small skewer inserted comes out with moist crumbs and no wet batter.
6. Remove the pan and allow the bread to cool in the pan.
7. Meanwhile, in a medium bowl, mix the maple syrup, cream cheese, and remaining vinegar until smooth.
8. Remove the bread onto a cutting board and spread the topping on top. Garnish with the lemon zest and pistachios. Slice and serve.

Nutrition:

- Calories: 573 Cal
- Fat: 26 g
- Carbs: 4 g
- Protein: 18 g
- Fiber: 5 g

136. Herby Goat Cheese Frittata

Preparation Time: 15 Minutes

Cooking Time: 15 Minutes

Servings: 4

Ingredients:

- 1 tablespoon. avocado oil for frying
- 2 oz. (56 g) bacon slices, chopped
- 1 medium red bell pepper, deseeded and chopped
- 1 small yellow onion, chopped
- 2 scallions, chopped
- 1 tablespoon. chopped fresh chives
- Salt and black pepper to taste
- 8 eggs, beaten
- 1 tablespoon. unsweetened almond milk
- 1 tablespoon. chopped fresh parsley
- 3 ½ oz. (100 g) goat cheese, divided
- ¾ oz. (20 g) grated Parmesan cheese

Directions:

1. Preheat the oven to 350°F/175°C.
2. Heat the avocado oil in a medium cast-iron pan and cook the bacon for 5 minutes or until golden brown. Stir in the bell pepper, onion, scallions, and chives. Cook for 3 to 4 minutes or until the vegetables soften. Season with salt and black pepper.
3. In a bowl, beat the eggs with the almond milk and parsley. Pour the mixture over the vegetables, stirring to spread out well. Share half of the goat cheese on top.
4. Once the eggs start to set, divide the remaining goat cheese on top, season with salt, black pepper, and place the pan in the oven. Bake for 5 to 6 minutes or until the eggs set all around.

5. Take out the pan, scatter the Parmesan cheese on top, slice, and serve warm.

Nutrition:

- Calories: 494 Cal Fat: 27g Carbs: 5 g
- Protein: 19 g Fiber: 5 g

137. Healthy 2 Ingredient Breakfast Cookies

Preparation Time: 4 minutes

Cooking Time: 15 minutes

Servings: 1

Ingredients:

- 1 ¾ cup of quick oats
- 2 large ripe bananas
- 4 teaspoon peanut butter
- 1/3 cup crushed nuts of your choice
- ½ teaspoon pure vanilla extract
- ¼ cup shredded coconut

Directions:

1. Preheat your oven to 350 degrees Fahrenheit.
2. Mash the bananas in a bowl and add the oats and mix them well to combine. Fold any optional add ins such as ¼ cup chocolate chips. You can add honey to taste.
3. Line your baking tray with parchment paper and drop one teaspoon of cookie dough per cookie into your tray. Press down with a metal spoon into the shape of the cookies.
4. Bake for 20 minutes depending on your oven or cook them until they are golden brown on top.
5. Remove and allow to cool before serving.

Nutrition:

Calories 24 Carbohydrates 5g

Proteins 1gCalcium: 4mg

Potassium: 29mg.

138. Grilled Avocado Caprese Crostini

Preparation Time: 10 minutes

Cooking Time: 20 minutes

Servings: 2

Ingredients:

- 1 avocado thinly sliced
- 9 ounces ripened cherry tomatoes
- ounces fresh bocconcini in water
- 2 teaspoon balsamic glaze
- 8 pieces Italian baguette
- ½ a cup basil leaves

Directions:

1. Preheat your oven to 375 degrees Fahrenheit
2. Arrange your baking sheet properly before spraying them on top with olive oil.
3. Bake your item of choice until they are well done or golden brown. Rub your crostini with the cut side of garlic while they are still warm and you can season them with pepper and salt.
4. Divide the basil leaves on each side of bread and top up with tomato halves, avocado slices and bocconcini. Season it with pepper and salt.
5. Broil it for 4 minutes and when the cheese starts to melt through remove and drizzle balsamic glaze before serving.

Nutrition:

Calories 278

Fat 10g

Carbohydrates 37g

Proteins 10g

Sodium: 342 Mg

Potassium: 277mg

139. Caprese Stuffed Garlic Butter Portobellos

Preparation Time: 5 minutes

Cooking Time: 10 minutes

Servings: 6

Ingredients:

- For Garlic butter
- 2 teaspoon of butter
- 2 cloves garlic 1 teaspoon parsley finely chopped
- For the mushrooms
- 6 large portobello mushrooms, washed and dried well with paper towel.
- 6 mozzarella cheese balls thinly sliced
- 1 cup grape tomatoes thinly sliced
- Fresh basil for garnishing
- For balsamic glaze
- 2 teaspoon brown sugar
- ¼ cup balsamic vinegar

Directions:

1. Preheat the oven to broil setting on high heat. Arrange the oven shelf and place it in the right direction.

2. Combine the garlic butter ingredients in a small pan and melt until the garlic begins to be fragrant. Brush the bottoms of the mushroom and place them on the buttered section of the baking tray.

3. Flip and brush the remaining garlic over each cap. Fill each mushroom with tomatoes and mozzarella slices and grill until the cheese has melted. Drizzle the balsamic glaze and sprinkle some salt to taste.

4. If you are making the balsamic glaze from scratch, combine the sugar and vinegar in a small pan and reduce the heat to low.

Allow it to simmer for 6 minutes or until the mixture has thickened well.

Nutrition:

Calories 101

Fat 5g

Carbohydrates 12g

Proteins 2g

Sodium: 58mg

Potassium: 377 Mg

140. Cheesy Mashed Sweet Potato Cakes

Preparation Time: 10 minutes

Cooking Time: 30 minutes

Servings: 4

Ingredients:

- ¾ cup bread crumbs
- 4 cups mashed potatoes
- ½ cup onions
- 2 cup of grated mozzarella cheese
- ¼ cup fresh grated parmesan cheese
- 2 large cloves finely chopped
- 1 egg
- 2 teaspoon finely chopped parsley
- Salt and pepper to taste

Directions:

1. Line your baking sheet with foil. Wash, peel and cut the sweet potatoes into 6 pieces. Arrange them inside the baking sheet and drizzle a small amount of oil on top before seasoning with salt and pepper.

2. Cover with a baking sheet and bake it for 45 minutes. Once cooked transfer them into a mixing bowl and mash them well with a potato masher.

3. To the sweet potatoes in a bowl add green onions, parmesan, mozzarella, garlic, egg,

parsley and bread crumbs. Mash and combine the mixture together using the masher.

4. Put the remaining ¼ cup of the breadcrumbs in a place. Scoop a teaspoon of mixture into your palm and form round patties around ½ and inch thick. Dredge your patties in the breadcrumbs to cover both sides and set them aside.

5. Heat a tablespoon of oil in a medium nonstick pan. When the oil is hot begin to cook the patties in batches 4 or 5 per session and cook each side for 6 minutes until they turn golden brown. Using a spoon or spatula flip them. Add oil to prevent burning.

Nutrition:

Calories 126

Fat 6g

Carbs 15g

Proteins 3g

Sodium: 400mg

141. Cheesy Garlic Sweet Potatoes

Preparation Time: 10 minutes

Cooking Time: 25 minutes

Servings: 4

Ingredients:

- Sea salt
- ¼ cup garlic butter melt
- ¾ cup shredded mozzarella cheese
- ½ cup of parmesan cheese freshly grated
- 4 medium sized sweet potatoes
- 2 teaspoon freshly chopped parsley

Directions:

1. Heat the oven to 400 degrees Fahrenheit and brush the potatoes with garlic butter

and season each with pepper and salt. Arrange the cut side down on a greased baking sheet until the flesh is tender or they turn golden brown.

2. Remove them from the oven, flip the cut side up and top up with parsley and parmesan cheese.

3. Change the settings of your instant fryer oven to broil and on medium heat add the cheese and melt it. Sprinkle salt and pepper to taste. Serve them warm

Nutrition:

Calories 356

Fat 9g

Carbohydrates 13g

Proteins 5g

Potassium: 232mg

Sodium: 252mg

142. Crispy Garlic Baked Potato Wedges

Preparation Time: 5 minutes

Cooking Time: 10 minutes

Servings: 3

Ingredients:

- 3 teaspoon salt
- 1 teaspoon minced garlic
- 6 large russet
- ¼ cup olive oil
- 1 teaspoon paprika
- 2/3 finely grated parmesan cheese
- 2 teaspoon freshly chopped parsley

Directions:

1. Preheat the oven into 350 degrees Fahrenheit and line the baking sheet with a parchment pepper.

2. Cut the potatoes into halfway length and cut each half in half lengthways again. Make 8 wedges.

3. In a small jug combine garlic, oil, paprika and salt and place your wedges in the baking sheets. Pour the oil mixture over the potatoes and toss them to ensure that they are evenly coated.

4. Arrange the potato wedges in a single layer on the baking tray and sprinkle salt and parmesan cheese if needed. Bake for 35 minutes turning the wedges once half side is cooked.

5. Flip the other side until they are both golden brown.

6. Sprinkle parsley and the remaining parmesan before serving.

Nutrition:

Calories 324

Fat 6g

Carbs 8g

Proteins 2g

Sodium: 51mg

Potassium: 120mg

143. Sticky Chicken Thai Wings

Preparation Time: 10 minutes

Cooking Time: 30 minutes

Servings: 6

Ingredients:

- 3 pounds chicken wings removed
- 1 teaspoon sea salt to taste
  For the glaze:
- ¾ cup Thai sweet chili sauce
- ¼ cup soy sauce
- 4 teaspoon brown sugar
- 4 teaspoon rice wine vinegar
- 3 teaspoon fish sauce
- 2 teaspoon lime juice
- 1 teaspoon lemon grass minced
- 2 teaspoon sesame oil
- 1 teaspoon garlic minced

1. **Directions:**

2. Preheat the oven to 350 degrees Fahrenheit. Lightly spray your baking tray with cooking tray and set it aside. To prepare the glaze combine the ingredients in a small bowl and whisk them until they are well combined. Pour half of the mixture into a pan and reserve the rest.

3. Trim any excess skin off the wing edges and season it with pepper and salt. Add the wings to a baking tray and pour the sauce over the wings tossing them for the sauce to evenly coat. Arrange them in a single layer and bake them for 15 minutes.

4. While the wings are in the oven, bring your glaze to simmer in medium heat until there are visible bubbles.

5. Once the wings are cooled on one side rotate each piece and bake for an extra 10 minutes. Baste them and return them into the oven to allow for more cooking until they are golden brown. Garnish with onion slices, cilantro, and chili flakes and sprinkle the remaining salt. Serving with glaze of your choice.

Nutrition:

Calories: 256

Fat: 16g

Carbohydrates 19g

Proteins: 20g

Potassium: 213mg

Sodium: 561mg

144. Coconut Shrimp

Preparation Time: 15 minutes

Cooking Time: 15 minutes

Servings: 6

Ingredients:

- Salt and pepper
- 1-pound jumbo shrimp peeled and deveined
- ½ cup all-purpose flour

For batter:

- ½ cup beer
- 1 teaspoon baking powder
- ½ cup all-purpose flour
- 1 egg

For coating:

- 1 cup panko bread crumbs
- 1 cup shredded coconut

Directions:

1. Line the baking tray with parchment paper.
2. In a shallow bowl add ½ cup flour for dredging and in another bowl whisk the batter ingredients. The batter should resemble a pancake consistency. If it is too thick add a little mineral or beer whisking in between. In another bowl mix together the shredded coconut and bread crumbs.
3. Dredge the shrimp in flour shaking off any excess before dipping in the batter and coat it with bread crumb mixture. Lightly press the coconut into the shrimp.
4. Place them into the baking sheet and repeat the process until you have several.
5. In a Dutch oven skillet heat vegetable oil until it is nice and hot fry the frozen shrimp batches for 3 minutes per side. Drain them on a paper towel lined plate.
6. Serve immediately with sweet chili sauce.

Nutrition:

Calories: 409

Fat 11g

Carbohydrates 46g

Proteins 30g

Sodium: 767mg

Potassium: 345mg

CHAPTER 8:

Dinner Recipes

145. Red Quinoa and Black Bean Soup

Preparation time: 5 minutes
Cooking time: 40 minutes
Servings: 6
Ingredients:

- 1 1/4 cup red quinoa
- 4 minced garlic cloves
- 1/2 tablespoon coconut oil
- 1 diced jalapeno
- 3 cups diced onion
- 2 teaspoon cumin
- 1 chopped sweet potato
- 1 teaspoon coriander
- 1 teaspoon chili powder
- 5 cups vegetable broth
- 15 ounces black beans
- 1/2 teaspoon cayenne pepper
- 2 cups spinach

Directions:

1. Begin by bringing the quinoa into a saucepan to boil with two cups of water. Allow the quinoa to simmer for twenty minutes. Next, remove the quinoa from the heat.
2. To the side, heat the oil, the onion, and the garlic together in a large soup pot.
3. Add the jalapeno and the sweet potato and sauté for an additional seven minutes.
4. Next, add all the spices and the broth and bring the soup to a simmer for twenty-five minutes. The potatoes should be soft.
5. Prior to serving, add the quinoa, the black beans, and the spinach to the mix. Season, and serve warm. Enjoy.

Nutrition:
Calories: 211
Carbs: 22g
Fat: 7g
Protein: 19g

146. October Potato Soup

Preparation time: 5 minutes
Cooking time: 20 minutes
Servings: 3
Ingredients:

- 4 minced garlic cloves
- 2 teaspoon coconut oil
- 3 diced celery stalks
- 1 diced onion
- 2 teaspoon yellow mustard seeds
- 5 diced Yukon potatoes
- 6 cups vegetable broth
- 1 teaspoon oregano

- 1 teaspoon paprika
- 1/2 teaspoon cayenne pepper
- 1 teaspoon chili powder
- Salt and pepper to taste

Directions:

1. Begin by sautéing the garlic and the mustard seeds together in the oil in a large soup pot.
2. Next, add the onion and sauté the mixture for another five minutes.
3. Add the celery, the broth, the potatoes, and all the spices, and continue to stir.
4. Allow the soup to simmer for thirty minutes without a cover.
5. Next, Position about three cups of the soup in a blender, and puree the soup until you've reached a smooth consistency. Pour this back into the big soup pot, stir, and serve warm. Enjoy.

Nutrition:

Calories: 203

Carbs: 12g

Fat: 7g

Protein: 9g

147. Chicken Relleno Casserole

Preparation Time: 19 minutes

Cooking Time: 29 minutes

Servings: 6

Ingredients:

- 6 Tortilla Factory low-carb whole wheat tortillas, torn into small pieces
- 1 ½ cups hand-shredded cheese, Mexican
- 1 beaten egg
- 1 cup milk
- 2 cups cooked chicken, shredded
- 1 can Ro-tel
- ½ cup salsa verde

Directions:

1. Grease an 8 x 8 glass baking dish
2. Heat oven to 375 degrees
3. Combine everything together, but reserve ½ cup of the cheese
4. Bake it for 29 minutes
5. Take it out of oven and add ½ cup cheese
6. Broil for about 2 minutes to melt the cheese

Nutrition:

Calories: 265

Total Fat: 16g

Protein: 20g

Total Carbs: 18g

Dietary Fiber: 10g

Sugar: 0g

Sodium: 708mg

148. Italian Chicken with Asparagus and Artichoke Hearts

Preparation Time: 9 minutes

Cooking Time: 40 minutes

Servings: 1

Ingredients:

- 1 can long asparagus spears, drained
- 1 c red peppers, roasted, drained
- 1 c artichoke hearts, drained
- 6 oz. of boneless chicken breast, pounded thin or sliced thinly
- 2 T parmesan cheese
- 1 T Bisquick
- ½ teaspoon oregano

- ½ teaspoon garlic powder
- ½ cup fresh sliced mushrooms
- 2 T red wine vinegar
- 2 T butter
- 3 T olive oil

Directions:

1. Place in a small blender container (or bowl) the oregano, garlic powder, vinegar, and 1 T oil. Place to the side.
2. Combine the Bisquick and Parmesan cheese.
3. Roll the chicken in the Bisquick and Parmesan mix.
4. Heat the butter in a skillet.
5. Brown the chicken on both sides and cook until done, approximately 4 minutes.
6. Emulsify or quickly whip the wet ingredients you have placed to the side. This is your dressing.
7. Place the chicken on the plate.
8. Surround with the vegetables and drizzle them with the dressing.

Nutrition:

Calories: 435 Total Fat: 18g

Protein: 38gTotal Carbs: 16g

Dietary Fiber: 7g

Sugar: 1g

Sodium: 860mg

149. Kabobs with Peanut Curry Sauce

Preparation Time: 9 minutes

Cooking Time: 9 minutes

Servings: 4

Ingredients:

- 1 cup Cream
- 4 teaspoon Curry Powder
- 1 1/2 teaspoon Cumin
- 1 1/2 teaspoon Salt
- 1 T minced garlic
- 1/3 cup Peanut Butter, sugar-free
- 2 T Lime Juice
- 3 T Water
- 1/2 small Onion, diced
- 2 T Soy Sauce
- 1 packet Splenda
- 8 oz. boneless, cooked Chicken Breast
- 8 oz. pork tenderloin

Directions:

1. Blend together cream, onion, 2 teaspoon. garlic, curry and cumin powder, and salt.
2. Slice the meats into 1 inch pieces.
3. Place the cream sauce into a bowl and put in the chicken and tenderloin to marinate. Let rest in sauce for 14 minutes.
4. Blend peanut butter, water, 1 teaspoon. garlic, lime juice, soy sauce, and Splenda. This is your peanut dipping sauce.
5. Remove the meats and thread on skewers. Broil or grill 4 minutes per side until meat is done.
6. Serve with dipping sauce.

Nutrition:

Calories: 530

Total Fat: 29g

Protein: 37g

Total Carbs: 6g

Dietary Fiber: 4g

Sugar: 2g

Sodium: 1538mg

150. Pizza

Preparation Time: 4 minutes

Cooking Time: 4 minutes

Servings: 1

Ingredients:

- 1 Tortilla Factory low carb whole wheat tortilla
- ¼ cup mozzarella cheese, hand-shredded
- ¼ cup tomato paste
- sprinkle of Italian seasoning
- sprinkle of garlic salt
- Cut the broccoli, spinach, mushrooms, peppers, and onions you like for toppings

Directions:

1. Turn broiler on in oven, or toaster oven
2. Spread tortilla with tomato paste
3. Sprinkle seasoning on the paste
4. Add the cheese
5. Add the veggies
6. Broil or toast 1-4 minutes until crust is crunchy and cheese melted

Nutrition:

Calories: 155 Total Fat: 7g

Protein: 13g Total Carbs: 18g

Dietary Fiber: 10g Sugar: 2g

Sodium: 741mg

151. Salmon with Bok-Choy

Preparation Time: 9 minutes

Cooking Time: 9 minutes

Servings: 4

Ingredients:

- 1 c red peppers, roasted, drained
- 2 cups chopped bok-choy
- 1 T salted butter
- 5 oz. salmon steak
- 1 lemon, sliced very thinly
- 1/8 teaspoon black pepper
- 1 T olive oil
- 2 T sriracha sauce

Directions:

1. Place oil in skillet
2. Place all but 4 slices of lemon in the skillet.
3. Sprinkle the bok choy with the black pepper.
4. Stir fry the bok-choy with the lemons.
5. Remove and place on four plates.
6. Place the butter in the skillet and stir fry the salmon, turning once.
7. Place the salmon on the bed of bok-choy.
8. Divide the red peppers and encircle the salmon.
9. Place a slice of lemon atop the salmon.
10. Drizzle with sriracha sauce.

Nutrition:

Calories: 410 Total Fat: 30g

Protein: 30g Total Carbs: 7g

Dietary Fiber: 2g Sugar: 0g

Sodium: 200mg

152. Sriracha Tuna Kabobs

Preparation Time: 4 minutes

Cooking Time: 9 minutes

Servings: 4

Ingredients:

- 4 T Huy Fong chili garlic sauce
- 1 T sesame oil infused with garlic
- 1 T ginger, fresh, grated
- 1 T garlic, minced
- 1 red onion, cut into quarters and separated by petals
- 2 cups bell peppers, red, green, yellow

- 1 can whole water chestnuts, cut in half
- ½ pound fresh mushrooms, halved
- 32 oz. boneless tuna, chunks or steaks
- 1 Splenda packet
- 2 zucchini, sliced 1 inch thick, keep skins on

Directions:

1. Layer the tuna and the vegetable pieces evenly onto 8 skewers.
2. Combine the spices and the oil and chili sauce, add the Splenda
3. Quickly blend, either in blender or by quickly whipping.
4. Brush onto the kabob pieces, make sure every piece is coated
5. Grill 4 minutes on each side, check to ensure the tuna is cooked to taste.
6. Serving size is two skewers.

Nutrition:

Calories: 467 Total Fat: 18g

Protein: 56g Total Carbs: 21g

Dietary Fiber: 3.5g Sugar: 6g

Sodium: 433mg

153. Steak Salad with Asian Spice

Preparation Time: 4 minutes

Cooking Time: 4 minutes

Servings: 2

Ingredients:

- 2 T sriracha sauce
- 1 T garlic, minced
- 1 T ginger, fresh, grated
- 1 bell pepper, yellow, cut in thin strips
- 1 bell pepper, red, cut in thin strips
- 1 T sesame oil, garlic

- 1 Splenda packet
- ½ teaspoon curry powder
- ½ teaspoon rice wine vinegar
- 8 oz. of beef sirloin, cut into strips
- 2 cups baby spinach, stemmed
- ½ head butter lettuce, torn or chopped into bite-sized pieces

Directions:

1. Place the garlic, sriracha sauce, 1 teaspoon sesame oil, rice wine vinegar, and Splenda into a bowl and combine well.
2. Pour half of this mix into a zip-lock bag. Add the steak to marinade while you are preparing the salad.
3. Assemble the brightly colored salad by layering in two bowls.
4. Place the baby spinach into the bottom of the bowl.
5. Place the butter lettuce next.
6. Mix the two peppers and place on top.
7. Remove the steak from the marinade and discard the liquid and bag.
8. Heat the sesame oil and quickly stir fry the steak until desired doneness, it should take about 3 minutes.
9. Place the steak on top of the salad.
10. Drizzle with the remaining dressing (other half of marinade mix).
11. Sprinkle sriracha sauce across the salad.

Nutrition:

Calories: 350

Total Fat: 23g

Protein: 28g

Total Carbs: 7g

Dietary Fiber: 3.5

Sugar: 0

Sodium: 267mg

154. Tilapia and Broccoli

Preparation Time: 4 minutes

Cooking Time: 14 minutes

Servings: 1

Ingredients:

- 6 oz. tilapia, frozen is fine
- 1 T butter
- 1 T garlic, minced or finely chopped
- 1 teaspoon of lemon pepper seasoning
- 1 cup broccoli florets, fresh or frozen, but fresh will be crisper

Directions:

1. Set the pre-warmed oven for 350 degrees.
2. Place the fish in an aluminum foil packet.
3. Arrange the broccoli around the fish to make an attractive arrangement.
4. Sprinkle the lemon pepper on the fish.
5. Close the packet and seal, bake for 14 minutes.
6. Combine the garlic and butter. Set aside.
7. Remove the packet from the oven and transfer ingredients to a plate.
8. Place the butter on the fish and broccoli.

Nutrition:

Calories: 362 Total Fat: 25g

Protein: 29g Total Carbs: 3.5g

Dietary Fiber: 3g Sugar: 0g

Sodium: 0mg

155. Brown Basmati Rice Pilaf

Preparation Time: 10 minutes

Cooking Time: 3 minutes

Servings: 2

Ingredients:

- ½ tablespoon vegan butter
- ½ cup mushrooms, chopped
- ½ cup brown basmati rice
- 2-3 tablespoons water
- 1/8 teaspoon dried thyme
- Ground pepper to taste
- ½ tablespoon olive oil
- ¼ cup green onion, chopped
- 1 cup vegetable broth
- ¼ teaspoon salt
- ¼ cup chopped, toasted pecans

Directions:

1. Place a saucepan over medium-low heat. Add butter and oil.
2. When it melts, add mushrooms and cook until slightly tender.
3. Stir in the green onion and brown rice. Cook for 3 minutes. Stir constantly.
4. Stir in the broth, water, salt, and thyme.
5. When it begins to boil, lower the heat and cover with a lid. Simmer until rice is cooked. Add more water or broth if required.
6. Stir in the pecans and pepper.
7. Serve.

Nutrition:

Calories 189 Fats 11 g

Carbohydrates 19 g Proteins 4 g

156. Walnut and Date Porridge

Preparation Time: 10 minutes

Cooking Time: 0 minutes

Servings: 1

Ingredients:

- Strawberries, ½ cup (hulled)

- Milk or dairy-free alternative, 200 ml
- Buckwheat flakes, ½ cup
- Medjool date, 1 (chopped)
- Walnut butter, 1 teaspoon, or chopped walnut halves

Directions:
1. Place the date and the milk in a pan, heat gently before adding the buckwheat flakes. Then cook until the porridge gets to your desired consistency.
2. Add the walnuts, stir, then top with the strawberries.
3. Serve.

Nutrition:
Calories: 254 Protein: 65 g
Fat: 4 g
Vitamin B

157. Vietnamese Turmeric Fish with Mango and Herbs Sauce

Preparation Time: 15 minutes
Cooking Time: 30 minutes
Servings: 4
Ingredients:
For the Fish:

- Coconut oil to fry the fish, 2 tablespoons
- Fresh codfish, skinless and boneless, 1 ¼ lbs. (cut into 2-inch piece wide)
- Pinch of sea salt, to taste

Fish Marinade:

- Chinese cooking wine, 1 tablespoon
- Turmeric powder, 1 tablespoon
- Sea salt, 1 teaspoon
- Olive oil, 2 tablespoons
- Minced ginger, 2 teaspoons

Mango Dipping Sauce:

- Juice of ½ lime
- Medium-sized ripe mango, 1
- Rice vinegar, 2 tablespoons
- Dry red chili pepper, 1 teaspoon (stir in before serving)
- Garlic clove, 1
- Infused scallion and dill oil
- Fresh dill, 2 cups
- Scallions, 2 cups (slice into long thin shape)
- A pinch of sea salt, to taste.

Toppings

- Nuts (pine or cashew nuts)
- Lime juice (as much as you like)
- Fresh cilantro (as much as you like)

Directions:

1. Add all the ingredients under "Mango Dipping Sauce" into your food processor. Blend until you get your preferred consistency.

2. Add two tablespoons of coconut oil in a large non-stick frying pan and heat over high heat. Once hot, add the pre-marinated fish. Add the slices of the fish

into the pan individually. Divide into batches for easy frying, if necessary.

3. Once you hear a loud sizzle, reduce the heat to medium-high.

4. Do not move or turn the fish until it turns golden brown on one side; then turn it to the other side to fry, about 5 minutes on each side. Add more coconut oil to the pan if needed. Season with the sea salt.

5. Transfer the fish to a large plate. You will have some oil left in the frypan, which you will use to make your scallion and dill infused oil.

6. Using the remaining oil in the frypan, set to medium-high heat, add 2 cups of dill, and 2 cups of scallions.

7. Put off the heat after you have added the dill and scallions. Toss them gently for about 15 seconds, until the dill and scallions have wilted. Add a dash of sea salt to season.

8. Pour the dill, scallion, and infused oil over the fish. Serve with mango dipping sauce, nuts, lime, and fresh cilantro.

Nutrition:
Calories: 234 Fat: 23 g
Protein: 76 g
Sugar: 5 g

158. Chicken and Kale Curry

Preparation Time: 20 min
Cooking Time: 1 hour
Servings: 3
Ingredients:

- Boiling water, 250 ml
- Skinless and boneless chicken thighs, 7 oz.
- Ground turmeric, 2 tablespoons
- Olive oil, 1 tablespoon
- Red onions, 1 (diced)
- Bird's eye chili, 1 (finely chopped)
- Freshly chopped ginger, ½ tablespoon
- Curry powder, ½ tablespoon
- Garlic, 1 ½ cloves (crushed)
- Cardamom pods, 1
- Tinned coconut milk, light, 100 ml
- Chicken stock, 2 cups
- Tinned chopped tomatoes, 1 cup

Direction:

1. Place the chicken thighs in a non-metallic bowl, add one tablespoon of turmeric and one teaspoon of olive oil. Mix together and keep aside to marinate for approx. 30 minutes.

2. Fry the chicken thighs over medium heat for about 5 minutes until well cooked and brown on all sides. Remove from the pan and set aside.

3. Add the remaining oil into a frypan on medium heat. Then add the

onion, ginger, garlic, and chili. Fry for about 10 minutes until soft.

4. Add one tablespoon of the turmeric and half a tablespoon of curry powder to the pan and cook for another 2 minutes.

5. Then add the cardamom pods, coconut milk, tomatoes, and chicken stock. Allow simmering for thirty minutes.

6. Add the chicken once the sauce has reduced a little into the pan, followed by the kale. Cook until the kale is tender and the chicken is warm enough.

7. Serve with buckwheat.

8. Garnish with the chopped coriander.

Nutrition:

Calories: 313 g

Protein: 13 g

Fat: 6 g

Carbohydrate: 23 g

159. Mediterranean Baked Penne

Preparation Time: 25 minutes

Cooking Time: 1 hour 20 minutes

Servings: 8

Ingredients:

- Extra-virgin olive oil, 1 tablespoon
- Fine dry breadcrumbs, ½ cup
- Small zucchini, 2 (chopped)
- Medium eggplant, 1 (chopped)
- Medium onion, 1 (chopped)
- Red bell pepper, 1 (seeded and chopped)
- Celery, 1 stalk (sliced)
- Garlic, 1 clove (minced)
- Salt and freshly ground pepper to taste
- Dry white wine, ¼ cup
- Plum tomatoes, 28-ounces (drained and coarsely chopped, juice reserved)
- Freshly grated Parmesan cheese, 2 tablespoons
- Large eggs, 2 (lightly beaten)
- Coarsely grated part-skim mozzarella cheese, 1 ½ cups
- Dried penne rig ate or rigatoni, 1 pound

Directions:

1. Preheat your oven to 375 degrees F. Apply nonstick spray on a 3-quart baking dish. Then coat the dish with ¼ cup of breadcrumbs, tapping out the excess.

2. Heat the oil in a large non-stick skillet over medium-high heat. Then add the onion, celery, bell pepper, eggplant, and zucchini.

3. Cook for about 10 minutes, occasionally stirring, until smooth. Then add the garlic and cook for another minute. Add the wine, stir and cook for about 2 minutes, long enough for the wine to almost evaporate.

4. Then add the juice and tomatoes. Bring to a simmer, then cook for about 10 to 15 minutes, until thickened, season with pepper and salt.

5. Transfer to a large bowl and allow to cool.

6. Pour water into a pot, add some salt, and then allow to boil. Add the penne into the boiling salted water to cook for about 10 minutes, until al dente.

7. Drain and rinse the pasta under running water. Toss the pasta with the vegetable mixture, then stir in the mozzarella.

8. Scoop the pasta mixture and place into the prepared baking dish. Drizzle the broken eggs evenly over the top.

9. Mix the Parmesan and ¼ cups of breadcrumbs in a small bowl, then sprinkle evenly over the top of the dish.

10. Place the dish into the oven to bake for about 40 to 50 minutes, until bubbly and golden.

11. Allow to rest for 10 min before you serve.

Nutrition:

Calories: 372

Protein: 45 g

Fat: 8 g

Sugar: 2 g

160. Prawn Arrabbiata

Preparation Time: 35 minutes

Cooking Time: 30 minutes

Servings: 1

Ingredients:

- Raw or cooked prawns, 1 cup
- Extra virgin olive oil, 1 tablespoon
- Buckwheat pasta, ½ cup
- Chopped parsley, 1 tablespoon
- Celery, ¼ cup (finely chopped)
- Tinned chopped tomatoes, 2 cups
- Red onion, 1/3 cup (finely chopped)
- Garlic clove, 1 (finely chopped)
- Extra virgin olive oil, 1 teaspoon
- Dried mixed herbs, 1 teaspoon
- Bird's eye chili, 1 (finely chopped)
- White wine, 2 tablespoons (optional)

Directions:

1. Add the olive oil into your fry-pan and fry the dried herbs, celery, and onions over medium-low heat for about two minutes.

2. Increase heat to medium, add the wine and cook for another min.

3. Add the tomatoes to the pan and allow to simmer for about 30 minutes, over medium-low heat, until you get a nice creamy consistency.

4. Add a little water if the sauce gets too thick.

5. While the sauce is cooking, cook the pasta following the instruction on the packet. Drain the water once the pasta is done cooking, toss with the olive oil, and set aside until needed.

6. If using raw prawns, add them to your sauce and cook for another four

minutes, until the prawns turn opaque and pink, then add the parsley. If using cooked prawns, add them at the same time with the parsley and allow the sauce to boil.

7. Add the already cooked pasta to the sauce, mix them, and serve.

Nutrition:

Calories: 321

Protein: 19 g

Fat: 2 g

Carbohydrate: 23 g

161. Air Fryer Asparagus

Preparation Time: 5 minutes

Cooking Time: 8 minutes

Servings: 1

Ingredients:

- Nutritional yeast
- Olive oil non-stick spray
- One bunch of asparagus

Directions:

1. Wash the asparagus. Do not forget to trim off thick, woody ends.

2. Spray with olive oil spray and sprinkle with yeast.

3. In your Instant Crisp Air Fryer, lay the asparagus in a singular layer. Set the temperature to 360°F. Limit the time to eight minutes.

Nutrition:

Calories: 17

Fat: 4 g

Protein: 9 g

162. Avocado Fries

Preparation Time: 10 minutes

Cooking Time: 7 minutes

Servings: 1

Ingredients:

- One avocado
- 1/8 tsp. salt
- 1/4 cup of panko breadcrumbs
- Bean liquid (aquafaba) from a 15-ounce can of white or garbanzo beans

Directions:

1. Peel, pit, and slice up avocado.

2. Toss salt and breadcrumbs together in a bowl. Place the aquafaba into another bowl.

3. Dredge slices of avocado first in the aquafaba and then in panko, making sure you are evenly coating.

4. Place coated avocado slices into a single layer in the Instant Crisp Air Fryer. Set temperature to 390°F and set time to 5 minutes.

5. Serve with your favorite Keto dipping sauce!

Nutrition:

Calories: 102

Fat: 22g

Protein: 9g

Sugar: 1g

163. Bell-Pepper Corn Wrapped in Tortilla

Preparation Time: 5 minutes

Cooking Time: 15 minutes

Servings: 1

Ingredients:

- 1/4 small red bell pepper, chopped
- 1/4 small yellow onion, diced
- 1/4 tablespoon water
- 1/2 cobs grilled corn kernels
- One large tortilla
- One-piece commercial vegan nuggets, chopped
- Mixed greens for garnish

Directions:

1. Preheat the Instant Crisp Air Fryer to 400°F.

2. In a skillet heated over medium heat, sauté the vegan nuggets and the onions, bell peppers, and corn kernels. Set aside.

3. Place filling inside the corn tortillas.

4. Lock the air fryer lid. Fold the tortillas and place inside the Instant Crisp Air Fryer, cook for 15 minutes until the tortilla wraps are crispy.

5. Serve with mixed greens on top.

Nutrition:

Calories: 548

Fat: 20.7g

Protein: 46g

164. Cauliflower Rice

Preparation Time: 5 minutes

Cooking Time: 20 minutes

Servings: 1

Ingredients:

Round 1:

- 1/2 tsp. turmeric
- 1/2 cup of diced carrot
- 1/8 cup of diced onion
- 1/2 tbsp. low-sodium soy sauce
- 1/8 block of extra firm tofu

Round 2:

- 1/2 cup of frozen peas
- 1/4 minced garlic cloves
- 1/2 cup of chopped broccoli
- 1/2 tbsp. minced ginger
- 1/4 tbsp. rice vinegar
- 1/4 tsp. toasted sesame oil
- 1/2 tbsp. reduced-sodium soy sauce
- 1/2 cup of riced cauliflower

Directions:

1. Crush tofu in a large bowl and toss with all the Round one ingredient.

2. Lock the air fryer lid — preheat the Instant Crisp Air Fryer to 370 degrees. Also, set the temperature to 370°F, set time to 10 minutes, and cook 10 minutes, making sure to shake once.

3. In another bowl, toss ingredients from Round 2 together.

4. Add Round 2 mixture to Instant Crisp Air Fryer and cook another 10 minutes to shake 5 minutes.

5. Enjoy!

Nutrition:

Calories: 67

Fat: 8 g

Protein: 3 g

Sugar: 0 g

165. Stuffed Bacon Mushrooms

Preparation Time: 7 minutes

Cooking Time: 8 minutes

Servings: 1

Ingredients:

- 1/2 rashers bacon, diced
- 1/2 onion, diced
- 1/2 bell pepper, diced
- 1/2 small carrot, diced
- 2 medium size mushrooms (separate the caps and stalks)
- 1/4 cup shredded cheddar plus extra for to top
- 1/4 cup sour cream

Directions:

1. Chop the mushrooms stalks finely and fry them up with the bacon, onion, pepper, and carrot at 350 ° for 8 minutes.

2. Also, check when the veggies are tender, stir in the sour cream and the cheese. Keep on the heat until the cheese has melted, and everything is mixed nicely.

3. Now grab the mushroom caps and heap a plop of filling on each one.

4. Place in the fryer basket and top with a little extra cheese.

Nutrition:

Calories: 285

Fat: 20.5 g

Protein: 8.6 g

166. Zucchini Omelet

Preparation Time: 10 minutes

Cooking Time: 10 minutes

Servings: 1

Ingredients:

- 1/2 teaspoon butter
- 1/2 zucchini, julienned
- One egg
- 1/8 teaspoon fresh basil, chopped
- 1/8 teaspoon red pepper flakes, crushed
- Salted and newly ground black pepper, to taste

Directions:

1. Preheat the Instant Crisp Air Fryer to 355 degrees F.

2. Melt butter on a medium heat using a skillet.

3. Add zucchini and cook for about 3-4 minutes.

4. In a bowl, add the eggs, basil, red pepper flakes, salt, and black pepper and beat well.

5. Add cooked zucchini and gently stir to combine.

6. Transfer the mixture into the Instant Crisp Air Fryer pan. Lock the air fryer lid.

7. Cook for about 10 minutes. Also, you may opt to wait until it is done thoroughly.

Nutrition:

Calories: 285

Fat: 20.5 g

Protein: 8.6 g

167. Cheesy Cauliflower Fritters

Preparation Time: 10 minutes

Cooking Time: 7 minutes

Servings: 1

Ingredients:

- 1/2 cup of chopped parsley
- 1 cup of Italian breadcrumbs
- 1/3 cup of shredded mozzarella cheese
- 1/3 cup of shredded sharp cheddar cheese
- One egg
- Two minced garlic cloves
- Three chopped scallions
- One head of cauliflower

Directions:

1. Cut the cauliflower up into florets. Wash well and pat dry. Place into a food processor and pulse 20-30 seconds till it looks like rice.

2. Place the cauliflower rice in a bowl and mix with pepper, salt, egg, cheeses, breadcrumbs, garlic, and scallions.

3. With hands, form 15 patties of the mixture, and then add more breadcrumbs if needed.

4. With olive oil, spritz patties, and put the fitters into your Instant Crisp Air Fryer. Pile it in a single layer. Lock the air fryer lid. Set temperature to 390°F, and set time to 7 minutes, flipping after 7 minutes.

Nutrition:

Calories: 209

Fat: 17 g

Protein: 6 g

Sugar: 0.5 g

168. Zucchini Parmesan Chips

Preparation Time: 10 minutes

Cooking Time: 8 minutes

Servings: 1

Ingredients:

- 1/2 tsp. paprika
- 1/2 cup of grated parmesan cheese
- 1/2 cup of Italian breadcrumbs
- One lightly beaten egg
- Two thinly sliced zucchinis

Directions:

1. Use a very sharp knife or mandolin slicer to slice the zucchini as thinly as you can. Pat off extra moisture.

2. Beat the egg with a pinch of pepper and salt and a bit of water.

3. Combine paprika, cheese, and breadcrumbs in a bowl.

4. Dip slices of zucchini into the egg mixture and then into breadcrumb mixture. Press gently to coat.

5. With olive oil cooking spray, mist encrusted zucchini slices. Put into your Instant Crisp Air Fryer in a single layer. Latch the air fryer lid. Set temperature to 350°F and set time to 8 minutes.

6. Sprinkle with salt and serve with salsa.

Nutrition:

Calories: 211 Fat: 16 g

Protein: 8 g Sugar: 0 g

169. Jalapeno Cheese Balls

Preparation Time: 10 minutes

Cooking Time: 8 minutes

Servings: 1

Ingredients:

- 1-ounce cream cheese
- 1/6 cup shredded mozzarella cheese
- 1/6 cup shredded Cheddar cheese
- 1/2 jalapeños, finely chopped
- 1/2 cup breadcrumbs
- Two eggs
- 1/2 cup all-purpose flour
- Salt
- Pepper
- Cooking oil

Directions:

1. Combine the cream cheese, mozzarella, Cheddar, and jalapeños in a medium bowl. Mix well.

2. Form the cheese mixture into balls about an inch thick. You may also use a small ice cream scoop. It works well.

3. Arrange the cheese balls on a sheet pan and place in the freezer for 15 minutes. It will help the cheese balls maintain their shape while frying.

4. Spray the Instant Crisp Air Fryer basket with cooking oil.

5. Place the breadcrumbs in a small bowl. In another small bowl, beat the eggs. In the third small bowl, combine the flour with salt and pepper to taste, and mix well.

6. Remove the cheese balls from the freezer. Plunge the cheese balls in the flour, then the eggs, and then the breadcrumbs.

7. Place the cheese balls in the Instant Crisp Air Fryer. Spray with cooking oil. Lock the air fryer lid. Cook for 8 minutes.

8. Open the Instant Crisp Air Fryer and flip the cheese balls. I recommend flipping them instead of shaking, so the balls maintain their form. Cook an additional 4 minutes.

9. Cool before serving.

Nutrition:

Calories: 96 Fat: 6 g

Protein: 4 g Sugar: 0 g

170. Crispy Roasted Broccoli

Preparation Time: 10 minutes

Cooking Time: 8 minutes

Servings: 1

Ingredients:

- 1/4 tsp. Masala

- 1/2 tsp. red chili powder
- 1/2 tsp. salt
- 1/4 tsp. turmeric powder
- 1 tbsp. chickpea flour
- 1 tbsp. yogurt
- 1/2-pound broccoli

Directions:

1. Cut broccoli up into florets. Immerse in a bowl of water with two teaspoons of salt for at least half an hour to remove impurities.
2. Take out broccoli florets from water and let drain. Wipe down thoroughly.
3. Mix all other ingredients to create a marinade.
4. Toss broccoli florets in the marinade. Cover and chill 15-30 minutes.
5. Preheat the Instant Crisp Air Fryer to 390 degrees. Place marinated broccoli florets into the fryer, lock the air fryer lid, set the temperature to 350°F, and set time to 10 minutes. Florets will be crispy when done.

Nutrition:

Calories: 96

Fat: 1.3 g

Protein: 7 g

Sugar: 4.5 g

171. Coconut Battered Cauliflower Bites

Preparation Time: 5 minutes

Cooking Time: 20 minutes

Servings: 1

Ingredients:

- Salt and pepper to taste
- One flax egg or one tablespoon flaxseed meal + 3 tablespoon water
- One small cauliflower, cut into florets
- One teaspoon mixed spice
- 1/2 teaspoon mustard powder
- Two tablespoons maple syrup
- One clove of garlic, minced
- Two tablespoons soy sauce
- 1/3 cup oats flour
- 1/3 cup plain flour
- 1/3 cup desiccated coconut

Directions:

1. In a mixing bowl, mix oats, flour, and desiccated coconut. Season with salt and pepper to taste. Set aside.
2. In another bowl, place the flax egg and add a pinch of salt to taste. Set aside.
3. Season the cauliflower with mixed spice and mustard powder.
4. Dredge the florets in the flax egg first, then in the flour mixture.
5. Place it inside the Instant Crisp Air Fryer, lock the air fryer lid, and cook at 400°F or 15 minutes.
6. Meanwhile, place the maple syrup, garlic, and soy sauce in a saucepan and heat over medium flame. Wait for it to boil and adjust the heat to low until the sauce thickens.
7. After 15 minutes, take out the Instant Crisp Air Fryer's florets and place them in the saucepan.

8. Toss to coat the florets and place inside the Instant Crisp Air Fryer and cook for another 5 minutes.

Nutrition:
Calories: 154 Fat: 2.3 g Protein: 4.69 g

172. Crispy Jalapeno Coins

Preparation Time: 10 minutes
Cooking Time: 5 minutes
Servings: 1
Ingredients:

- One egg
- 2/3 tbsp. coconut flour
- One sliced and seeded jalapeno
- Pinch of garlic powder
- Pinch of onion powder
- Bit of Cajun seasoning (optional)
- Pinch of pepper and salt

Directions:

1. Ensure your Instant Crisp Air Fryer is preheated to 400 degrees.
2. Mix all dry ingredients.
3. Pat jalapeno slices dry. Dip them into the egg wash and then into the dry mixture. Toss to coat thoroughly.
4. Add coated jalapeno slices to Instant Crisp Air Fryer in a singular layer. Spray with olive oil.
5. Lock the air fryer lid. Set temperature to 350°F and set time to 5 minutes. Cook just till crispy.

Nutrition:
Calories: 128 Fat: 8 g
Protein: 7 g
Sugar: 0 g

173. Beauty School Ginger Cucumbers

Preparation time: 10 minutes
Cooking time: 5 minutes
Servings: 14 slices.
Ingredients:

- 1 sliced cucumber
- 3 teaspoon rice wine vinegar
- 1 1/2 tablespoon sugar
- 1 teaspoon minced ginger

Directions:

1. Bring all of the above **Ingredients:** together in a mixing bowl, and toss the **Ingredients:** well. Enjoy!

Nutrition:
Calories: 210
Carbs: 14g Fat: 7g
Protein: 19g

174. Mushroom Salad

Preparation time: 10 minutes
Cooking time: 20 minutes
Servings: 2
Ingredients:

- 1 tablespoon butter
- 1/2 pound cremini mushrooms, chopped
- 2 tablespoon extra-virgin olive oil
- Salt and black pepper to taste
- 2 bunches arugula
- 4 slices prosciutto
- 1 tablespoon apple cider vinegar
- 4 sundried tomatoes in oil, drained and chopped
- Parmesan cheese, shaved
- Fresh parsley leaves, chopped

Directions:

1. Heat a pan with butter and half of the oil.
2. Add the mushrooms, salt, and pepper. Stir-fry for 3 minutes. Reduce heat. Stir again, and cook for 3 minutes more.
3. Add rest of the oil and vinegar. Stir and cook for 1 minute.
4. Place arugula on a platter, add prosciutto on top, add the mushroom mixture, sundried tomatoes, more salt and pepper, parmesan shavings, parsley, and serve.

Nutrition:

Calories: 191

Carbs: 6g

Fat: 7g

Protein: 17g

175. Easy Pork Ribs

Preparation Time: 10 minutes

Cooking Time: 15 minutes

Servings: 6

Ingredients:

- 3 pounds boneless pork ribs
- ½ cup soy sauce
- ¼ cup ketchup
- 2 tablespoons olive oil
- Black pepper to taste

Directions:

1. Pour oil into your PPCXL and hit "chicken/meat," leaving the lid off.
2. When oil is hot, add ribs and sear till golden on both sides.
3. In a bowl, mix black pepper, soy sauce, and ketchup.

4. Pour over ribs and seal the lid.
5. Adjust cook time to 15 minutes.
6. When the timer beeps, hit "cancel" and wait 5 minutes before quick-releasing.
7. Make sure pork is at least 145-degrees before serving.

Nutrition:

Total calories: 570

Protein: 65

Carbs: 0

Fat: 27

Fiber: 0

176. Pineapple-BBQ Pork

Preparation Time: 10 minutes

Cooking Time: 6 minutes

Servings: 4

Ingredients:

- 4 bone-in pork loin chops
- One 8-ounce can of undrained crushed pineapple
- 1 cup honey BBQ sauce
- 2 tablespoons chili sauce
- 1 tablespoon olive oil

Directions:

1. Mix can of pineapple, BBQ sauce, and chili sauce.
2. Turn your PPCXL to "chicken/meat" and heat.
3. When hot, add olive oil.
4. When the oil is sizzling, sear pork chops on both sides, 3-4 minutes per side.
5. When brown, pour sauce over the pork and seal the lid.
6. Adjust time to 6 minutes.

7. When time is up, hit "cancel" and wait 5 minutes before quick-releasing.

8. Pork should be cooked to 145-degrees.

9. Serve with sauce.

Nutrition:

Total calories: 370

Protein: 28

Carbs: 37

Fat: 13

Fiber: 0

177. Apple-Garlic Pork Loin

Preparation Time: 5 minutes

Cooking Time: 25 minutes

Servings: 12

Ingredients:

- One 3-pound boneless pork loin roast
- One 12-ounce jar of apple jelly
- 1/3 cup water
- 1 tablespoon Herbs de Provence
- 2 teaspoons minced garlic

Directions:

1. Put pork loin in your cooker. Cut in half if necessary.
2. Mix garlic, water, and jelly.
3. Pour over pork.
4. Season with Herbs de Provence.
5. Seal the lid.
6. Hit "chicken/meat" and adjust time to 25 minutes.
7. When time is up, hit "cancel" and wait 10 minutes before quick-releasing.

8. Pork should be served at 145-degrees. If not cooked through yet, hit "chicken/meat" and cook with the lid off until temperature is reached.

9. Rest for 15 minutes before slicing.

Nutrition:

Total calories: 236

Protein: 26 Carbs: 19

Fat: 6 Fiber: 0

178. Pork with Cranberry-Honey Gravy

Preparation Time: 10 minutes

Cooking Time: 72 minutes

Servings: 4

Ingredients:

- 2 ½ pounds bone-in pork shoulder
- One 15-ounce can of whole-berry cranberry sauce
- ¼ cup minced onion
- ¼ cup honey
- Salt to taste

Directions:

1. Add all the ingredients into your pressure cooker and seal the lid.
2. Hit "chicken/meat" and adjust time to 1 hour, 12 minutes.
3. When time is up, hit "cancel" and wait 10 minutes for a natural pressure release.
4. Remove the shoulder and de-bone.
5. Serve pork with gravy!

Nutrition:

Total calories: 707 Protein: 43

Carbs: 61 Fat: 30

Fiber: 0

179. Mexican-Braised Pork with Sweet Potatoes

Preparation Time: 10 minutes

Cooking Time: 25 minutes

Servings: 4

Ingredients:

- 3 pounds pork loin
- 2 peeled and diced sweet potatoes
- 1 cup tomato salsa
- ½ cup chicken stock
- 1/3 cup Mexican spice blend

Directions:

1. Season the pork all over with the spice blend.
2. Turn your cooker to "chicken/meat" and heat.
3. When hot, sear the pork on both sides. If the meat sticks, pour in a little chicken stock.
4. When the pork is golden, pour in stock and salsa.
5. Tumble sweet potatoes on one side of the pot and seal the lid.
6. Adjust time to 25 minutes.
7. When the timer beeps, hit "cancel" and wait 10 minutes before quick-releasing.
8. The pork should be cooked to 145-degrees, and the potatoes should be tender.
9. Remove the pork and rest 8-10 minutes before serving.

Nutrition:

Total calories: 513 Protein: 73

Carbs: 17 Fat: 14 Fiber: 1

180. Peach-Mustard Pork Shoulder

Preparation Time: 2 minutes

Cooking Time: 55 minutes

Servings: 8

Ingredients:

- 4 pounds pork shoulder
- 1 cup peach preserving:
- 1 cup white wine
- 1/3 cup salt
- 1 tablespoon grainy mustard

Directions:

1. Season the pork well with salt.
2. Mix mustard and peach, and rub on the pork.
3. Pour wine into cooker and add pork.
4. Seal the lid.
5. Hit "chicken/meat" and adjust time to 55 minutes.
6. When time is up, hit "cancel" and wait 10 minutes before quick-releasing.
7. Pork should be cooked to at least 145-degrees.
8. Move pork to a plate and tent with foil for 15 minutes before slicing and serving.

Nutrition:

Total calories: 583

Protein: 44

Carbs: 26

Fat: 32

Fiber: 0

CHAPTER 9:

Side Dish Recipes

181. Parmesan Sweet Potato Casserole

Preparation Time: 15 minutes

Cooking Time: 35 minutes

Servings: 2

Ingredients:

- 2 sweet potatoes, peeled
- ½ yellow onion, sliced
- ½ cup cream
- ¼ cup spinach
- 2 oz. Parmesan cheese, shredded
- ½ teaspoon salt
- 1 tomato
- 1 teaspoon olive oil

Directions:

1. Chop the sweet potatoes.
2. Chop the tomato.
3. Chop the spinach.
4. Spray the air fryer tray with the olive oil.
5. Then place on the layer of the chopped sweet potato.
6. Add the layer of the sliced onion.
7. After this, sprinkle the sliced onion with the chopped spinach and tomatoes.
8. Sprinkle the casserole with the salt and shredded cheese.
9. Pour cream.
10. Preheat the air fryer to 390 F.
11. Cover the air fryer tray with the foil.
12. Cook the casserole for 35 minutes.
13. When the casserole is cooked – serve it. Enjoy!

Nutrition: Calories: 93 Fat: 1.8g Fiber: 3.4g Carbs: 20.3g Protein: 1.8g

182. Spicy Zucchini Slices

Preparation Time: 10 minutes

Cooking Time: 6 minutes

Servings: 2

Ingredients:

- 1 teaspoon cornstarch
- 1 zucchini
- ½ teaspoon chili flakes
- 1 tablespoon flour
- 1 egg
- ¼ teaspoon salt

Directions:

1. Slice the zucchini and sprinkle with the chili flakes and salt.

2.   Crack the egg into the bowl and whisk it.

3.   Dip the zucchini slices in the whisked egg.

4.   Combine together cornstarch with the flour. Stir it.

5.   Coat the zucchini slices with the cornstarch mixture.

6.   Preheat the air fryer to 400 F.

7.   Place the zucchini slices in the air fryer tray.

8.   Cook the zucchini slices for 4 minutes.

9.   After this, flip the slices to another side and cook for 2 minutes more.

10.   Serve the zucchini slices hot.

11.   Enjoy!

Nutrition: Calories: 67 Fat: 2.4g Fiber: 1.2g Carbs: 7.7g Protein: 4.4g

183. Cheddar Potato Gratin

Preparation Time: 15 minutes

Cooking Time: 20 minutes

Servings: 2

Ingredients:

- 2 potatoes
  - 1/3 cup half and half
  - 1 tablespoon oatmeal flour
  - ¼ teaspoon ground black pepper
  - 1 egg
  - 2 oz. Cheddar cheese

Directions:

1.   Wash the potatoes and slice them into thin pieces.

2.   Preheat the air fryer to 365 F.

3.   Put the potato slices in the air fryer and cook them for 10 minutes.

4.   Meanwhile, combine the half and half, oatmeal flour, and ground black pepper.

5.   Crack the egg into the liquid and whisk it carefully.

6.   Shred Cheddar cheese.

7.   When the potato is cooked – take 2 ramekins and place the potatoes on them.

8.   Pour the half and half mixture.

9.   Sprinkle the gratin with shredded Cheddar cheese.

10.   Cook the gratin for 10 minutes at 360 F.

11.   Serve the meal immediately.

12.   Enjoy!

Nutrition: Calories: 353 Fat: 16.6g Fiber: 5.4g Carbs: 37.2g Protein: 15g

184. Salty Lemon Artichokes

Preparation Time: 15 minutes

Cooking Time: 45 minutes

Servings: 2

Ingredients:

- 1 lemon
- 2 artichokes
- 1 teaspoon kosher salt

- 1 garlic head
- 2 teaspoons olive oil

Directions:

1. Cut off the edges of the artichokes.
2. Cut the lemon into the halves.
3. Peel the garlic head and chop the garlic cloves roughly.
4. Then place the chopped garlic in the artichokes.
5. Sprinkle the artichokes with the olive oil and kosher salt.
6. Then squeeze the lemon juice into the artichokes.
7. Wrap the artichokes in the foil.
8. Preheat the air fryer to 330 F.
9. Place the wrapped artichokes in the air fryer and cook for 45 minutes.
10. When the artichokes are cooked – discard the foil and serve. Enjoy!

Nutrition: Calories: 133 Fat: 5g Fiber: 9.7g Carbs: 21.7g Protein: 6g

185. Asparagus & Parmesan

Preparation Time: 10 minutes

Cooking Time: 6 minutes

Servings: 2

Ingredients:

- 1 teaspoon sesame oil
- 11 oz. asparagus
- 1 teaspoon chicken stock

- ½ teaspoon ground white pepper
- 3 oz. Parmesan

Directions:

1. Wash the asparagus and chop it roughly.
2. Sprinkle the chopped asparagus with the chicken stock and ground white pepper.
3. Then sprinkle the vegetables with the sesame oil and shake them.
4. Place the asparagus in the air fryer basket.
5. Cook the vegetables for 4 minutes at 400 F.
6. Meanwhile, shred Parmesan cheese.
7. When the time is over – shake the asparagus gently and sprinkle with the shredded cheese.
8. Cook the asparagus for 2 minutes more at 400 F.
9. After this, transfer the cooked asparagus in the serving plates.
10. Serve and taste it!

Nutrition: Calories: 189 Fat: 11.6g Fiber: 3.4g Carbs: 7.9g Protein: 17.2g

186. Carrot Lentil Burgers

Preparation Time: 10 minutes

Cooking Time: 12 minutes

Servings: 2

Ingredients:

- 6 oz. lentils, cooked
- 1 egg

- 2 oz. carrot, grated
- 1 teaspoon semolina
- ½ teaspoon salt
- 1 teaspoon turmeric
- 1 tablespoon butter

Directions:

1. Crack the egg into the bowl and whisk it.
2. Add the cooked lentils and mash the mixture with the help of the fork.
3. Then sprinkle the mixture with the grated carrot, semolina, salt, and turmeric.
4. Mix it up and make the medium burgers.
5. Put the butter into the lentil burgers. It will make them juicy.
6. Preheat the air fryer to 360 F.
7. Put the lentil burgers in the air fryer and cook for 12 minutes. Flip the burgers into another side after 6 minutes of cooking. Then chill the cooked lentil burgers and serve them.
8. Enjoy!

Nutrition: Calories: 404 Fat: 9g Fiber: 26.9g Carbs: 56g Protein: 25.3g

187. Corn on Cobs

Preparation Time: 10 minutes
Cooking Time: 10 minutes
Servings: 2
Ingredients:

- 2 fresh corn on cobs
  - 2 teaspoon butter

- 1 teaspoon salt
- 1 teaspoon paprika
- ¼ teaspoon olive oil

Directions:

1. Preheat the air fryer to 400 F.
2. Rub the corn on cobs with the salt and paprika.
3. Then sprinkle the corn on cobs with the olive oil.
4. Place the corn on cobs in the air fryer basket.
5. Cook the corn on cobs for 10 minutes.
6. When the time is over – transfer the corn on cobs in the serving plates and rub with the butter gently.
7. Serve the meal immediately.
8. Enjoy!

Nutrition: Calories: 122 Fat: 5.5g Fiber: 2.4g Carbs: 17.6g Protein: 3.2g

188. Sugary Carrot Strips

Preparation Time: 10 minutes
Cooking Time: 10 minutes
Servings: 2
Ingredients:

- 2 carrots
  - 1 teaspoon brown sugar
  - 1 teaspoon olive oil
  - 1 tablespoon soy sauce
  - 1 teaspoon honey
  - ½ teaspoon ground black pepper

Directions:

1. Peel the carrot and cut it into the strips.

2. Then put the carrot strips in the bowl.

3. Sprinkle the carrot strips with the olive oil, soy sauce, honey, and ground black pepper.

4. Shake the mixture gently.

5. Preheat the air fryer to 360 F.

6. Cook the carrot for 10 minutes.

7. After this, shake the carrot strips well.

8. Enjoy!

Nutrition: Calories: 67 Fat: 2.4g Fiber: 1.7g Carbs: 11.3g Protein: 1.1g

189. Onion Green Beans

Preparation Time: 10 minutes

Cooking Time: 12 minutes

Servings: 2

Ingredients:

- 11 oz. green beans
  - 1 tablespoon onion powder
  - 1 tablespoon olive oil
  - ½ teaspoon salt
  - ¼ teaspoon chili flakes

Directions:

1. Wash the green beans carefully and place them in the bowl.

2. Sprinkle the green beans with the onion powder, salt, chili flakes, and olive oil.

3. Shake the green beans carefully.

4. Preheat the air fryer to 400 F.

5. Put the green beans in the air fryer and cook for 8 minutes.

6. After this, shake the green beans and cook them for 4 minutes more at 400 F.

7. When the time is over – shake the green beans.

8. Serve the side dish and enjoy!

Nutrition: Calories: 1205 Fat: 7.2g Fiber: 5.5g Carbs: 13.9g Protein: 3.2g

190. Mozzarella Radish Salad

Preparation Time: 10 minutes

Cooking Time: 20 minutes

Servings: 2

Ingredients:

- 8 oz. radish
  - 4 oz. Mozzarella
  - 1 teaspoon balsamic vinegar
  - ½ teaspoon salt
  - 1 tablespoon olive oil
  - 1 teaspoon dried oregano

Directions:

1. Wash the radish carefully and cut it into the halves.

2. Preheat the air fryer to 360 F.

3. Put the radish halves in the air fryer basket.

4. Sprinkle the radish with the salt and olive oil.

5. Cook the radish for 20 minutes.

6. Shake the radish after 10 minutes of cooking.

7. When the time is over – transfer the radish to the serving plate.

8. Chop Mozzarella roughly.

9. Sprinkle the radish with Mozzarella, balsamic vinegar, and dried oregano.

10. Stir it gently with the help of 2 forks.

11. Serve it immediately.

Nutrition: Calories: 241 Fat: 17.2g Fiber: 2.1g Carbs: 6.4g Protein: 16.9g

5. Put the mushrooms in the air fryer and cook for 2 minutes.

6. Shake the mushrooms well and sprinkle with the coconut milk and balsamic vinegar.

7. Cook the mushrooms for 4 minutes more at 400 F.

8. Then skewer the mushrooms on the wooden sticks and serve.

9. Enjoy!

Nutrition: Calories 116 Fat: 9.5g Fiber: 1.3g Carbs: 5.6g Protein: 3g

191. Cremini Mushroom Satay

Preparation Time: 10 minutes

Cooking Time: 6 minutes

Servings: 2

Ingredients:

- 7 oz. cremini mushrooms
  - 2 tablespoon coconut milk
  - 1 tablespoon butter
  - 1 teaspoon chili flakes
  - ½ teaspoon balsamic vinegar
  - ½ teaspoon curry powder
  - ½ teaspoon white pepper

Directions:

1. Wash the mushrooms carefully.

2. Then sprinkle the mushrooms with the chili flakes, curry powder, and white pepper.

3. Preheat the air fryer to 400 F.

4. Toss the butter in the air fryer basket and melt it.

192. Eggplant Ratatouille

Preparation Time: 15 minutes

Cooking Time: 15 minutes

Servings: 2

Ingredients:

- 1 eggplant
  - 1 sweet yellow pepper
  - 3 cherry tomatoes
  - 1/3 white onion, chopped
  - ½ teaspoon garlic clove, sliced
  - 1 teaspoon olive oil
  - ½ teaspoon ground black pepper
  - ½ teaspoon Italian seasoning

Directions:

1. Preheat the air fryer to 360 F.

2. Peel the eggplants and chop them.

3. Put the chopped eggplants in the air fryer basket.

4. Chop the cherry tomatoes and add them to the air fryer basket.

5. Then add chopped onion, sliced garlic clove, olive oil, ground black pepper, and Italian seasoning.

6. Chop the sweet yellow pepper roughly and add it to the air fryer basket.

7. Shake the vegetables gently and cook for 15 minutes.

8. Stir the meal after 8 minutes of cooking.

9. Transfer the cooked ratatouille in the serving plates.

10. Enjoy!

Nutrition: Calories: 149 Fat: 3.7g Fiber: 11.7g Carbs: 28.9g Protein: 5.1g

193. Cheddar Portobello Mushrooms

Preparation Time: 15 minutes

Cooking Time: 6 minutes

Servings: 2

Ingredients:

- 2 Portobello mushroom hats
  - 2 slices Cheddar cheese
  - ¼ cup panko breadcrumbs
  - ½ teaspoon salt
  - ½ teaspoon ground black pepper
  - 1 egg
  - 1 teaspoon oatmeal
  - 2 oz. bacon, chopped cooked

Directions:

1. Crack the egg into the bowl and whisk it.

2. Combine the ground black pepper, oatmeal, salt, and breadcrumbs in the separate bowl.

3. Dip the mushroom hats in the whisked egg.

4. After this, coat the mushroom hats in the breadcrumb mixture.

5. Preheat the air fryer to 400 F.

6. Place the mushrooms in the air fryer basket tray and cook for 3 minutes.

7. After this, put the chopped bacon and sliced cheese over the mushroom hats and cook the meal for 3 minutes.

8. When the meal is cooked – let it chill gently.

9. Enjoy!

Nutrition: Calories: 376 Fat: 24.1g Fiber: 1.8g Carbs: 14.6g Protein: 25.2g

194. 600. Salty Edamame

Preparation Time: 15 minutes

Cooking Time: 6 minutes

Servings: 2

Ingredients:

- 1 cup of edamame, inside a shell
- The salt, for taste

Directions:

1. Over a medium-low heat, place a large saucepan. Add 2 quarts of edamame and water. Cover and simmer for about 5-8 minutes, until tender.

2. Drain and add salt to sprinkle.

Nutrition: Calories: 376 Fat: 24.1g Fiber: 1.8g Carbs: 14.6g Protein: 25.2g

195. Parsley Zucchini and Radishes

Preparation time: 5 minutes

Cooking time: 15 minutes

Servings: 4

Ingredients

- 1 pound zucchinis, cubed
- 1 cup radishes, halved
- 1 tablespoon olive oil
- 1 tablespoon balsamic vinegar
- 2 tomatoes, cubed
- 3 tablespoons parsley, chopped
- Salt and black pepper to the taste

Directions

1. In a pan that fits your air fryer, mix the zucchinis with the radishes, oil and the other ingredients, toss, introduce in the fryer and cook at 350 degrees F for 15 minutes.
2. Divide between plates and serve as a side dish.

Nutrition: Calories 170, Fat 6, Fiber 2, Carbs 5, Protein 6

196. Cherry Tomatoes Sauté

Preparation time: 5 minutes

Cooking time: 15 minutes

Servings: 4

Ingredients

- 1 tablespoon olive oil
- 1 pound cherry tomatoes, halved
- Juice of 1 lime
- 2 tablespoons parsley, chopped
- A pinch of salt and black pepper

Directions

1. In a pan that fits the air fryer, mix the tomatoes with the oil and the other ingredients, toss, introduce the pan in the machine and cook at 360 degrees F for 15 minutes.
2. Divide between plates and serve.

Nutrition: Calories 141, Fat 6, Fiber 2, Carbs 4, Protein 7

197. Creamy Eggplant

Preparation time: 5 minutes

Cooking time: 20 minutes

Servings: 4

Ingredients

2 pounds eggplants, roughly cubed

1 cup heavy cream

2 tablespoons butter, melted

Salt and black pepper to the taste

½ teaspoon chili powder

½ teaspoon turmeric powder

Directions

1. In a pan that fits the air fryer, mix the eggplants with the cream, butter and the other ingredients, toss, introduce in the machine and cook at 370 degrees F for 20 minutes.

2. Divide between plates and serve as a side dish.

Nutrition: Calories 151, Fat 3, Fiber 2, Carbs 4, Protein 6

198. Eggplant and Carrots Mix

Preparation time: 5 minutes

Cooking time: 25 minutes

Servings: 4

Ingredients

- 1 pound eggplants, roughly cubed
- 1 pound baby carrots
- 1 cup heavy cream
- ½ teaspoon chili powder
- 1 teaspoon garlic powder
- 1 tablespoon chives, chopped
- A pinch of salt and black pepper

Directions

1. In a pan that fits your air fryer, mix the eggplants with the carrots, cream and the other ingredients, toss, introduce in the air fryer and cook at 370 degrees F for 25 minutes.
2. Divide between plates and serve as a side dish.

Nutrition: Calories 129, Fat 6, Fiber 2, Carbs 5, Protein 8

199. Parmesan Eggplants

Preparation time: 5 minutes

Cooking time: 20 minutes

Servings: 4

Ingredients

- 1 pound eggplants, roughly cubed
- 1 tablespoon olive oil
- 1 teaspoon garlic powder
- 1 cup parmesan, grated
- A pinch of salt and black pepper
- Cooking spray

Directions

1. In the air fryer's pan, mix the eggplants with the oil and the other ingredients except the parmesan and toss.
2. Sprinkle the parmesan on top, put the pan in the machine and cook at 370 degrees F for 20 minutes.
3. Divide between plates and serve as a side dish.

Nutrition: calories 183, fat 6, fiber 2, carbs 3, protein 8

200. Kale Sauté

Preparation time: 5 minutes

Cooking time: 15 minutes

Servings: 4

Ingredients

- 1 tablespoon avocado oil
- 1 pound baby kale
- ½ cup heavy cream
- Salt and black pepper to the taste

- ¼ teaspoon chili powder
- 1 tablespoon dill, chopped
- ¼ cup walnuts, chopped

Directions

1. In a pan that fits the air fryer, mix the kale with the oil, cream and the other ingredients, toss, introduce the pan in the machine and cook at 360 degrees F for 15 minutes.
2. Divide between plates and serve as a side dish.

Nutrition: Calories 160, Fat 7, Fiber 2, Carbs 4, Protein 5

201. Carrots Sauté

Preparation time: 5 minutes

Cooking time: 20 minutes

Servings: 4

Ingredients 2 pounds baby carrots, peeled

- 1 tablespoon balsamic vinegar
- 2 tablespoons olive oil
- Salt and black pepper to the taste
- 1 tablespoon lemon juice
- 1/3 cup almonds, chopped
- ½ cup walnuts, chopped

Directions

1. In a pan that fits the air fryer, mix the carrots with the vinegar, oil and the other ingredients, toss, introduce the pan in the machine and cook at 380 degrees F for 20 minutes.
2. Divide between plates and serve as a side dish.

Nutrition: Calories 121, Fat 9, Fiber 2, Carbs 4, Protein 5

202. Bok Choy and Sprouts

Preparation time: 5 minutes

Cooking time: 20 minutes

Servings: 4

Ingredients

- 1 tablespoon avocado oil
- 1 pound Brussels sprouts, trimmed and halved
- 2 bok choy heads, trimmed and cut into strips
- 1 tablespoon balsamic vinegar
- A pinch of salt and black pepper
- 1 tablespoon dill, chopped

Directions

1. In a pan that fits your air fryer, mix the sprouts with the bok choy and the other ingredients, toss, introduce the pan in the air fryer and cook at 380 degrees F for 20 minutes.
2. Divide between plates and serve as a side dish.

Nutrition: Calories 141, Fat 3, Fiber 2, Carbs 4, Protein 3

203. Balsamic Radishes

Preparation time: 10 minutes

Cooking time: 20 minutes

Servings: 4

Ingredients

- 1 pound radishes, halved
- 1 tablespoon balsamic vinegar

- 1 teaspoon chili powder
- 1 tablespoon avocado oil
- Salt and black pepper to the taste

Directions

1. In a pan that fits the air fryer, combine the radishes with the vinegar and the other ingredients, toss, introduce the pan in the air fryer and cook at 380 degrees F for 20 minutes.
2. Divide between plates and serve as a side dish.

Nutrition: Calories 151, Fat 2, Fiber 3, Carbs 5, Protein 5

204. Spaghetti Squash Casserole

Preparation time: 10 minutes

Cooking time: 20 minutes

Servings: 4

Ingredients

- 12 oz spaghetti squash
- 1 teaspoon ground cinnamon
- ½ teaspoon salt
- 1 sweet potato, grated
- 1 tablespoon almond flour
- 2 eggs
- 1 tablespoon olive oil
- 1 onion, diced
- ¼ teaspoon thyme

Directions

1. Peel the spaghetti squash and chop it into the ½ inch chunks.
2. Then place the squash in the air fryer basket.
3. Add salt and ground cinnamon.
4. Cook the sweet potatoes for 5 minutes at 380 F.
5. After this, make the layer of the grated potato over the sweet potato.
6. Beat the eggs in the bowl and whisk them.
7. Add almond flour and stir the mixture.
8. Then add olive oil, diced onion, and thyme.
9. Stir the mixture.
10. Pour it over the grated potato.
11. Cook the casserole for 15 minutes at 365 F.
12. When the time is over and casserole is cooked – let it chill little and serve!

Nutrition: Calories 166, Fat 9.8, Fiber 2.6, Carbs 16.5, Protein 5.7

205. Cinnamon Baby Carrot

Preparation time: 8 minutes

Cooking time: 15 minutes

Servings: 4

Ingredients

- 1-pound baby carrot
- 1 tablespoon ground cinnamon
- 1 teaspoon ground ginger
- ¼ cup almond milk
- 1 tablespoon olive oil

Directions

1. Wash the baby carrot carefully and sprinkle with the ground cinnamon, ground ginger, and olive oil.
2. Stir the vegetables and transfer them to the air fryer basket.
3. Cook the baby carrot for 10 minutes at 380 F.
4. Then stir the baby carrots and add almond milk.
5. Stir the vegetables again and cook for 5 minutes more at the same temperature.
6. Let the cooked carrot chill little and serve it!

Nutrition: Calories 110, Fat 7.3, Fiber 4.6, Carbs 11.9, Protein 1.2

206. Eggplant Tongues

Preparation time: 10 minutes
Cooking time: 14 minutes
Servings: 2
Ingredients

- 2 eggplants
- 1 teaspoon minced garlic
- 1 teaspoon olive oil
- ¼ teaspoon ground black pepper

Directions

1. Wash the eggplants carefully and slice them.
2. Rub every eggplant slice with the minced garlic, olive oil, and ground black pepper.
3. Place the eggplants in the air fryer basket and cook for 7 minutes from each side at 375 F.
4. When the eggplant tongues are cooked – serve them immediately!

Nutrition: Calories 160, Fat 3.3, Fiber 19.4, Carbs 32.9, Protein 5.5

207. Super Tasty Onion Petals

Preparation time: 10 minutes
Cooking time: 15 minutes
Servings: 4
Ingredients

- 13 oz onion, peeled
- 1 teaspoon basil, dried
- 1 teaspoon ground coriander
- 1 tablespoon olive oil
- ¼ teaspoon ground nutmeg
- ¾ teaspoon turmeric

Directions

1. Cut the onion into the petals and sprinkle with the basil, ground coriander, olive oil, ground nutmeg, and turmeric.
2. Mix the onion petals and transfer them to the air fryer basket.
3. Cook the petals for 15 minutes at 375 F. Stir the petals every 3 minutes.
4. When the onion petals are cooked – they will have a soft texture.
5. Serve the side dish immediately!

Nutrition: Calories 69, Fat 3.7, Fiber 2.1, Carbs 9, Protein 1.

208. Eggplant Garlic Salad with Tomatoes

Preparation time: 10 minutes

Cooking time: 15 minutes

Servings: 6

Ingredients

- 3 tomatoes, chopped
- 2 eggplants, chopped
- 1 tablespoon olive oil
- 1 teaspoon avocado oil
- 1 tablespoon vinegar
- ½ teaspoon ground black pepper
- ½ teaspoon dried basil
- 2 garlic cloves, chopped

Directions

1. Place the chopped eggplants in the air fryer.
2. Sprinkle the eggplants with the olive oil, ground black pepper, and dried basil.
3. Stir the eggplants and cook for 15 minutes at 390 F. Stir the vegetables every 5 minutes.
4. Then place the tomatoes in the bowl.
5. Add cooked eggplants, vinegar, and chopped garlic.
6. Then sprinkle the salad with the avocado oil and stir it.
7. Serve the cooked salad or keep it in the fridge!

Nutrition: Calories 80, Fat 2.9, Fiber 7.3, Carbs 13.6, Protein 2.4

209. Curry Eggplants

Preparation time: 10 minutes

Cooking time: 14 minutes

Servings: 2

Ingredients

- 2 eggplants
- 1 teaspoon vinegar
- 1 tablespoon olive oil
- 1 teaspoon curry powder
- 1 garlic clove
- 3 tablespoons chicken stock

Directions

1. Peel the eggplants and cut them into the cubes.
2. Sprinkle the eggplants with the curry powder and chicken stock.
3. Put the vegetables in the air fryer and cook for 14 minutes at 390 F.
4. Stir the eggplants every 5 minutes.
5. When the eggplants are cooked – let them chill till the room temperature.
6. Sprinkle the vegetables with the olive oil and vinegar. Stir and serve!

Nutrition: Calories 204, Fat 8.2, Fiber 19.7, Carbs 33.4, Protein 5.7

210. Eggplants Pizzas

Preparation time: 15 minutes

Cooking time: 15 minutes

Servings: 2

Ingredients

- 1 eggplant
- 1 tomato, sliced
- 1 tablespoon fresh basil, chopped
- ½ teaspoon cilantro, dried
- 1 oz ground chicken
- 1 teaspoon olive oil
- ¾ teaspoon salt

Directions

1. Slice the eggplant and sprinkle every slice with the salt and olive oil.
2. Place the sliced eggplants in the air fryer basket.
3. After this, mix up together the dried cilantro, basil, and ground chicken. Stir it.
4. Place the ground chicken over every sliced tomato.
5. Then place the ground chicken over the tomatoes.
6. Cook the pizzas for 15 minutes at 390 F.
7. When the ground chicken is cooked – the pizza is ready to eat.
8. Enjoy!

Nutrition: Calories 110, Fat 3.9, Fiber 8.5, Carbs 14.7, Protein 6.7

211. Radishes and Walnuts Mix

Preparation time: 5 minutes

Cooking time: 15 minutes

Servings: 4

Ingredients

- 1 pound radishes, halved
- 1 cup walnuts, chopped
- Juice of 1 lime
- 1 tablespoon olive oil
- Salt and black pepper to the taste
- 3 teaspoons black sesame seeds
- 1 tablespoon chives, chopped

Directions

1. In the air fryer's pan, mix the radishes with the walnuts, lime juice and the other ingredients, toss, put the pan in the machine and cook at 380 degrees F for 15 minutes.
2. Divide between plates and serve as a side dish.

Nutrition: Calories 150, Fat 4, Fiber 2, Carbs 3, Protein 5

212. Protein Pumpkin Spiced Donuts

Preparation Time: 10 minutes

Cooking Time: 25 minutes

Servings: 8

Ingredients:

- Oat flour (1 cup)
- Xylitol (3/4 cup)
- Vanilla protein (1 scoop, powdered)
- Flaxseed (1 tbsp, ground)

- Cinnamon (1 tbsp, ground)
- Baking powder (2 tsp.)
- Sea salt (1 tsp.)
- Eggs (3, beaten)
- Pumpkin (1/2 cup, canned)
- Coconut oil (1 tbsp, melted)
- Vanilla (2 tsp., pure)
- Apple cider vinegar (1 tsp.)

<u>Ingredients for the frosting:</u>

- Cream cheese (1/2 cup, whipped)
- Liquid stevia (1/2 tsp.)

Directions:

1. Place the xylitol, oat flour, ground flaxseed, powdered protein, baking powder, ground cinnamon and a dash of sea salt in a large bowl. Preheat your oven to 350 degrees Fahrenheit.
2. Add the egg (beaten) into another bowl (large) along with the pumpkin (canned), pure vanilla and vinegar and coconut oil (melted)
3. Whisk until mixed (evenly) then pour mixture into the flour. Stir until thoroughly mixed.
4. Using cooking spray grease a large donut pan.
5. Pour batter into the donut pan (greased).
6. Place batter into the oven and bake for approximately 10 minutes until thoroughly baked.
7. Remove from heat and set donuts onto a wire rack to cool.
8. Add in the cream cheese (whipped) and liquid stevia in a small bowl, whisk until becomes smooth.
9. Frost donuts using the frosting and serve with a sprinkle of cinnamon (ground) over the top.

Nutrients:

Calories 95kcal

Fats 0.3 g

Carbohydrates 9.3 g

Protein 12.5 g

213. Taco Zucchini Boats

Preparation Time: 20 minutes

Cooking Time: 70 minutes

Servings: 4

Ingredients:

- 4 medium zucchinis cut in half lengthwise
- 1/4 cup fresh cilantro, chopped
- 1/2 cup cheddar cheese, shredded
- 1/4 cup water
- 4 oz. tomato sauce
- 2 tbsp bell pepper, mined
- 1/2 small onion, minced
- 1/2 tsp. oregano
- 1 tsp. paprika
- 1 tsp. chili powder
- 1 tsp. cumin
- 1 tsp. garlic powder
- 1 lb. lean ground turkey
- 1/2 cup salsa
- 1 tsp. kosher salt

Directions:

1. Preheat the oven to 400 F. Add 1/4 cup of salsa in the bottom of the baking dish.
2. Using a spoon hollow out the center of the zucchini halves.
3. Chop the scooped-out flesh of zucchini and set aside 3/4 of a cup chopped meat.

4. Add zucchini halves in the boiling water and cook for 1 minute.
5. Remove zucchini halves from water.
6. Add ground turkey in a large pan and cook until meat is no longer pink.
7. Add spices and mix well.
8. Add reserved zucchini flesh, water, tomato sauce, bell pepper, and onion.
9. Stir well and cover, simmer over low heat for 20 minutes.
10. Stuff zucchini boats with taco meat and top each with one tablespoon of shredded cheddar cheese.
11. Place zucchini boats in baking dish.
12. Cover dish with foil and bake in preheated oven for 35 minutes.
13. Top with remaining salsa and chopped cilantro.
14. Serve and enjoy.

Nutrition:

Calories: 297 Cal Fat: 13.7 g

Carbohydrates: 17.2 g

Sugar: 9.3 g

Protein: 30.2 g

Cholesterol: 96 mg

214. Creamy Coconut Kiwi Drink

Preparation Time: 5 minutes

Cooking Time: 3 minutes

Servings: 4

Ingredients:

- 5 kiwis, pulp scooped
- 2 tbsp erythritol
- 2 cups unsweetened coconut milk
- 2 cups coconut cream
- 7 ice cubes
- Mint leaves to garnish

Directions:

1. In a blender, process the kiwis, erythritol, milk, cream, and ice cubes until smooth, about 3 minutes.
2. Pour into four serving glasses, garnish with mint leaves, and serve.

Nutrition:

Calories: 351 Cal

Fat: 28 g

Carbohydrates: 9.7 g

Protein: 16 g

215. Easy One-Pot Vegan Marinara

Preparation Time: 5 minutes

Cooking Time: 15 minutes

Servings: 2

Ingredients:

1 cup water

- 1 cup tomato paste
- 2 tablespoons maple syrup
- 1 teaspoon dried oregano
- 1 teaspoon dried thyme
- 1 teaspoon garlic powder
- 1 teaspoon onion powder
- 1/2 teaspoon dried basil
- 1/4 teaspoon red pepper flakes

Directions:

1. In a medium saucepan, bring the water to a rolling boil over high heat.
2. Reduce the heat to low, and whisk in the tomato paste, maple syrup, oregano, thyme, garlic powder, onion powder, basil, and red pepper flakes.
3. Cover and simmer for 10 minutes, stirring occasionally. Serve warm.

Nutrition: Fat: 0g Carbohydrates: 17 g Fiber: 3 g Protein: 3 g

216. Sunflower Parmesan Cheese

Preparation Time: 5 minutes

Cooking Time: 30 minutes

Servings: 1

Ingredients:

- 1/2 cup sunflower seeds
- 2 tablespoons nutritional yeast
- 1/2 teaspoon garlic powder

Directions:

1. In a food processor or blender, combine the sunflower seeds, nutritional yeast, and garlic powder.

2. Process on low for 30 to 45 seconds, or until the sunflower seeds have been broken down to the size of coarse sea salt.

3. Store in a refrigerator-safe container for up to 2 months.

Nutrition:

Fat: 4 g

Carbohydrates: 3 g

Fiber: 1 g

Protein: 3 g

CHAPTER 10:

Dessert Recipes

217. Chocolate Bars

Preparation Time: 10 minutes

Cooking Time: 20 minutes

Servings: 16

Ingredients:

- 15 oz cream cheese, softened
- 15 oz unsweetened dark chocolate
- 1 tsp vanilla
- 10 drops liquid stevia

Directions:

1. Grease 8-inch square dish and set aside.
2. In a saucepan dissolve chocolate over low heat.
3. Add stevia and vanilla and stir well.
4. Remove pan from heat and set aside.
5. Add cream cheese into the blender and blend until smooth.
6. Add melted chocolate mixture into the cream cheese and blend until just combined.
7. Transfer mixture into the prepared dish and spread evenly and place in the refrigerator until firm.
8. Slice and serve.

Nutrition:

Calories: 230 Fat: 24 g

Carbs: 7.5 g Sugar: 0.1 g

Protein: 6 g Cholesterol: 29 mg

218. Blueberry Muffins

Preparation Time: 15 minutes

Cooking Time: 35 minutes

Servings: 12

Ingredients:

- 2 eggs
- 1/2 cup fresh blueberries
- 1 cup heavy cream
- 2 cups almond flour
- 1/4 tsp lemon zest
- 1/2 tsp lemon extract
- 1 tsp baking powder
- 5 drops stevia
- 1/4 cup butter, melted

Directions:

1. heat the cooker to 350 F. Line muffin tin with cupcake liners and set aside.
2. Add eggs into the bowl and whisk until mix.
3. Add remaining ingredients and mix to combine.

4. Pour mixture into the prepared muffin tin and bake for 25 minutes. Serve and enjoy.

Nutrition: Calories: 190 Fat: 17 g Carbs: 5 g Sugar: 1 g Protein: 5 g Cholesterol: 55 mg

219. Chia Pudding

Preparation Time: 20 minutes

Cooking Time: 0 minutes

Servings: 2

Ingredients:

- 4 tbsp chia seeds
  - 1 cup unsweetened coconut milk
  - 1/2 cup raspberries

Directions:

1. Add raspberry and coconut milk into a blender and blend until smooth.
2. Pour mixture into the glass jar.
3. Add chia seeds in a jar and stir well.
4. Seal the jar with a lid and shake well and place in the refrigerator for 3 hours.
5. Serve chilled and enjoy.

Nutrition: Calories: 360 Fat: 33 g Carbs: 13 g Sugar: 5 g Protein: 6 g Cholesterol: 0 mg

220. Avocado Pudding

Preparation Time: 20 minutes

Cooking Time: 0 minutes

Servings: 8

Ingredients:

- 2 ripe avocados, pitted and cut into pieces
  - 1 tbsp fresh lime juice
  - 14 oz can coconut milk

- 2 tsp liquid stevia
- 2 tsp vanilla

Directions:

1. Inside the blender Add all ingredients and blend until smooth.
2. Serve immediately and enjoy.

Nutrition: Calories: 317 Fat: 30 g Carbs: 9 g Sugar: 0.5 g Protein: 3 g Cholesterol: 0 mg

221. Delicious Brownie Bites

Preparation Time: 20 minutes

Cooking Time: 0 minutes

Servings: 13

Ingredients:

- 1/4 cup unsweetened chocolate chips
- 1/4 cup unsweetened cocoa powder
- 1 cup pecans, chopped
- 1/2 cup almond butter
- 1/2 tsp vanilla
- 1/4 cup monk fruit sweetener
- 1/8 tsp pink salt

Directions:

1. Add pecans, sweetener, vanilla, almond butter, cocoa powder, and salt into the food processor and process until well combined.
2. Transfer brownie mixture into the large bowl. Add chocolate chips and fold well.
3. Make small round shape balls from brownie mixture and place onto a baking tray.

4. Place in the freezer for 20 minutes. Serve and enjoy.

Nutrition: Calories: 108 Fat: 9 g Carbs: 4 g Sugar: 1 g Protein: 2 g Cholesterol: 0 mg

222. Pumpkin Balls

Preparation Time: 15 minutes

Cooking Time: 0 minutes

Servings: 18

Ingredients: 1 cup almond butter

- 5 drops liquid stevia
- 2 tbsp coconut flour
- 2 tbsp pumpkin puree
- 1 tsp pumpkin pie spice

Directions:

1. Mix together pumpkin puree in a large bowl, and almond butter until well combined.
2. Add liquid stevia, pumpkin pie spice, and coconut flour and mix well.
3. Make small balls from mixture and place onto a baking tray.
4. Place in the freezer for 1 hour.
5. Serve and enjoy.

Nutrition: Calories: 96 Fat: 8 g Carbs: 4 g Sugar: 1 g Protein: 2 g Cholesterol: 0 mg

223. Smooth Peanut Butter Cream

Preparation Time: 10 minutes

Cooking Time: 0 minutes

Servings: 8

Ingredients:

- 1/4 cup peanut butter

- 4 overripe bananas, chopped
- 1/3 cup cocoa powder
- 1/4 tsp vanilla extract
- 1/8 tsp salt

Directions:

1. In the blender add all the listed ingredients and blend until smooth.
2. Serve immediately and enjoy.

Nutrition: Calories: 101 Fat: 5 g Carbs: 14 g Sugar: 7 g Protein: 3 g Cholesterol: 0 mg

224. Vanilla Avocado Popsicles

Preparation Time: 20 minutes

Cooking Time: 0 minutes

Servings: 6

Ingredients: 2 avocadoes

- 1 tsp vanilla - 1 cup almond milk
- 1 tsp liquid stevia
- 1/2 cup unsweetened cocoa powder

Directions:

1. In the blender add all the listed ingredients and blend smoothly.
2. Pour blended mixture into the Popsicle molds and place in the freezer until set.
3. Serve and enjoy.

Nutrition: Calories: 130 Fat: 12 g Carbs: 7 g Sugar: 1 g Protein: 3 g Cholesterol: 0 mg

225. Chocolate Popsicle

Preparation Time: 20 minutes

Cooking Time: 10 minutes

Servings: 6

Ingredients:

- 4 oz unsweetened chocolate, chopped

- 6 drops liquid stevia
- 1 1/2 cups heavy cream

Directions:

1. Add heavy cream into the microwave-safe bowl and microwave until just begins the boiling.
2. Add chocolate into the heavy cream and set aside for 5 minutes.
3. Add liquid stevia into the heavy cream mixture and stir until chocolate is melted.
4. Pour mixture into the Popsicle molds and place in freezer for 4 hours or until set.
5. Serve and enjoy.

Nutrition: Calories: 198 Fat: 21 g Carbs: 6 g Sugar: 0.2 g Protein: 3 g Cholesterol: 41 mg

226. Raspberry Ice Cream

Preparation Time: 10 minutes
Cooking Time: 0 minutes
Servings: 2
Ingredients:

- 1 cup frozen raspberries
  - 1/2 cup heavy cream
  - 1/8 tsp stevia powder

Directions:

1. Blend all the listed ingredients in a blender until smooth.
2. Serve immediately and enjoy.

Nutrition: Calories: 144 Fat: 11 g Carbs: 10 g Sugar: 4 g Protein: 2 g Cholesterol: 41 mg

227. Chocolate Frosty

Preparation Time: 20 minutes
Cooking Time: 0 minutes
Servings: 4
Ingredients:

- 2 tbsp unsweetened cocoa powder
  - 1 cup heavy whipping cream
  - 1 tbsp almond butter
  - 5 drops liquid stevia
  - 1 tsp vanilla

Directions:

1. Add cream into the medium bowl and beat using the hand mixer for 5 minutes.
2. Add remaining ingredients and blend until thick cream form.
3. Pour in serving bowls and place them in the freezer for 30 minutes.
4. Serve and enjoy.

Nutrition: Calories: 137 Fat: 13 g Carbs: 3 g Sugar: 0.5 g Protein: 2 g Cholesterol: 41 mg

228. Chocolate Almond Butter Brownie

Preparation Time: 10 minutes
Cooking Time: 16 minutes
Servings: 4
Ingredients:

- 1 cup bananas, overripe
  - 1/2 cup almond butter, melted
  - 1 scoop protein powder
  - 2 tbsp unsweetened cocoa powder

Directions:

1. Preheat the air fryer to 325 F. Grease air fryer baking pan and set aside.

2. Blend all ingredients in a blender until smooth.

3. Pour batter into the prepared pan and place in the air fryer basket and cook for 16 minutes.

4. Serve and enjoy.

Nutrition: Calories: 82 Fat: 2 g Carbs: 11 g Sugar: 5 g Protein: 7 g Cholesterol: 16 mg

229. Peanut Butter Fudge

Preparation Time: 10 minutes

Cooking Time: 10 minutes

Servings: 20

Ingredients:

- 1/4 cup almonds, toasted and chopped
- 12 oz smooth peanut butter
- 15 drops liquid stevia
- 3 tbsp coconut oil
- 4 tbsp coconut cream
- Pinch of salt

Directions:

1. Line baking tray with parchment paper.

2. Melt coconut oil in a pan over low heat. Add peanut butter, coconut cream, stevia, and salt in a saucepan. Stir well.

3. Pour fudge mixture into the prepared baking tray and sprinkle chopped almonds on top.

4. Place the tray in the refrigerator for 1 hour or until set.

5. Slice and serve.

Nutrition: Calories: 131 Fat: 12 g Carbs: 4 g Sugar: 2 g Protein: 5 g Cholesterol: 0 mg

230. Almond Butter Fudge

Preparation Time: 10 minutes

Cooking Time: 10 minutes

Servings: 18

Ingredients:

- 3/4 cup creamy almond butter
- 1 1/2 cups unsweetened chocolate chips

Directions:

1. Line 8*4-inch pan with parchment paper and set aside.

2. Add chocolate chips and almond butter into the double boiler and cook over medium heat until the chocolate-butter mixture is melted. Stir well. Place mixture into the prepared pan and place in the freezer until set.

3. Slice and serve.

Nutrition: Calories: 197 Fat: 16 g Carbs: 7 g Sugar: 1 g Protein: 4 g Cholesterol: 0 mg

231. Bounty Bars

Preparation Time: 20 minutes

Cooking Time: 0 minutes

Servings: 12

Ingredients:

- 1 cup coconut cream
- 3 cups shredded unsweetened coconut

- 1/4 cup extra virgin coconut oil
- 1/2 teaspoon vanilla powder
- 1/4 cup powdered erythritol
- 1 1/2 oz. cocoa butter
- 5 oz. dark chocolate

Directions:

1. Heat the oven at 350 °F and toast the coconut in it for 5-6 minutes. Remove from the oven once toasted and set aside to cool.

2. Take a bowl of medium size and add coconut oil, coconut cream, vanilla, erythritol, and toasted coconut. Mix the ingredients well to prepare a smooth mixture.

3. Make 12 bars of equal size with the help of your hands from the prepared mixture and adjust in the tray lined with parchment paper.

4. Place the tray in the fridge for around one hour and, in the meantime, put the cocoa butter and dark chocolate in a glass bowl.

5. Heat a cup of water in a saucepan over medium heat and place the bowl over it to melt the cocoa butter and the dark chocolate.

6. Remove from the heat once melted properly, mix well until blended and set aside to cool.

7. Take the coconut bars and coat them with dark chocolate mixture one by one using a wooden stick. Adjust on the tray lined with parchment paper and drizzle the remaining mixture over them.

8. Refrigerate for around one hour before you serve the delicious bounty bars.

Nutrition:
Calories: 230 Fat: 25 g
Carbohydrates: 5 g Protein: 32 g

232. Optavia Granola

Preparation Time: 5 minutes
Cooking Time: 8 minutes
Servings: 3
Ingredients:

- 1 package Medifast or Optavia Oatmeal
- 1 packet stevia
- 1 teaspoon vanilla extract
- 1/2 teaspoon apple spice or pumpkin pie spice

Directions:

1. Preheat the oven to 4000F. In a bowl, combine all ingredients and add enough water to get the granola to stick together.

2. Drop the granola onto a cookie sheet lined with parchment paper.

3. Bake for 8 minutes, but make sure to give the granola a fair shake for even browning halfway through the cooking time.

Nutrition: Calories per serving: 209 Cal
Protein: 5.8 g Carbohydrates: 42 g
Fat: 3.2 g Sugar: 6.2 g

233. No Bake Optavia Fueling Peanut Butter Brownies

Preparation Time: 5 minutes

Cooking Time: 30 minutes

Servings: 6

Ingredients:

- 3 tablespoons peanut butter
- 1 cup water
- 6 packets Optavia Double Chocolate Brownie Fueling

Directions:

1. Put all ingredients in a bowl and mix until all elements are well incorporated.
2. Pour into silicone molds and place in the freezer.
3. Freeze for 30 minutes before eating.

Nutrition:

Calories per serving: 906 Cal

Protein: 8.7 g

Carbohydrates: 157 g

Fat: 31.8 g

Sugar: 1.5 g

234. Peanut Butter Brownie Ice Cream Sandwiches

Preparation Time: 2 minutes

Cooking Time: 2 minutes

Servings: 2

Ingredients:

- 1 packet Medifast Brownie Mix
- 3 tablespoons water
- 1 Peanut Butter Crunch Bar or any bar of your choice
- 2 tablespoons Peanut Butter Powder
- 1 tablespoon water
- 2 tablespoons cool whip

Directions:

1. Melt the Brownie Mix with water.
2. Add in the Peanut Butter Crunch until a dough is formed.
3. Spoon 4 dough balls on a plate and flatten using the palm of your hands.
4. Make sure that the dough is 1/4 inch thick.
5. Place in a microwave oven and cook for 2 minutes.
6. Meanwhile, mix the Peanut Butter Powder and water to form a paste.
7. Add cool whip. Set aside in the fridge to chill for at least 1 hour.
8. Take the cookies out from the microwave oven and allow to cool.
9. Once cooled, spoon the Peanut Butter ice cream in between two cookies.
10. Serve immediately.

Nutrition:

Calories per serving: 410 Cal

Protein: 8.3 g Carbohydrates: 57.6 g

Fat: 13.2 g

Sugar: 5.3g

235. Cranberry Salad

Preparation Time: 5 minutes

Cooking Time: 5 minutes

Servings: 2

Ingredients:

- 1 Sugar free cranberry jello pack (1/2 cup for snacks allowed)
- 1/2 cup celery chopped (1 green)
- 7 Half Cut Walnut (1 snack)

Directions:

1. Jello mix according to the instructions of the box.
2. Attach walnuts and celery.
3. Allow setting.

4. Shake until serving.
5. Requires servings in 4-1/2 cups.

Nutrition:

Fats: 11 g Sodium: 73 mg

Potassium: 212 mg Carbohydrates: 54 g

Protein: 4.1 g

236. Chicken Salad with Pineapple and Pecans

Preparation Time: 10 minutes

Cooking Time: 5 minutes

Servings: 4

Ingredients:

- (6-ounce) Boneless, skinless, cooked and cubed chicken breast
- Tablespoons of celery hacked
- Cut 1/4 cup of pineapple
- 1/4 cup orange peeled segments
- Tablespoon of pecans hacked
- 1/4 cup seedless grapes
- Salt and black chili pepper, to taste
- Cups cut from roman lettuce

Directions:

1. Put chicken, celery, pineapple, grapes, pecans, and raisins in a medium dish.
2. Kindly blend until mixed with a spoon, then season with salt and pepper.
3. Create a bed of lettuce on a plate.
4. Cover with mixture of chicken and serve.

Nutrition:

Calories: 386 Cal Carbohydrates: 20 g

Fat: 19 g

Protein: 25 g

237. Cobb Salad with Blue Cheese Dressing

Preparation Time: 15 minutes

Cooking Time: 30 minutes

Servings: 6

Ingredients:

Dressing:

- 1/2 cup buttermilk
- 1 cup mayonnaise
- 2 tbsp Worcestershire sauce
- 1/2 cup sour cream
- 1 1/2 cup crumbled blue cheese
- Salt and black pepper to taste
- 2 tbsp chopped chives

Salad:

- 6 eggs
- 2 chicken breasts, boneless and skinless
- 5 strips bacon
- 1 iceberg lettuce, cut into chunks
- 1 romaine lettuce, chopped
- 1 bibb lettuce, cored and leaves removed
- 2 avocado, pitted and diced
- 2 large tomatoes, chopped
- 1/2 cup crumbled blue cheese
- 2 scallions, chopped

Directions:

1. In a bowl, whisk the buttermilk, mayonnaise, Worcestershire sauce, and sour cream.
2. Stir in the blue cheese, salt, black pepper, and chives. Place in the refrigerator to chill until ready to use.
3. Bring the eggs to boil in salted water over medium heat for 10 minutes.
4. Once ready, drain the eggs and transfer to the ice bath. Peel and chop the eggs. Set aside.

5. Preheat the grill pan over high heat. Season the chicken with salt and pepper.
6. Grill for 3 minutes on each side. Remove to a plate to cool for 3 minutes, and cut into bite-size chunks.
7. Fry the bacon in another pan set over medium heat until crispy, about 6 minutes. Remove, let cool for 2 minutes, and chop.
8. Arrange the lettuce leaves in a salad bowl and add the avocado, tomatoes, eggs, bacon, and chicken in single piles.
9. Sprinkle the blue cheese over the salad as well as the scallions and black pepper.
10. Drizzle the blue cheese dressing on the salad and serve with low carb bread.

Nutrition:
Calories: 122 Cal
Fats: 14 g
Carbohydrates: 2 g
Protein: 23 g

238. Dark Chocolate Mochaccino Ice Bombs

Preparation Time: 5 minutes
Cooking Time: 10 minutes
Servings: 4
Ingredients:

- 1/2 pound cream cheese
- 4 tbsp powdered sweetener
- 2 ounces strong coffee
- 2 tbsp cocoa powder, unsweetened
- 1 ounce cocoa butter, melted
- 2 1/2 ounces dark chocolate, melted

Directions:
1. Combine cream cheese, sweetener, coffee, and cocoa powder, in a food processor.
2. Roll 2 tbsp of the mixture and place on a lined tray.
3. Mix the melted cocoa butter and chocolate, and coat the bombs with it.
4. Freeze for 2 hours.

Nutrition:
Calories: 127 Cal Fats: 13g
Carbohydrates: 1.4 g Protein: 1.9 g

239. Chocolate Bark with Almonds

Preparation Time: 5 minutes
Cooking Time: 10 minutes
Servings: 12
Ingredients:

- 1/2 cup toasted almonds, chopped
- 1/2 cup butter
- 10 drops stevia
- 1/4 tsp. salt
- 1/2 cup unsweetened coconut flakes
- 4 ounces dark chocolate

Directions:
1. Melt together the butter and chocolate, in the microwave, for 90 seconds.
2. Remove and stir in stevia.
3. Line a cookie sheet with waxed paper and spread the chocolate evenly.
4. Scatter the almonds on top, coconut flakes, and sprinkle with salt.
5. Refrigerate for one hour.

Nutrition:
Calories: 161 Cal Fats: 15.3 g
Carbohydrates: 1.9 g

Protein: 1.9 g

240. Optavia Fueling Mousse

Preparation Time: 3 minutes

Cooking Time: 3 minutes

Servings: 2

Ingredients:

- 1 packet Medifast or Optavia hot cocoa
- 1/2 cup sugar-free gelatin
- 1 tablespoon light cream cheese
- 2 tablespoons cold water
- 1/4 cup crushed ice

Directions:

1. Place all ingredients in a blender.
2. Pulse until smooth.
3. Pour into glass and place in the fridge to set.
4. Serve chilled.

Nutrition:

Calories per serving: 156 Cal

Protein: 5.7 g

Carbs: 17.6 g

Fat: 3.7 g

Sugar: 4.5 g

241. Protein Brownies

Preparation Time: 10 minutes

Cooking Time: 40 minutes

Servings: 8

Ingredients:

- Almond milk (1/2 cup)
- Egg whites (1/2 cup, chocolate flavored)
- Apple sauce (1/2 cup, unsweetened)
- Yogurt (1/2 cup+1 tbsp, nonfat, Greek)
- Flour (1 cup, oat)
- Chocolate protein (2-3 scoops, powdered)
- Cocoa (3 tbsp, powdered unsweetened)
- Baking powder (1 tsp., baker style)
- Salt (1/2 tsp.)

Ingredients for the frosting:

- Greek yogurt (1/2 cup, nonfat)
- Cherries (1/4 cup)
- Sweetener (optional)

Directions:

1. First step is to heat an oven to 350 degrees Fahrenheit then lightly spray a baking dish using cooking spray.
2. Add the egg whites and whisk well until beaten lightly.
3. Add the protein powder, oat flour, sweetener, powdered cocoa and the baking powder separately.
4. Stir well until mixed evenly then pour milk mixture (almond) into flour mixture.
5. Stir well until thoroughly mixed and set batter aside for approximately 5 minutes.
6. Pour batter into the dish and place into the oven to bake for approximately 25 minutes until thoroughly cooked.
7. Remove brownie from heat then set aside to cool.
8. Add all the frosting ingredients in a food processor then process on the highest setting until becomes smooth.
9. Spread frosting over the top of brownies. Serve

Nutrition:

Carbohydrates: 6 g Protein: 16 g

Fat: 12 g Potassium: 4 mg

242. Raspberry Flax Seed Dessert

Preparation Time: 3 minutes

Cooking Time: 5 minutes

Servings: 4

Ingredients:

- 2 cups raspberries, reserve a few for topping
- 3 cups unsweetened vanilla almond milk
- 1 cup heavy cream
- 1/2 cup chia seeds
- 1/2 cup flaxseeds, ground
- 4 tsp. liquid stevia
- Chopped mixed nuts for topping

Directions:

1. In a medium bowl, crush the raspberries with a fork until pureed.
2. Pour in the almond milk, heavy cream, chia seeds, and liquid stevia.
3. Mix and refrigerate the pudding overnight.
4. Spoon the pudding into serving glasses, top with raspberries, mixed nuts, and serve

Nutrition:

Calories: 390 Cal

Fats: 33.5 g

Carbohydrates: 3 g

Protein: 13 g

243. Chocolate Matcha Balls

Preparation Time: 10 minutes

Cooking Time: 15 minutes

Servings: 15

Ingredients:

- 2 tbsp unsweetened cocoa powder
- 3 tbsp oats, gluten-free
- 1/2 cup pine nuts
- 1/2 cup almonds
- cup dates, pitted
- tbsp matcha powder

Directions:

1. Add oats, pine nuts, almonds, and dates into a food processor and process until well combined.
2. Place matcha powder in a small dish.
3. Make small balls from mixture and coat with matcha powder.

Serve and enjoy.

Nutrition:

Calories: 150 Fat: 8g

Carbs: 17g

Protein: 2g

244. Chia Almond Butter Pudding

Preparation Time: 10 minutes

Cooking Time: 10 minutes

Servings: 1

Ingredients:

- 1/4 cup chia seeds
- cup unsweetened almond milk
- 1/2 tbsp maple syrup
- 1/2 tbsp almond butter

Directions:

1. Add almond milk, maple syrup, and almond butter in a bowl and stir well.
2. Add chia seeds and stir to mix.
3. Pour pudding mixture into the Mason jar and place in the refrigerator for overnight.
4. Serve and enjoy.

Nutrition:

Calories: 230 Fat: 9g Carbs: 34g

Protein: 5g

245. Summer Fruit Granita

Preparation Time: 10 minutes

Cooking Time: 1 hour and 30 minutes

Servings: 4

Ingredients

- 1/4 cup sugar
- 1 cup fresh strawberries
- 1 cup fresh raspberries
- 1 cup fresh blackberries
- 1 teaspoon freshly squeezed lemon juice

Directions

1. In a small saucepan, bring 1 cup water to a boil over high heat. Add the sugar and stir well until dissolved.
2. Remove the pan from the heat, add the berries and lemon juice, and cool to room temperature. Once cooled, place the fruit in a blender and smoothen it.
3. Pour the mixture into a shallow glass baking dish and place in the freezer for 1 hour. Stir with a fork and freeze for 30 minutes, then repeat.
4. To serve, use an ice cream scoop to portion the granita into dessert dishes.

Nutrition:

Calories: 75 Fat: 0g

Carbs: 17g Protein: 1g

246. Red Grapefruit Granita

Preparation Time: 10 minutes

Cooking Time: 1 hour and 30 minutes

Servings: 6

Ingredients

- 3 cups red grapefruit sections
- 1 cup freshly squeezed red grapefruit juice

- 1/4 cup honey
- 1 tablespoon freshly squeezed lime juice
- Fresh basil leaves for garnish
- Directions
1. Remove as much pith (white part) and membrane as possible from the grapefruit segments.
2. Combine all ingredients except the basil in a blender or food processor and pulse just until smooth.
3. Pour the mixture into a shallow glass baking dish and place in the freezer for 1 hour. Stir with a fork and freeze for another 30 minutes, then repeat.
4. To serve, scoop into small dessert glasses and garnish with fresh basil leaves.

Nutrition:

Calories: 69

Fat: 0g

Carbs: 17g

Protein: 1g

247. Grilled Pineapple and Melon

Preparation Time: 10 minutes

Cooking Time: 7 minutes

Servings: 4

Ingredients

- 8 fresh pineapple rings, rind removed
- 8 watermelon triangles, with rind
- 1 tablespoon honey
- 1/2 teaspoon freshly ground black pepper

Directions

1. Preheat an outdoor grill or a grill pan over high heat.

2. Drizzle the fruit slices with honey and sprinkle one side of each piece with pepper.
3. Grill for 5 minutes, turn, and grill for another 2 minutes. Serve.

Nutrition:

Calories: 54

Fat: 0g

Carbs: 11g

Protein: 1g

248. Baked Pears in Red Wine Sauce

Preparation Time: 10 minutes

Cooking Time: 25 minutes

Servings: 4

Ingredients

- 4 just-ripe firm pears, such as Bosc or Anjou
- 1 cup sweet red wine, such as port or Beaujolais Nouveau
- 1 cinnamon stick
- 2 teaspoons light brown sugar
- 1/2 teaspoon pure almond extract
- 4 mint sprigs for garnish

Directions

1. Preheat the oven to 325°F.
2. Peel the pears, leaving the core and stem intact. Cut a slice from the bottom of each to allow them to stand easily. Place the pears in a small baking dish.
3. In a small saucepan, combine the red wine, cinnamon stick, and brown sugar and heat over low heat just until it reaches a simmer.
4. Stir in the almond extract, remove the cinnamon stick, and pour the liquid into the baking dish. Slide the

dish into the oven, being careful not to tip the pears.
5. Bake until the pears are golden and fork-tender, about 1 hour. The bottom one-third to one-half will be a deep red.
6. Gently transfer the pears to a platter and pour the red wine mixture back into the saucepan. Heat over medium heat and simmer until reduced by half, about 15 minutes.
7. Remove the pan from the heat and allow the sauce to cool for 10 minutes.
8. To serve, place each pear in a shallow dessert bowl and pour a little red wine sauce around it. Garnish with fresh mint.

Nutrition:

Calories: 124

Fat: 0g

Carbs: 29g

Protein: 1g

249. Avocado & Sweet Potato Cupcakes

Preparation Time: 15 minutes

Cooking Time: 15 minutes

Servings: 12

For the butter:

- Cup + 2 tablespoons sweet potato, mashed
- 1 cup whole wheat flour
- 3/4 cup caster sugar
- 1/2 cup unsalted butter, room temperature
  Eggs
- Tablespoons brown sugar
- 1 teaspoon baking powder

- 1/2 teaspoon cinnamon
- 1/4 teaspoon vanilla extract
- 1/4 teaspoon baking soda
- For the frosting:
- 2 avocados, mashed
- 1/2 cup agave nectar
- 1/2 cup cocoa powder
- 1/2 teaspoon vanilla extract

Directions:

1. Preheat oven to 350 degrees Fahrenheit.
2. Line a 12-insert cupcake tray with cupcake cups and set aside.
3. Whisk together the whole wheat flour, baking powder, and baking soda in a medium-sized bowl until well combined. Set this aside for later.
4. In a separate bowl, beat together the caster sugar and butter until well combined.
5. Once the caster sugar and butter are well combined, crack in the eggs and beat them in as well.
6. Once the eggs are thoroughly distributed, dump in the mashed sweet potato and vanilla extract. Mix this in until well incorporated.
7. Add the dry mixture to the wet mixture and fold it in until well combined.
8. Scoop your cupcake batter into the inserts, dividing evenly as you go, and place the cupcake tray in the oven for 10-15 minutes or until the tops of the cupcakes are golden-brown and bouncy.
9. Remove the cupcake tray from the oven and let the cupcakes sit to cool for a couple minutes.
10. Once the cupcakes are cool enough to touch, transfer them to a cooling rack to finish cooling.
11. While the cupcakes finish cooling, you can prepare the avocado frosting. Begin by placing the mashed avocados, agave nectar, cocoa powder, and vanilla extract in a bowl.
12. Beat the frosting ingredients together until smooth and well combined. Tip: You'll know you're done when the green of the avocados is no longer visible!
13. Once the cupcakes are completely cool, spread the avocado frosting overtop, dividing it evenly as you go. Plate, serve, and enjoy!
14. Nutrition:

Calories: 140

Fat: 0g

Carbs: 32g

Protein: 2g

250. Poached Cherries

Preparation Time: 10 minutes

Cooking Time: 10 minutes

Servings: 12

Ingredients

- pound fresh and sweet cherries, rinsed, pitted
- strips (1x3 inches each) orange zest,
- strips (1x3 inches each) lemon zest,
- 2/3 cup sugar
- 15 peppercorns
- 1/4 vanilla bean, split but not scraped
- 3/4 cups water

Directions:

1. In a saucepan, mix the water, citrus zest, sugar, peppercorns, and vanilla bean; bring to a boil, stirring until the sugar is dissolved.
2. Add the cherries; simmer for about 10 minutes until the cherries are soft, but not falling apart.
3. Skim any foam from the surface and let the poached cherries cool.
4. Refrigerate with the poaching liquid. Before serving, strain the cherries.

Nutrition:

Calories: 170 Fat: 1g

Carbs: 42g

Protein: 1g

251. Roasted Honey-Cinnamon Apples

Preparation Time: 10 minutes

Cooking Time: 30 minutes

Servings: 2

Ingredients

- 1 teaspoon extra-virgin olive oil
- firm apples, peeled, cored, and sliced
- 1/2 teaspoon salt
- 1/2 teaspoons ground cinnamon, divided
- 2 tablespoons low-fat milk
- 2 tablespoons honey

Directions

1. Preheat the oven to 375°F. Grease a small casserole dish with the olive oil.
2. In a medium bowl, toss the apple slices with the salt and 1/2 teaspoon of the cinnamon. Spread the apples in the baking dish and bake for 20 minutes.
3. Meanwhile, in a small saucepan, heat the milk, honey, and remaining 1 teaspoon cinnamon over medium heat, stirring frequently. When it reaches a simmer, remove the pan from the heat and cover to keep warm.
4. Divide the apple slices between 2 dessert plates and pour the sauce over the apples. Serve warm.

Nutrition:

Calories: 130

Fat: 4g

Carbs: 23g

Protein: 2g

Conclusion

The Optavia diet's main plan is to help people reduce weight and obesity by controlled portion meals and snacks with low in calories and carbohydrates.

The 5&1 plan limits calories split between six portioned-controlled foods to 800-1,000 calories each day. Although the evidence is mixed, several reports have demonstrated stronger weight reduction of complete or partial meal replacement programs relative to conventional calorie-restricted diets.

The low calorie, low sugar, high protein plan of the Optavia diet includes coaching assistance, which has been proven good, to contribute to short-term weight loss. Its long-term efficacy is uncertain, though. Packaged foods provide convenience.

- Achieves fast weight reduction
- Takes away guesswork about whether to eat
- Offers mutual assistance

The Optavia diet is a series of three plans, two of which concentrate on weight reduction and better at managing weight. The program's foods are lower in calories and carbs and higher in protein to promote weight reduction. Each strategy demands that you consume at least half of your food in the form of Optavia pre-packaged food. Since the menu calls for eating carbs, protein, and healthy fat to be eaten, it is a reasonably healthy diet for healthy food. As far as weight reduction goes, experts agree that Optavia can benefit because its diet is low in calories, for the positive. Still, it's unlikely to change your eating habits significantly. You're likely to regain weight once you quit your diet.

Hence optavia diet has proven to be extremely helpful in controlling and maintaining weight. Still, when optavia lean & green food merges with air frying, it can make this diet much easier for people to follow. Air frying food cuts the cooking time in half and makes the food more nutritious.

You can get many benefits if you follow optavia lean & green air frying recipes along with targeted weight reduction.

Other Advantages

There are additional advantages to the Optavia diet that can improve weight reduction and general health.

Simple to Follow Diet

Since the diet depends primarily on pre-packaged foods, on the 5&1 program, you are only liable for cooking one meal each day. Furthermore, to make things easy to execute, each schedule comes with meal plans and sample meal plans. Although you are expected to prepare 1-3 Lean & Green meals every day, they are quick to create depending on the diet, since the package provides unique recipes and a selection of food choices.

Besides, to supplement lean & green foods, many that are not involved in cooking should purchase prepared meals called "Flavors of Home."

Blood pressure can also be improved

Via weight loss and restricted consumption of sodium, Optavia programs can help improve blood pressure. Optavia can eventually help you lose excess weight. Still, it is in your best interest to develop good-for-your behaviors for long-term results and sticking to a tried-and-tested balanced eating plan like changing your lifestyle for good. If anyone tries to lose weight, it is advised for the long run to care about lifestyle improvements, rather than fast solutions. After all, you're going to have to make those visits to the grocery store for healthy living.

2

250+ OPTAVIA DIET COOKBOOK

Introduction

The Optavia diet is a weight loss program considered by many to be the most effective. Dr. Nathaniel Greats developed it. It is based on principles of the Theory of Relative Deprivation (TRD).

With TRD, by the time you have reached your target weight, your satisfaction level with your new body will be a 100 percent. Your newly found body will not only feel good for you, it will feel good for everyone else.

Following the Optavia program requires you to feed on low calorie and reduced carb foods. You will need a combination of packaged foods and homemade meals to lose weight effectively. If you don't enjoy cooking or are an active type and don't have enough time to cook your meals, the Optavia diet will be great for you as it doesn't require you to do prolonged cooking.

It is important to note that while Medifast does not require one-on-one coaching, the Optavia diet requires.

Optavia diet enhances weight loss through branded products known as fueling. At the same time, the homemade entrées are referred to as the Lean and Green meals. The fuelings are made up of over 60 items specifically low carbs but are high in probiotic cultures and Protein. The fuelings ultimately contain friendly bacteria that can help to boost gut health. They include; cookies, bars, puddings, shakes, soups, cereals, and pasta.

Looking at the listed foods, you might think they are quite high in carbs, which is understandable. Still, the fuelings are composed so that they are lower in sugar and carbs than the traditional versions of the similar foods. The company does this by using small portion sizes and sugar substitutes. Many of the fuelings are packed with soy protein isolate and whey protein powder in furtherance. Those interested in the Optavia diet plan but are not interested or got no chance to cook are provided with pre-made low-carb meals. These meals are referred to as Flavors of Home, and they can sufficiently replacing the Lean and Green Meals.

The company explicitly states that by working with its team of coaches and following the Optavia diet as required, you will achieve a "lifelong transformation, one healthy habit at a time."

Therefore, to record success with this diet plan, you have to stick to the fuelings supplemented by veggie, meat, and healthy fat entrée daily. You will be full and nourished. Although you will be consuming low calories, you will not be losing a lot of muscle since you will be feeding on lots of fibre, protein, and other vital nutrients. Your calories as an adult will not exceed 800-1,000. You can lose 12 pounds in 12 weeks if you follow the optimal weight 5&1 plan option.

Since you will curb your carb intake while on this diet plan, you will naturally shed fat because the carb is the primary source of energy, therefore, if it is not readily available, the body finds a fat alternative, which implies that the body will have to break down your fats for energy and keep burning fat.

Summary: The Optavia diet is an idea of Medifast, and it comprises of pre-purchased portioned snacks and meals, low carb Lean and Green (homemade) meals, and continuous coaching that is based on facilitating fat and weight loss.

CHAPTER 1:

Fundamentals of Optavia Diet

The Optavia diet is a practice that aims to reduce or maintain current weight. It is a diet that recommends eating a combination of processed foods called fuellings and home-cooked meals (lean and green meals). It is believed that it sticks to the brand product (input) and supplements it with meat, vegetables, and fatty snacks; this will keep you satisfied and nourished. You don't need to worry much about losing muscles because you are eating enough protein and consuming too few calories. And that way, the individual who practices the diet can lose around 12 pounds in just 12 weeks using the ideal 5&1 weight plan.

In short, the Optavian diet is a program that focuses on cutting calories and reducing carbohydrates in meals. To do this effectively, combine packaged foods called fuels with home-cooked meals, which encourages weight loss.

The Optavia Diet encourages people to limit the number of calories that they should take daily. Under this program, dieters are encouraged to consume between 800 and 1000 calories daily. To make this possible, dieters are encouraged to choose healthier foods and meal replacements. But, unlike other types of commercial diets, the Optavia diet comes in several variations. Currently, there are three variations of the Optavia diet plan that you can choose from based on your needs.

What Are the Benefits?

Optavia's program may be a solid match for you on the off chance that you need a diet plan that is clear and simple to follow, that will assist you with getting in shape rapidly, and offers worked in social help.

When embarking on any new diet regimen, you may experience some difficulties along the way. Below are why this diet regimen is considered the easiest to follow among all commercial diet regimens.

Accomplishes Rapid Weight Loss

Most solid individuals require around 1600 to 3000 calories for each day to keep up their weight. Limiting that number to as low as 800 ensures weight loss for a great many people.

Optavia's 5&1 Plan is intended for brisk weight loss, making it a strong choice for somebody with a clinical motivation to shed pounds quick.

You enter the fat-loss stage in just 3 days. Look for Weight loss story on YouTube to see how many people out there are losing an impressing amount of weight, even 20 or more pounds in a week.

The average of 12 pounds in 12 weeks on the website counts all the people that do it by themselves, and nobody knows how many times they actually follow the plan, how many times they cheat, how much water they drink, exercise, etc.

Easy to Follow

As the diet depend on generally a prepackaged Fuelings, you are only accountable for doing one meal a day on the 5&1 Plan.

Although you are encouraged to prepare 1 to 3 green and lean foods a day, depending on your strategy, they are very simple to prepare, as the program will include detailed recipes and a list of food options to choose from.

Also, those who don't like to cook can purchase packaged meals called Flavors of Home to replace Lean and Green meals.

Bundled Items Offer Comfort

In spite of the fact that you should search for your own elements for "lean and green" dinners, the home conveyance choice for Optavia's "Fuelings" spares time and vitality.

When the items show up, they're anything but difficult to get ready and make phenomenal snatch and go suppers.

Packaged Products

They will be delivered directly at home, and they are quick-to-make and grab-and-go.

Social Support and Coaching

Stay motivated, do not cheat. Point out how people on coaching achieve a much faster and more massive weight loss.

Offers Social Help

Social help is a crucial part of achievement with any weight loss plan. Optavia's training project and gathering can give worked in consolation and backing for clients.

Optavia's health coaches are available throughout the weight loss and maintenance programs.

Eliminates the Guesswork

You don't have to worry about what to eat all day, just cook it once a day or every other day.

Some people find that the hardest part of the diet is the psychological effort required to understand what to eat every day, or even every dinner.

Optavia reduces the pressure of party planning and "running out of options" by offering customers set foods with "supplies" and rules for "simple and green" meals.

It's Not a Ketogenic Diet

Carbs are allowed and higher than the majority of weight-loss diets out there, just not the refined ones.

No Counting Calories

You don't really need to count your calories when following this type of diet, just as long as you stick with the rule of Fuelings, meals, snacks and water intake depending on your preference may it be 5&1, 4&2&1 or 3&3.

Food to eat and food to avoid

There are a lot many foods that you can eat while following the Optavia Diet. However, you must know these foods by heart. This is particularly true if you are just new to this diet, and you have to follow the 5&1 Optavia Diet Plan strictly. Thus, this section is dedicated to the types of foods that are recommended and those to avoid while following this diet regimen.

Food allowed

There are numerous categories of foods that can be eaten under this diet regimen. This section will break down the Lean and Green foods that you can eat while following this diet regime.

Lean Foods

Leanest Foods - These foods are considered to be the leanest as it has only up to 4 grams of total fat. Moreover, dieters should eat a 7-ounce cooked portion of these foods. Consume these foods with 1 healthy fat serving.

- **Fish:** Flounder, cod, haddock, grouper, Mahi, tilapia, tuna (yellowfin fresh or canned), and wild catfish.
- **Shellfish:** Scallops, lobster, crabs, shrimp
- **Game meat:** Elk, deer, buffalo
- **Ground turkey or other meat:** Should be 98% lean
- **Meatless alternatives:** 14 egg whites, 2 cups egg substitute, 5 ounces seitan, 1 ½ cups 1% cottage cheese, and 12 ounces non-fat 0% Greek yogurt

Leaner Foods - These foods contain 5 to 9 grams of total fat. Consume these foods with 1 healthy fat serving. Make sure to consume only 6 ounces of a cooked portion of these foods daily:

- **Fish:** Halibut, trout, and swordfish
- **Chicken:** White meat such as breasts as long as the skin is removed
- **Turkey:** Ground turkey as long as it is 95% to 97% lean.
- **Meatless options:** 2 whole eggs plus 4 egg whites, 2 whole eggs plus one cup egg substitute, 1 ½ cups 2% cottage cheese, and 12 ounces low fat 2% plain Greek yogurt

Lean Foods - These are foods that contain 10g to 20g total fat. When consuming these foods, there should be no serving of healthy fat. These include the following:

- **Fish:** Tuna (bluefin steak), salmon, herring, farmed catfish, and mackerel
- **Lean beef:** Ground, steak, and roast
- **Lamb:** All cuts
- **Pork:** Pork chops, pork tenderloin, and all parts. Make sure to remove the skin
- **Ground turkey and other meats:** 85% to 94% lean
- **Chicken:** Any dark meat
- **Meatless options:** 15 ounces extra-firm tofu, 3 whole eggs (up to two times per week), 4 ounces reduced-fat skim cheese, 8 ounces part-skim ricotta cheese, and 5 ounces tempeh

Healthy Fat Servings - Healthy fat servings are allowed under this diet. They should contain 5 grams of fat and less than grams of carbohydrates. Regardless of what type of Optavia Diet plan you follow, make sure that you add between 0 and 2 healthy fat servings daily. Below are the different healthy fat servings that you can eat:

- 1 teaspoon oil (any kind of oil)
- 1 tablespoon low carbohydrate salad dressing
- 2 tablespoons reduced-fat salad dressing
- 5 to 10 black or green olives
- 1 ½ ounce avocado
- 1/3-ounce plain nuts including peanuts, almonds, pistachios
- 1 tablespoon plain seeds such as chia, sesame, flax, and pumpkin seeds
- ½ tablespoon regular butter, mayonnaise, and margarine

Green Foods

This section will discuss the green servings that you still need to consume while following the Optavia Diet Plan. These include all kinds of vegetables that have been categorized from lower, moderate, and high in terms of carbohydrate content. One serving of vegetables should be at ½ cup unless otherwise specified.

Lower Carbohydrate - These are vegetables that contain low amounts of carbohydrates. If you are following the 5&1 Optavia Diet plan, then these vegetables are good for you.

- A cup of green leafy vegetables, such as collard greens (raw), lettuce (green leaf, iceberg, butterhead, and romaine), spinach (raw), mustard greens, spring mix, bok choy (raw), and watercress.
- ½ cup of vegetables including cucumbers, celery, radishes, white mushroom, sprouts (mung bean, alfalfa), arugula, turnip greens, escarole, nopales, Swiss chard (raw), jalapeno, and bok choy (cooked).

Moderate Carbohydrate - These are vegetables that contain moderate amounts of carbohydrates. Below are the types of vegetables that can be consumed in moderation:

- **½ cup of any of the following vegetables** such as asparagus, cauliflower, fennel bulb, eggplant, portabella mushrooms, kale, cooked spinach, summer squash (zucchini and scallop).

Higher Carbohydrates - Foods that are under this category contain a high amount of starch. Make sure to consume limited amounts of these vegetables.

- **½ cup of the following vegetables** like chayote squash, red cabbage, broccoli, cooked collard and mustard greens, green or wax beans, kohlrabi, kabocha squash, cooked leeks, any peppers, okra, raw scallion, summer squash such as straightneck and crookneck, tomatoes, spaghetti squash, turnips, jicama, cooked Swiss chard, and hearts of palm.

- **Foods to avoid**

The following foods are to be avoided, except it's included in the fuelings — they include:

•Fried foods: meats, fish, shellfish, vegetables, desserts like baked goods

•Refined grains: white bread, pasta, scones, hotcakes, flour tortillas, wafers, white rice, treats, cakes, cakes

•Certain fats: margarine, coconut oil, strong shortening

•Whole fat dairy: milk, cheddar, yogurt

•Alcohol: all varieties, no exception

•Sugar-sweetened beverages: pop, natural product juice, sports drinks, caffeinated drinks, sweet tea

The accompanying nourishments are beyond reach while on the 5&1 plan, however, included back during the 6-week progress stage and permitted during the 3&3 plan:

•Fruit: all kinds of fresh fruits

•Low fat or without fat dairy: yogurt, milk, cheddar

CHAPTER 2:

How does Optavia work?

The Optavia diet is considered a high-protein diet, having a protein that counts up to 10–35% of a person's daily calories. Nevertheless, powdered, processed substances can result in some unpleasant consequences.

According to London, "The additives and protein isolate plus can give you some unnecessary GI side effects that can make an individual feel bloated, making it a lot better with a sugar-free Greek yogurt that contains protein in a smoothie." Also, according to London, "there is no regulation of dietary supplements like powders and shakes for safety by the FDA as there is for foods. Protein blends and powders can contain unwanted ingredients and can interfere with your medication. This makes it important to inform your doctor about what you are trying to indulge yourself in".

Like many commercial plans, Optavia involves buying most of the foods permitted on a diet in packaged form. The company deals on a wide range of food products that they call "fuelings"—on its website. These include pancakes, shakes, pasta dishes, soups, cookies, mashed potatoes, and popcorn.

Users pick the plan that best suits them. The 5 & 1 Plan entails eating five small meals per day. The meals can be selected from more than 60 substitutable fuelings, including one "lean and green" meal, probably veggies or protein that you will prepare by yourself. The Optimal Essential Kit, costing $356.15, provides 119 servings, or about 20 days' worth.

A flexible option is the 4 & 2 & 1 plan. It just contains four supplies a day; you can choose and create two of your "lean and green" meals and one of the snacks purchased from Optavia. Plus, with a similar mix of prepared foods, a 140-serving kit costs $ 399.00

Is Optavia And Medifast The Same?

Relatively, Medifast Inc. is known as the parent company of Optavia. It also the owner and the one that operates the Medifast program. The program is already present in the '80s and '90s with doctors who prescribe meals to their clients. Optavia makes use of identical foods with a similar macronutrient profile. Consumers can sign up online for the plan by themselves.

How Much Does Optavia Cost?

In comparison, the United States Department of Agriculture estimates that a woman whose ages range from 10-50 can follow a nutritious diet while spending as little as $166.40 per month on groceries. As long as she is preparing all her meals at home.

How Nutritious Is Optavia Diet

Below is the breakdown comparison of meals' nutritional content on the Optavial Weight 5&1 Plan and the federal government's 2015 Dietary Guidelines for Americans.

	Optimal Weight 5&1 Plan	Federal Government Recommendation
Calories	800-1,000	Men 19-25: 2,800 26-45: 2,600 46-65: 2,400 65+: 2,200 Women 19-25: 2,200 26-50: 2,000 51+: 1,800
Total fat % of Calorie Intake	20%	20%-35%
Total Carbohydrates % of Calorie Intake	40%	45%-65%
Sugars	10%-20%	N/A
Fiber	25 g – 30 g	Men 19-30: 34 g. 31-50: 31 g. 51+: 28 g. Women 19-30: 28 g. 31-50: 25 g. 51+: 22 g.
Protein	40%	10%-35%
Sodium	Under 2,300 mg	Under 2,300 mg.
Potassium	Average 3,000 mg	At least 4,700 mg.
Calcium	1,000 mg – 1,200 mg	Men 1,000 mg. Women 19-50: 1,000 mg. 51+: 1,200 mg.

CHAPTER 3:

The Medifast Optavia diets plan

The Optavia Diet encourages people to limit the number of calories that they should take daily. Under this program, dieters are encouraged to consume between 800 and 1000 calories daily. To make this possible, dieters are encouraged to choose healthier foods and meal replacements. But, unlike other types of commercial diets, the Optavia diet comes in several variations. Currently, there are three variations of the Optavia diet plan that you can choose from based on your needs.

- **5&1 Optavia Diet Plan:** This is the most common version of the Optavia Diet, and it involves eating five prepackaged meals from the Optimal Health Fuelings and one home-made balanced meal.

- **4&2&1 Octavia Diet Plan:** This diet plan is designed for people who want to have flexibility while following this regimen. Under this program, dieters are encouraged to eat more calories and have more flexible food choices. This means that they can consume 4 prepackaged Optimal Health Fuelings food, three home-cooked meals from the Lean and Green, and one snack daily.

- **5&2&2 Optavia Diet Plan:** This diet plan is perfect for individuals who prefer to have a flexible meal plan in order to achieve a healthy weight. It is recommended for a wide variety of people. Under this diet regimen, dieters are required to eat 5 fuelings, 2 lean and green meals, and 2 healthy snacks.

- **3&3 Optavia Diet Plan:** This particular Diet plan is created for people who have moderate weight problems and merely want to maintain a healthy body. Under this diet plan, dieters are encouraged to consume 3 prepackaged Optimal Health Fuelings and three home-cooked meals.

- **Optavia for Nursing Mothers:** This diet regimen is designed for nursing mothers with babies of at least two months old. Aside from supporting breastfeeding mothers, it also encourages gradual weight loss.

- **Optavia for Diabetes:** This Optavia Diet plan is designed for people who have Type 1 and Type 2 diabetes. The meal plans are designed so that dieters consume more green and lean meals, depending on their needs and condition.

- **Optavia for Gout:** This diet regimen incorporates a balance of foods that are low in purines and moderate in protein.

- **Optavia for Seniors (65 years and older):** Designed for seniors, this Optavia Diet plan has some variations following the components of Fuelings depending on the needs and activities of the senior dieters.

- **Optavia for Teen Boys and Optavia for Teen Girls (13-18 years old):** Designed for active teens, the Optavia for Teens Boys and Optavia for Teens Girls provide the right nutrition to growing teens.

Regardless of which type of Optavia Diet plan you choose, it is important that you talk with a coach to help you determine which plan is right for you based on your individual goals.

- **How to Start This Diet**

The Optavia Diet is comprised of different phases. A certified coach will educate you on the steps that you need to undertake if you want to follow this regimen., below are some the things you need to know, especially when you are still starting with this diet regimen.

Initial Steps

During this phase, people are encouraged to consume800 to 1,000 calories to help you shed off at least 12 pounds within the next 12 weeks. For instance, if you are following the 5&1 Optavia Diet Plan, then you need to eat 1 meal every 2 or 3 hours and include a 30-minute moderate workout most days of your week. You need to consume not more than 100 grams of Carbs daily during this phase.

Further, consuming meals are highly encouraged. This phase also encourages the dieter to include 1 optional snack per day, such as ½ cup sugar-free gelatin,3 celery sticks, and 12 ounces nuts. Aside from these things, below are other things that you need to remember when following this phase:

- Make sure that the portion size recommendations are for cooked weight and not the raw weight of your ingredients

- Opt for meals that are baked, grilled, broiled, or poached. Avoid frying foods, as this will increase your calorie intake.

- Eat at least 2 servings of fish rich in Omega-3 fatty acids. These include fishes like tuna, salmon, trout, mackerel, herring, and other cold-water fishes.

- Choose meatless alternatives like tofu and tempeh.

- Follow the program even when you are dining out. Keep in mind that drinking alcohol is discouraged when following this plan.

Maintenance Phase

As soon as you have attained your desired weight, the next phase is the transition stage. It is a 6-week stage that involves increasing your calorie intake to 1,550 per day. This is also the phase when you are allowed to add more varieties into your meal, such as whole grains, low-fat dairy, and fruits.

After six weeks, you can now move into the 3&3 Optavia Diet plan, so you are required to eat three Lean and Green meals and 3 Fueling foods.

CHAPTER 4:

Breakfast and Smoothies Recipes

1. Bacon and Brussels Sprout Breakfast

Preparation Time: 10 minutes

Cooking Time: 15 minutes

Servings: 3

Ingredients:

- Apple cider vinegar, 1½ tbsps.
- Salt
- Minced shallots, 2
- Minced garlic cloves, 2
- Medium eggs, 3
- Sliced Brussels sprouts, 12 oz.
- Black pepper
- Chopped bacon, 2 oz.
- Melted butter, 1 tbsp.

Directions:

1. Over medium heat, quick fry the bacon until crispy then reserve on a plate
2. Set the pan on fire again to fry garlic and shallots for 30 seconds
3. Stir in apple cider vinegar, Brussels sprouts, and seasoning to cook for five minutes
4. Add the bacon to cook for five minutes then stir in the butter and set a hole at the center
5. Crash the eggs to the pan and let cook fully
6. Enjoy

Nutrition:

Calories: 275

Fat: 16.5

Fiber: 4.3

Carbs: 17.2

Protein: 17.4

2. Gluten-Free Pancakes

Preparation Time: 5 minutes

Cooking Time: 2 minutes

Servings: 2

Ingredients:

- 6 eggs
- 1 cup low-fat cream cheese
- 1 1/12; teaspoons baking powder
- 1 scoop protein powder
- 1/4 cup almond meal
- 1/4 teaspoon salt

Directions:

1. Combine dry ingredients in a food processor. Add the eggs one after another and then the cream cheese. Mix it well.
2. Lightly grease a skillet with cooking spray and place over medium-high heat.
3. Pour the batter into the pan. Turn the pan gently to create round pancakes.
4. Cook for about 2 minutes on each side.
5. Serve pancakes with your favorite topping.

Nutrition: Dietary Fiber: 1 g Net Carbs: 5 g Protein: 25 g Total Fat: 14 g Calories: 288

3. Mushroom & Spinach Omelet

Preparation Time: 20 minutes

Cooking Time: 20 minutes

Servings: 3

Ingredients:

- 2 tablespoons butter, divided

- 6-8 fresh mushrooms, sliced, 5 ounces
- Chives, chopped, optional
- Salt and pepper, to taste
- 1 handful baby spinach, about 1/2 ounce
- Pinch garlic powder
- 4 eggs, beaten
- 1-ounce shredded Swiss cheese

Directions:

1. In a very large saucepan, sauté the mushrooms in one tablespoon of butter until soft. Season with salt, pepper, and garlic.
2. Remove the mushrooms from the pan and keep warm. Heat the remaining tablespoon of butter in the same skillet over medium heat.
3. Beat the eggs with a little salt and pepper and add to the hot butter. Turn the pan over to coat the entire bottom of the pan with egg. Once the egg is almost out, place the cheese over the middle of the tortilla.
4. Fill the cheese with spinach leaves and hot mushrooms. Let cook for about a minute for the spinach to start to wilt. Fold the empty side of the tortilla carefully over the filling and slide it onto a plate and sprinkle with chives, if desired.
5. Alternatively, you can make two tortillas using half the mushroom, spinach, and cheese filling in each.

Nutrition:

Calories: 321 Fat: 26 g

Protein: 19 g

Carbohydrate: 4 g

Dietary Fiber: 1 g

4. Alkaline Blueberry Spelt Pancakes

Preparation Time: 6 minutes

Cooking Time: 20 minutes

Servings: 3

Ingredients:

- 2 cups Spelt Flour
- 1 cup Coconut Milk
- 1/2 cup Alkaline Water
- 2 tbsps. Grapeseed Oil
- 1/2 cup Agave
- 1/2 cup Blueberries
- 1/4 tsp. Sea Moss

Directions:

1. Mix the spelt flour, agave, grapeseed oil, hemp seeds, and the sea moss together in a bowl.
2. Add in 1 cup of hemp milk and alkaline water to the mixture, until you get the consistency mixture you like.
3. Crimp the blueberries into the batter.
4. Heat the skillet to moderate heat then lightly coat it with the grapeseed oil.
5. Pour the batter into the skillet then let them cook for approximately 5 minutes on every side.
6. Serve and Enjoy.

Nutrition:

Calories: 203 kcal

Fat: 1.4g

Carbs: 41.6g

Proteins: 4.8g

5. Alkaline Blueberry Muffins

Preparation Time: 5 Minutes

Cooking Time: 20 minutes

Servings: 3

Ingredients:

- 1 cup Coconut Milk
- 3/4 cup Spelt Flour
- 3/4 Teff Flour
- 1/2 cup Blueberries
- 1/3 cup Agave
- 1/4 cup Sea Moss Gel
- 1/2 tsp. Sea Salt
- Grapeseed Oil

Directions:

1. Adjust the temperature of the oven to 365 degrees.
2. Grease 6 regular-size muffin cups with muffin liners.
3. In a bowl, mix together sea salt, sea moss, agave, coconut milk, and flour gel until they are properly blended.
4. You then crimp in blueberries.
5. Coat the muffin pan lightly with the grapeseed oil.
6. Pour in the muffin batter.
7. Bake for at least 30 minutes until it turns golden brown.
8. Serve.

Nutrition:

Calories: 160 kcal

Fat: 5g

Carbs: 25g

Proteins: 2g

6. Crunchy Quinoa Meal

Preparation Time: 5 minutes

Cooking Time: 25 minutes

Servings: 2

Ingredients:

- 3 cups coconut milk
- 1 cup rinsed quinoa
- 1/8 tsp. ground cinnamon
- 1 cup raspberry
- 1/2 cup chopped coconuts

Directions:

1. In a saucepan, pour milk and bring to a boil over moderate heat.
2. Add the quinoa to the milk and then bring it to a boil once more.
3. You then let it simmer for at least 15 minutes on medium heat until the milk is reduced.
4. Stir in the cinnamon then mix properly.
5. Cover it then cook for 8 minutes until the milk is completely absorbed.
6. Add the raspberry and cook the meal for 30 seconds.
7. Serve and enjoy.

Nutrition:

Calories: 271 kcal Fat: 3.7g

Carbs: 54g Proteins: 6.5g

7. Coconut Pancakes

Preparation Time: 5 minutes

Cooking Time: 15 minutes

Servings: 4

Ingredients:

- 1 cup coconut flour
- 2 tbsps. arrowroot powder
- 1 tsp. baking powder

- 1 cup coconut milk
- 3 tbsps. coconut oil

Directions:

1. In a medium container, mix in all the dry ingredients.
2. Add the coconut milk and 2 tbsps. of the coconut oil then mix properly.
3. In a skillet, melt 1 tsp. of coconut oil.
4. Pour a ladle of the batter into the skillet then swirl the pan to spread the batter evenly into a smooth pancake.
5. Cook it for like 3 minutes on medium heat until it becomes firm.
6. Turn the pancake to the other side then cook it for another 2 minutes until it turns golden brown.
7. Cook the remaining pancakes in the same process.
8. Serve.

Nutrition:

Calories: 377 kcal Fat: 14.9g
Carbs: 60.7g
Protein: 6.4g

8. Quinoa Porridge

Preparation Time: 5 minutes
Cooking Time: 25 minutes
Servings: 2
Ingredients:

- 2 cups coconut milk
- 1 cup rinsed quinoa
- 1/8 tsp. ground cinnamon
- 1 cup fresh blueberries

Directions:

1. In a saucepan, boil the coconut milk over high heat.

2. Add the quinoa to the milk then bring the mixture to a boil.
3. You then let it simmer for 15 minutes on medium heat until the milk is reduces.
4. Add the cinnamon then mix it properly in the saucepan.
5. Cover the saucepan and cook for at least 8 minutes until milk is completely absorbed.
6. Add in the blueberries then cook for 30 more seconds.
7. Serve.

Nutrition:

Calories: 271 kcal Fat: 3.7g
Carbs: 54g Protein:6.5g

9. Banana Barley Porridge

Preparation Time: 15 minutes
Cooking Time: 5 minutes
Servings: 2
Ingredients:

- 1 cup divided unsweetened coconut milk
- 1 small peeled and sliced banana
- 1/2 cup barley
- 3 drops liquid stevia
- 1/4 cup chopped coconuts

Directions:

1. In a bowl, properly mix barley with half of the coconut milk and stevia.
2. Cover the mixing bowl then refrigerate for about 6 hours.
3. In a saucepan, mix the barley mixture with coconut milk.
4. Cook for about 5 minutes on moderate heat.

5. Then top it with the chopped coconuts and the banana slices.

6. Serve.

Nutrition:

Calories: 159kcal

Fat: 8.4g

Carbs: 19.8g

Proteins: 4.6g

10. Zucchini Muffins

Preparation Time: 10 minutes

Cooking Time: 25 minutes

Servings: 16

Ingredients:

- 1 tbsp. ground flaxseed
- 3 tbsps. alkaline water
- 1/4 cup walnut butter
- 3 medium over-ripe bananas
- 2 small grated zucchinis
- 1/2 cup coconut milk
- 1 tsp. vanilla extract
- 2 cups coconut flour
- 1 tbsp. baking powder
- 1 tsp. cinnamon
- 1/4 tsp. sea salt

Directions:

1. Tune the temperature of your oven to 375°F.
2. Grease the muffin tray with the cooking spray.
3. In a bowl, mix the flaxseed with water.
4. In a glass bowl, mash the bananas then stir in the remaining ingredients.
5. Properly mix and then divide the mixture into the muffin tray.

6. Bake it for 25 minutes.
7. Serve.

Nutrition:

Calories: 127 kcal Fat: 6.6g

Carbs: 13g

Protein: 0.7g

11. Millet Porridge

Preparation Time: 10 minutes

Cooking Time: 20 minutes

Servings: 2

Ingredients:

- Sea salt
- 1 tbsp. finely chopped coconuts
- 1/2 cup unsweetened coconut milk
- 1/2 cup rinsed and drained millet
- 1-1/2 cups alkaline water
- 3 drops liquid stevia

Directions:

1. Sauté the millet in a non-stick skillet for about 3 minutes.
2. Add salt and water then stir.
3. Let the meal boil then reduce the amount of heat.
4. Cook for 15 minutes then add the remaining ingredients. Stir.
5. Cook the meal for 4 extra minutes.
6. Serve the meal with toping of the chopped nuts.

Nutrition:

Calories: 219 kcal

Fat: 4.5g Carbs: 38.2g

Protein: 6.4g

12. Jackfruit Vegetable Fry

Preparation Time: 5 minutes

Cooking Time: 5 minutes

Servings: 6

Ingredients:

- 2 finely chopped small onions
- 2 cups finely chopped cherry tomatoes
- 1/8 tsp. ground turmeric
- 1 tbsp. olive oil
- 2 seeded and chopped red bell peppers
- 3 cups seeded and chopped firm jackfruit
- 1/8 tsp. cayenne pepper
- 2 tbsps. chopped fresh basil leaves
- Salt

Directions:

1. In a greased skillet, sauté the onions and bell peppers for about 5 minutes.
2. Add the tomatoes then stir.
3. Cook for 2 minutes.
4. Then add the jackfruit, cayenne pepper, salt, and turmeric.
5. Cook for about 8 minutes.
6. Garnish the meal with basil leaves.
7. Serve warm.

Nutrition: Calories: 236 kcal Fat: 1.8g Carbs: 48.3g Protein: 7g

13. Zucchini Pancakes

Preparation Time: 15 minutes

Cooking Time: 8 minutes

Servings: 8

Ingredients:

- 12 tbsps. alkaline water

- 6 large grated zucchinis
- Sea salt
- 4 tbsps. ground Flax Seeds
- 2 tsps. olive oil
- 2 finely chopped jalapeño peppers
- 1/2 cup finely chopped scallions

Directions:

1. In a bowl, mix together water and the flax seeds then set it aside.
2. Pour oil in a large non-stick skillet then heat it on medium heat.
3. The add the black pepper, salt, and zucchini.
4. Cook for 3 minutes then transfer the zucchini into a large bowl.
5. Add the flax seed and the scallion's mixture then properly mix it.
6. Preheat a griddle then grease it lightly with the cooking spray.
7. Pour 1/4 of the zucchini mixture into griddle then cook for 3 minutes.
8. Flip the side carefully then cook for 2 more minutes.
9. Repeat the procedure with the remaining mixture in batches.
10. Serve.

Nutrition:

Calories: 71 kcal Fat: 2.8g

Carbs: 9.8g Protein: 3.7g

14. Squash Hash

Preparation Time: 2 minutes

Cooking Time: 10 minutes

Servings: 2

Ingredients:

- 1 tsp. onion powder
- 1/2 cup finely chopped onion

- 2 cups spaghetti squash
- 1/2 tsp. sea salt

Directions:

1. Using paper towels, squeeze extra moisture from spaghetti squash.
2. Place the squash into a bowl then add the salt, onion, and the onion powder.
3. Stir properly to mix them.
4. Spray a non-stick cooking skillet with cooking spray then place it over moderate heat.
5. Add the spaghetti squash to pan.
6. Cook the squash for about 5 minutes.
7. Flip the hash browns using a spatula.
8. Cook for 5 minutes until the desired crispness is reached.
9. Serve.

Nutrition:
Calories: 44 kcal Fat: 0.6g
Carbs: 9.7g Protein: 0.9g

15. Pumpkin Spice Quinoa

Preparation Time: 10 minutes
Cooking Time: 0 minutes
Servings: 2
Ingredients:

- 1 cup cooked quinoa
- 1 cup unsweetened coconut milk
- 1 large mashed banana
- 1/4 cup pumpkin puree
- 1 tsp. pumpkin spice
- 2 tsps. chia seeds

Directions:

1. In a container, mix all the ingredients.

2. Seal the lid then shake the container properly to mix.
3. Refrigerate overnight.
4. Serve.

Nutrition:
Calories: 212 kcal Fat: 11.9g
Carbs: 31.7g
Protein: 7.3g

16. Sweet Cashew Cheese Spread

Preparation Time: 5 minutes
Cooking Time: 5 minutes
Servings: 10 servings
Ingredients:

- Stevia (5 drops)
- Cashews (2 cups, raw)
- Water (1/2 cup)

Directions:

1. Soak the cashews overnight in water.
2. Next, drain the excess water then transfer cashews to a food processor.
3. Add in the stevia and the water.
4. Process until smooth.
5. Serve chilled. Enjoy.

Nutrition:
Fat: 7 g
Cholesterol: 0 mg
Sodium: 12.6 mg
Carbohydrates: 5.7 g

17. Mini Zucchini Bites

Preparation Time: 10 minutes
Cooking Time: 10 minutes
Servings: 6
Ingredients:

- 1 zucchini, cut into thick circles

181 | P a g .

- 3 cherry tomatoes, halved
- 1/2 cup parmesan cheese, grated
- Salt and pepper to taste
- 1 tsp. chives, chopped

Directions:

1. Preheat the oven to 390 degrees F.
2. Add wax paper on a baking sheet.
3. Arrange the zucchini pieces.
4. Add the cherry halves on each zucchini slice.
5. Add parmesan cheese, chives, and sprinkle with salt and pepper.
6. Bake for 10 minutes. Serve.

Nutrition:

Fat: 1.0 g

Cholesterol: 5.0 mg

Sodium: 400.3 mg

Potassium: 50.5 mg

Carbohydrates: 7.3 g

18. Beef with Broccoli on Cauliflower Rice

Preparation Time: 5 minutes

Cooking Time: 15 minutes

Servings: 2

Ingredients:

- 1 lb. raw beef round steak, cut into strips.
- 1 Tbsp + 2 tsp low sodium soy sauce
- 1 Splenda packet
- ½ C water
- 1 ½ C broccoli florets
- 1 tsp sesame or olive oil
- 2 Cups cooked, grated cauliflower or frozen riced cauliflower

Directions:

1. Stir steak with soy sauce and let sit about 15 minutes.
2. Heat oil over medium-high heat and stir fry beef for 3-5 minutes or until browned.
3. Remove from pan.
4. Place broccoli, Splenda and water. Cook for 5 minutes or until broccoli start to turn tender, stirring sometimes.
5. Add beef back in and heat up thoroughly.
6. Serve the dish with cauliflower rice.

Nutrition:

Calories 201

Protein 23g

Fat 4

Carbs 2

19. Asparagus & Crabmeat Frittata

Preparation Time: 5 minutes

Cooking Time: 15 minutes

Servings: 4

Ingredients:

- 2½ tbsp extra virgin olive oil
- 2 lbs. asparagus
- 1 tsp salt
- 1 ½ tsp black pepper
- 2 tsp sweet paprika
- 1 lb. lump crabmeat
- 1 tbsp finely cut chives
- ¼ cup basil chopped
- 4 cups liquid egg substitute

Directions:

1. Deter the tough ends of the asparagus and cut it into bite-sized pieces.
2. Preheat an oven to 375°F.
3. In a 12-Inch to a 14-inch oven-proof, non-stick skillet, warm the olive oil and sweat the asparagus until tender. Season with pepper, paprika, and salt.
4. In a mixing bowl, add the chives, crab and basil meat.
5. Pour in the liquid egg substitute and mix until combined.
6. Pour the crab and egg mixture into the skillet with the cooked asparagus and stir to combine. Bake over low to medium heat until the eggs start bubbling.
7. Place the skillet in the oven and bake for about 15-20 minutes until the eggs are golden brown. Serve the dish warm.

Nutrition: Calories: 340 Protein: 50 g
Carbohydrate: 14 g Fat: 10g

20. Grilled Chicken Power Bowl with Green Goddess Dressing

Preparation Time: 5 minutes
Cooking Time: 15 minutes
Servings: 4
Ingredients:

- 1 ½ boneless, skinless chicken breasts
- ¼ tsp each salt & pepper
- 1 cup riced or cubed kabocha squash
- 1 cup diced zucchini
- 1 cup riced yellow summer squash
- 1 cup riced broccoli
- 8 cherry tomatoes, halved
- 4 radishes, sliced thin
- 1 cup shredded red cabbage
- ¼ cup hemp or pumpkin seeds

Green Goddess Dressing:

- ½ cup low-fat plain Greek yogurt
- 1 cup fresh basil
- 1 clove garlic
- 4 tbsp lemon juice
- ¼ tsp each salt & pepper

Directions:

1. Pre-heat oven to 350°F.
2. Season chicken with salt and pepper.
3. Roast chicken for 12 minutes until it reaches a temperature of 165°F. When done, dismiss from oven and set aside to rest, about 5 minutes. Cut into bite-sized pieces and keep warm.
4. While the chicken rests, steam riced kabocha squash, yellow summer squash, zucchini, and broccoli in a covered microwave-proof bowl about 5 minutes till tender.
5. For the dressing, arrange the ingredients in a blender and puree till smooth.
6. To serve, place an equal amount of Veggie Mix into four individual bowls. Add an equal amount of cherry tomatoes, radishes, and chopped cabbage to each bowl along with a quarter of the chicken and a tablespoon of seeds. Dress up. Enjoy!

Nutrition:
Calories: 300 Protein: 43 g
Carbohydrate: 12 g Fat: 10 g

21. Bacon Cheeseburger

Preparation Time: 5 minutes

Cooking Time: 15 minutes

Servings: 4

Ingredients:

- 1 lb. lean ground beef
- ¼ cup chopped yellow onion
- 1 clove garlic, minced
- 1 Tbsp. yellow mustard
- 1 Tbsp. Worcestershire sauce
- ½ tsp salt
- Cooking spray
- 4 ultra-thin slices cheddar cheese, cut into 6 equal-sized rectangular pieces
- 3 pieces of turkey bacon, each cut into 8 evenly-sized rectangular pieces
- 24 dill pickle chips
- 4-6 green leaf
- lettuce leaves, torn into 24 small square-shaped pieces
- 12 cherry tomatoes, sliced in half

Directions:

1. Pre-heat oven to 400°F.
2. Combine the garlic, salt, onion, Worcestershire sauce, and beef in a medium-sized bowl, and mix well.
3. Form mixture into 24 small meatballs. Put meatballs onto a foil-lined baking sheet and cook for 12-15 minutes. Leave oven on.
4. Top every meatball with a piece of cheese, then go back to the oven till cheese melts, about 2 to 3 minutes. Let meatballs cool.
5. To assemble bites: on a toothpick layer a cheese-covered meatball, piece of bacon, piece of lettuce, pickle chip, and a tomato half.

Nutrition:

Calories 234 Protein 20g

Fat 3

Carbs 12

22. Cheeseburger Pie

Preparation Time: 25 minutes

Cooking Time: 90 minutes

Servings: 4

Ingredients:

- 1 large spaghetti squash
- 1 lb. lean ground beef
- ¼ cup diced onion
- 2 eggs
- 1/3 cup low-fat, plain Greek yogurt
- 2 Tbsp. Tomato sauce
- ½ tsp Worcestershire sauce
- 2/3 cup reduced-fat, shredded cheddar cheese
- 2 oz dill pickle slices
- Cooking spray

Directions:

1. Preheat oven to 400°F.
2. Slice spaghetti squash in half lengthwise; dismiss pulp and seeds. Spray cooking spray.
3. 3. Place the cut pumpkin halves on a foil-lined baking sheet and bake for 30 minutes. Once cooked, let it cool before scraping the pulp from the squash with a fork to remove the spaghetti-like strings. set aside.
4. Push squash strands in the bottom and up sides of the greased pie pan, creating an even layer.

5. Meanwhile, set up pie filling. In a lightly greased, medium-sized skillet, cook beef and onion over medium heat 8 to 10 minutes, sometimes stirring, until meat is brown. Drain and remove from heat.

6. whisk together the eggs, tomato paste, Greek yogurt and Worcestershire sauce and add the ground beef mixture. Pour the pie filling over the pumpkin rind.

7. Sprinkle the meat filling with cheese, then fill with pickled cucumber slices.

8. Bake for 40 minutes.

Nutrition:
Calories: 270
Protein: 23 g
Carbohydrate: 10 g
Fat: 23 g

23. Ancho Tilapia On Cauliflower Rice

Preparation Time: 15 minutes
Cooking Time: 30 minutes
Servings: 4
Ingredients:

- 2 lbs. tilapia
- 1 tsp lime juice
- 1 tsp salt
- 1 tbsp ground ancho pepper
- 1 tsp ground cumin
- 1 ½ tbsp. extra virgin olive oil
- ¼ cup toasted pumpkin seeds
- 6 cups cauliflower rice minutes
- 1 cup coarsely chopped fresh cilantro

Directions:
1. Preheat oven to 450°F.

2. Dress tilapia with lime juice and set aside.

3. Combine cumin, ancho pepper, and salt in a bowl. Season tilapia with spice mixture.

4. Lay tilapia on a baking sheet or casserole dish and bake for 7 minutes.

5. In the meantime, in a big skillet, sweat the cauliflower rice in olive oil till tender, about 2-3 minutes.

6. Blend the pumpkin seeds and cilantro into the rice. Dismiss from heat, and serve.

Nutrition:
Calories: 350
Fat: 13 g
Carbohydrate: 10 g
Protein: 51 g

24. Personal Biscuit Pizza

Preparation Time: 5 minutes
Cooking Time: 15 minutes
Servings: 1
Ingredients:

- 1 sachet OPTAVIA Select
- Buttermilk Cheddar Herb Biscuit
- 2 Tbsp cold water
- Cooking spray
- 2 Tbsp no-sugar-added tomato sauce
- ¼ cup reduced-fat shredded cheese

Directions:
1. Preheat oven to 350°F.

2. Mix biscuit and water, and spread mixture into a small, circular crust shape onto a greased, foil-lined baking sheet. Bake for 10 minutes.

3. Top with tomato sauce and cheese, and cook till cheese is melted about 5 minutes.

Nutrition:

Calories 301

Protein 13g

Fat 8

Carbs 7

25. Turkey Caprese Meatloaf Cups

Preparation Time: 20 minutes

Cooking Time: 45 minutes

Servings: 6

Ingredients:

- 1 large egg
- 2 pounds ground turkey breast
- 3 pieces of sun-dried tomatoes,
- drained and chopped
- ¼ cup fresh basil leaves, chopped
- 5 ounces low-fat fresh mozzarella, shredded
- ½ teaspoon garlic powder
- ¼ teaspoon salt and ½ teaspoon pepper, to taste

Directions:

1. Preheat oven to 400°F.
2. Beat the egg in a big mixing bowl.
3. Add the remaining ingredients and mix everything with your hands until evenly combined.
4. Spray a 12-cup muffin tin and divide the turkey mixture among the muffin cups, pressing the mix in. Cook in the preheated oven till the turkey is well-cooked for about 25-30 minutes.

5. Chill the meatloaves entirely and store them in a container in the fridge for up to 5 days.

Nutrition:

Calories 181

Protein 43g

Fat 11

Carbs 9

26. Zucchini Noodles with Creamy Avocado Pesto

Preparation Time: 10 minutes

Cooking Time: 20 minutes

Servings: 4

Ingredients:

- 6 c of spiralized zucchini
- 1 Tbsp olive oil
- 6 oz of avocado
- 1 basil leaves
- 3 garlic cloves
- 1/3 oz pine nuts
- 2 Tbsp lemon juice
- ½ tsp salt
- ¼ tsp black pepper

Directions:

1. Spiralize the courgettes and set them aside on paper towels so that the excess water is absorbed.
2. In a food processor, put avocados, lemon juice basil leaves garlic, pine nuts, and sea salt and pulse until chopped. Then put olive oil in a slow stream till emulsified and creamy.
3. Drizzle olive oil in a skillet over medium-high heat and put zucchini noodles, cooking for about 2 minutes till tender.

4. Put zucchini noodles to a big bowl and toss with avocado pesto. Season with cracked pepper and a little Parmesan and serve.

Nutrition:

Calories 115

Protein 30g

Fat 0

Carbs 3

27. Avocado Chicken Salad

Preparation Time: 5 minutes

Cooking Time: 10 minutes

Servings: 2

Ingredients:

- 10 oz diced cooked chicken
- ½ cup 2% Plain Greek yogurt
- 3 oz chopped avocado
- 12 tsp garlic powder
- ¼ tsp salt
- 1/8 tsp pepper
- 1 tbsp + 1 tsp lime juice
- ¼ cup fresh cilantro, chopped

Directions:

1. Combine all ingredients in a medium-sized bowl. Refrigerate until ready to serve.
2. Cut the chicken salad in half and serve with your favorite greens.

Nutrition:

Calories 265

Protein 35g

Fat 13

Carbs 5

28. Chicken Lo Mein

Preparation Time: 15 minutes

Cooking Time: 30 minutes

Servings: 4

Ingredients:

- 2 tbsp + 2 tsp sesame oil, divided
- 790g boneless. skinless chicken breasts, sliced
- ¼ tsp ground black pepper
- 2 tbsp soy sauce
- 2 tbsp oyster sauce
- 1 garlic clove, minced
- 2 tsp peeled and minced fresh ginger-root
- 2 spring onions, trimmed and
- sliced with white and green parts separated
- 110 g fresh mushrooms, divided
- 1 medium red bell pepper, membranes and seeds removed
- 2 medium zucchinis (400g), cut, sliced

Directions:

1. In a skillet, heat one teaspoon sesame oil over medium-high heat. Put the sliced chicken, season with black pepper, and cook until chicken is done (internal temperature about 165°F). Dismiss from wok or skillet and set aside.
2. While the chicken cooks, prepare the sauce by combining the oyster sauce, soy sauce, and 2 tablespoons sesame oil in a bowl and whisking together. Set aside.
3. With the same skillet used to cook the chicken, heat 1 teaspoon sesame oil and put the garlic, ginger, and

white spring onion pieces; cook until fragrant, about 1 minute. Put the mushrooms and bell peppers and continue to cook until just tender, about 3 minutes. Add zucchini noodles and toss to combine.

4. Pour in the sauce and put the chicken; cook until zucchini is tender and the mixture is heated for 5 minutes.

5. Garnish with green parts of spring onions.

Nutrition:
Calories: 312 Protein: 9g
Fat: 10 Carbs: 22

29. Avocado Blueberry Smoothie
Preparation Time: 5 minutes
Cooking Time: 5 minutes
Servings: 1
Ingredients:

- 1 tsp chia seeds
- ½ cup unsweetened coconut milk
- 1 avocado
- ½ cup blueberries

Directions:
1. Add all the listed ingredients to the blender and blend until smooth and creamy.
2. Serve immediately and enjoy.

Nutrition: Calories: 389 Fat: 34.6g
Carbs: 20.7g Protein: 4.8g Fiber: 0g

30. Vegan Blueberry Smoothie
Preparation Time: 5 minutes
Cooking Time: 5 minutes

Servings: 2
Ingredients:

- 2 cups blueberries
- 1 tbsp hemp seeds
- 1 tbsp chia seeds
- 1 tbsp flax meal
- 1/8 tsp orange zest, grated
- 1 cup fresh orange juice
- 1 cup unsweetened coconut milk

Directions:
1. Toss all your ingredients into your blender then process till smooth and creamy.
2. Serve immediately and enjoy.

Nutrition: Calories: 212 Fat: 6.6g Carbs: 36.9g Protein: 5.2g Fiber: 0g

31. Berry Peach Smoothie
Preparation Time: 5 minutes
Cooking Time: 5 minutes
Servings: 2
Ingredients:

- 1 cup coconut water
- 1 tbsp hemp seeds
- 1 tbsp agave
- ½ cup strawberries
- ½ cup blueberries
- ½ cup cherries - ½ cup peaches

Directions:
1. Toss all your ingredients into your blender then process till smooth and creamy.
2. Serve immediately and enjoy.

Nutrition: Calories: 117 Fat: 2.5g Carbs: 22.5g Protein: 3.5g Fiber: 0g

32. Cantaloupe Blackberry Smoothie

Preparation Time: 5 minutes

Cooking Time: 5 minutes

Servings: 2

Ingredients:

- 1 cup coconut milk yogurt
- ½ cup blackberries
- 2 cups fresh cantaloupe
- 1 banana

Directions:

1. Toss all your ingredients into your blender then process till smooth.
2. Serve and enjoy.

Nutrition: Calories: 160 Fat: 4.5g Carbs: 33.7g Protein: 1.8g Fiber: 0g

33. Cantaloupe Kale Smoothie

Preparation Time: 5 minutes

Cooking Time: 5 minutes

Servings: 2

Ingredients:

- 8 oz. water
- 1 orange, peeled
- 3 cups kale, chopped
- 1 banana, peeled
- 2 cups cantaloupe, chopped
- 1 zucchini, chopped

Directions:

1. Toss all your ingredients into your blender then process till smooth and creamy.
2. Serve immediately and enjoy.

Nutrition: Calories: 203 Fat: 0.5g Carbs: 49.2g Protein: 5.6g Fiber: 0g

34. Mix Berry Cantaloupe Smoothie

Preparation Time: 5 minutes

Cooking Time: 5 minutes

Servings: 2

Ingredients: 1 cup alkaline water

- 2 fresh Seville orange juices
- ¼ cup fresh mint leaves
- 1 ½ cups mixed berries
- 2 cups cantaloupe

Directions:

1. Toss all your ingredients into your blender then process till smooth.
2. Serve immediately and enjoy.

Nutrition: Calories: 122 Fat: 1g Carbs: 26.1g Protein: 2.4g Fiber: 0g

35. Avocado Kale Smoothie

Preparation Time: 5 minutes

Cooking Time: 5 minutes

Servings: 3

Ingredients:

- 1 cup water
- ½ Seville orange, peeled
- 1 avocado
- 1 cucumber, peeled
- 1 cup kale
- 1 cup ice cubes

Directions:

1. Toss all your ingredients into your blender then process till smooth and creamy.
2. Serve immediately and enjoy.

Nutrition: Calories: 160 Fat: 13.3g Carbs: 11.6g Protein: 2.4g Fiber: 0g

36. Apple Kale Cucumber Smoothie

Preparation Time: 5 minutes

Cooking Time: 5 minutes

Servings: 1

Ingredients:

- 3/4 cup water
- 1/2 green apple, diced
- 3/4 cup kale
- 1/2 cucumber

Directions:

3. Toss all your ingredients into your blender then process till smooth and creamy.
4. Serve immediately and enjoy.

Nutrition: Calories: 86 Fat: 0.5g Carbs: 21.7g Protein: 1.9g Fiber: 0g

CHAPTER 5:

Lunch Recipes

37. Almond Pancakes

Preparation Time: 10 minutes
Cooking Time: 13 minutes
Servings: 12
Ingredients:

- 6 eggs
- 1/4 cup almonds; toasted
- 2 ounces' cocoa chocolate
- 1 teaspoon almond extract
- 1/3 cup coconut; shredded
- 1/2 teaspoon baking powder
- 1/4 cup coconut oil
- 1/2 cup coconut flour
- 1/4 cup stevia
- 1 cup almond milk
- Cooking spray
- A pinch of salt

Directions:

1. Mix coconut flour with stevia, baking powder, salt and coconut and stir.
2. Add coconut oil, eggs, almond milk and the almond extract and stir well again.
3. Add chocolate and almonds and whisk well again.
4. Heat up a pan and add cooking spray; add 2 tablespoons batter, spread into a circle, cook until it's golden, flip, cook again until it's done and transfer to a pan.
5. Do the same for rest of the batter and serve your pancakes right away.

Nutrition:

Calories: 266

Fat: 13

Fiber: 8

Carbs: 10

Protein: 11

38. Mouth-watering Pie

Preparation Time: 15 minutes
Cooking Time: 45 minutes
Servings: 8
Ingredients:

- 3/4-pound beef; ground
- 1/2 onion; chopped.
- 1 pie crust
- 3 tablespoons taco seasoning
- 1 teaspoon baking soda
- Mango salsa for serving
- 1/2 red bell pepper; chopped.
- A handful cilantro; chopped.
- 8 eggs
- 1 teaspoon coconut oil
- Salt and black pepper to the taste.

Directions:

1. Heat up a pan, add oil, beef, cook until it browns and mixes with salt, pepper and taco seasoning.
2. Stir again, transfer to a bowl and leave aside for now.
3. Heat up the pan again over medium heat with cooking juices from the meat, add onion and pepper; stir and cook for 4 minutes
4. Add eggs, baking soda and some salt and stir well.
5. Add cilantro; stir again and take off heat.
6. Spread beef mix in pie crust, add veggies mix and spread over meat, heat oven at 350 degrees F and bake for 45 minutes
7. Leave the pie to cool down a bit, slice, divide between plates and serve with mango salsa on top.

Nutrition: Calories: 198 Fat: 11 Fiber: 1
Carbs: 12 Protein: 12

39. Chicken Omelet

Preparation Time: 5 minutes

Cooking Time: 15 minutes

Servings: 1

Ingredients:

- 2 bacon slices; cooked and crumbled
- 2 eggs
- 1 tablespoon homemade mayonnaise
- 1 tomato; chopped.
- 1-ounce rotisserie chicken; shredded
- 1 teaspoon mustard
- 1 small avocado; pitted, peeled and chopped.
- Salt and black pepper to the taste.

Directions:

1. In a bowl, mix eggs with some salt and pepper and whisk gently.
2. Heat up a pan over medium heat; spray with some cooking oil, add eggs and cook your omelet for 5 minutes
3. Add chicken, avocado, tomato, bacon, mayo and mustard on one half of the omelet.
4. Fold omelet, cover pan and cook for 5 minutes more
5. Transfer to a plate and serve

Nutrition:

Calories: 400 Fat: 32

Fiber: 6 Carbs: 4 Protein: 25

40. Special Almond Cereal

Preparation Time: 5 minutes

Cooking Time: 5 minutes

Servings: 1

Ingredients:

- 2 tablespoons almonds; chopped.
- 1/3 cup coconut milk
- 1 tablespoon chia seeds
- 2 tablespoon pepitas; roasted
- A handful blueberries
- 1 small banana; chopped.
- 1/3 cup water

Directions:

1. In a bowl, mix chia seeds with coconut milk and leave aside for 5 minutes
2. In your food processor, mix half of the pepitas with almonds and pulse them well.
3. Add this to chia seeds mix.
4. Also add the water and stir.
5. Top with the rest of the pepitas, banana pieces and blueberries and serve

Nutrition:

Calories: 200

Fat: 3

Fiber: 2 Carbs: 5

Protein: 4

41. Awesome Avocado Muffins

Preparation Time: 10 minutes

Cooking Time: 20 minutes

Servings: 12

Ingredients:

- 6 bacon slices; chopped.
- 1 yellow onion; chopped.
- 1/2 teaspoon baking soda
- 1/2 cup coconut flour
- 1 cup coconut milk
- 2 cups avocado; pitted, peeled and chopped.
- 4 eggs
- Salt and black pepper to the taste.

Directions:

1. Heat up a pan, add onion and bacon; stir and brown for a few minutes
2. In a bowl, mash avocado pieces with a fork and whisk well with the eggs
3. Add milk, salt, pepper, baking soda and coconut flour and stir everything.
4. Add bacon mix and stir again.
5. Add coconut oil to muffin tray, divide eggs and avocado mix into the tray, heat oven at 350 degrees F and bake for 20 minutes
6. Divide muffins between plates and serve them for breakfast.

Nutrition:

Calories: 200

Fat: 7

Fiber: 4

Carbs: 7

Protein: 5

42. Tasty WW Pancakes

Preparation Time: 12 minutes

Cooking Time: 3 minutes

Servings: 4

Ingredients:

- 2 ounces' cream cheese
- 1 teaspoon stevia
- 1/2 teaspoon cinnamon; ground
- 2 eggs
- Cooking spray

Directions:

1. Mix the eggs with the cream cheese, stevia, and cinnamon in a blender, and mix well.
2. Heat pan with cooking spray over medium high heat. add 1/4 of the batter, spread well, cook 2 minutes, invert and cook 1 minute more
3. Move to a plate and repeat with the rest of the dough.
4. Serve them right away.

Nutrition:

Calories: 344

Fat: 23

Fiber: 12

Carbs: 3

Protein: 16

43. WW Salad in A Jar

Preparation Time: 10 minutes

Cooking Time: 5 minutes

Servings: 1

Ingredients:

- 1 ounce favorite greens
- 1-ounce red bell pepper; chopped.
- 4 ounces' rotisserie chicken; roughly chopped.
- 4 tablespoons extra virgin olive oil
- 1/2 scallion; chopped.
- 1-ounce cucumber; chopped.
- 1-ounce cherry tomatoes; halved
- Salt and black pepper to the taste.

Directions:

1. In a bowl, mix greens with bell pepper, tomatoes, scallion, cucumber, salt, pepper and olive oil and toss to coat well.
2. Transfer this to a jar, top with chicken pieces and serve for breakfast.

Nutrition:

Calories: 180 Fat: 12

Fiber: 4 Carbs: 5

Protein: 17

44. WW Breakfast Cereal

Preparation Time: 10 minutes

Cooking Time: 3 minutes

Servings: 2

Ingredients:

- 1/2 cup coconut; shredded
- 1/3 cup macadamia nuts; chopped.
- 4 teaspoons ghee
- 2 cups almond milk
- 1 tablespoon stevia
- 1/3 cup walnuts; chopped.
- 1/3 cup flax seed
- A pinch of salt

Directions:

1. Heat a pot of mistletoe over medium heat. Add the milk, coconut, salt, macadamia nuts, walnuts, flax seeds, and stevia and mix well.
2. Cook for 3 minutes. Stir again, remove from heat for 10 minutes.
3. Divide into 2 bowls and serve

Nutrition:

Calories: 140 Fat: 3

Fiber: 2

Carbs: 1. 5

Protein: 7

45. Yummy Smoked Salmon

Preparation Time: 10 minutes

Cooking Time: 10 minutes

Servings: 3

Ingredients:

- 4 eggs; whisked
- 1/2 teaspoon avocado oil
- 4 ounces smoked salmon; chopped.

For the sauce:

- 1/2 cup cashews; soaked; drained

- 1/4 cup green onions; chopped.
- 1 teaspoon garlic powder
- 1 cup coconut milk
- 1 tablespoon lemon juice
- Salt and black pepper to the taste.

Directions:

1. In your blender, mix cashews with coconut milk, garlic powder and lemon juice and blend well.
2. Add salt, pepper and green onions, blend again well, transfer to a bowl and keep in the fridge for now.
3. Heat up a pan with the oil over medium-low heat; add eggs, whisk a bit and cook until they are almost done
4. Introduce in your preheated broiler and cook until eggs set.
5. Divide eggs on plates, top with smoked salmon and serve with the green onion sauce on top.

Nutrition:

Calories: 200 Fat: 10

Fiber: 2

Carbs: 11

Protein: 15

46. Almond Coconut Cereal

Preparation Time: 5 minutes

Cooking Time: 5 minutes

Servings: 2

Ingredients:

- Water, 1/3 cup.
- Coconut milk, 1/3 cup.
- Roasted sunflower seeds, 2 tbsps.
- Chia seeds, 1 tbsp.
- Blueberries, ½ cup.
- Chopped almonds, 2 tbsps.

Directions:

1. Set a medium bowl in position to add coconut milk and chia seeds then reserve for five minutes
2. Plug in and set the blender in position to blend almond with sunflower seeds
3. Stir the combination to chia seeds mixture then add water to mix evenly.
4. Serve topped with the remaining sunflower seeds and blueberries

Nutrition:

Calories: 181 Fat: 15.2

Fiber: 4 Carbs: 10.8

Protein: 3.7

47. Almond Porridge

Preparation Time: 10 minutes

Cooking Time: 5 minutes

Servings: 1

Ingredients:

- Ground cloves, ¼ tsp.
- Nutmeg, ¼ tsp.
- Stevia, 1 tsp.
- Coconut cream, ¾ cup.
- Ground almonds, ½ cup.
- Ground cardamom, ¼ tsp.
- Ground cinnamon, 1 tsp.

Directions:

1. Set your pan over medium heat to cook the coconut cream for a few minutes
2. Stir in almonds and stevia to cook for 5 minutes
3. Mix in nutmeg, cardamom, and cinnamon
4. Enjoy while still hot

Nutrition:

Calories: 695 Fat: 66.7

Fiber: 11.1 Carbs: 22

Protein: 14.3

48. Asparagus Frittata Recipe

Preparation Time: 20 minutes

Cooking Time: 20 minutes

Servings: 4

Ingredients:

- Bacon slices, chopped: 4
- Salt and black pepper
- Eggs (whisked): 8
- Asparagus (trimmed and chopped): 1 bunch

Directions:

1. Heat a pan, add bacon, stir and cook for 5 minutes.
2. Add asparagus, salt, and pepper, stir and cook for another 5 minutes.
3. Add the chilled eggs, spread them in the pan, let them stand in the oven and bake for 20 minutes at 350° F.
4. Share and divide between plates and serve for breakfast.

Nutrition:

Calories 251 carbs 16

fat 6

fiber 8 protein 7

49. Avocados Stuffed with Salmon

Preparation Time: 5 minutes

Cooking Time: 5 minutes

Servings: 2

Ingredients:

- Avocado (pitted and halved): 1
- Olive oil: 2 tablespoons
- Lemon juice: 1

- Smoked salmon (flaked): 2 ounces
- Goat cheese (crumbled): 1 ounce
- Salt and black pepper

Directions:

1. Combine the salmon with lemon juice, oil, cheese, salt, and pepper in your food processor and pulsate well.
2. Divide this mixture into avocado halves and serve.
3. Dish and Enjoy!

Nutrition:

Calories: 300

Fat: 15

Fiber: 5

Carbs: 8

Protein: 16

50. Beef with Broccoli or Cauliflower Rice

Preparation Time: 10 minutes

Cooking Time: 30 minutes

Servings: 2

Ingredients:

- 1 lb. raw beef round steak, cut into strips.
- 1 Tbsp + 2 tsp. low sodium soy sauce
- 1 Splenda packet
- 1/2 C water
- 1 1/2 C broccoli florets
- 1 tsp. sesame or olive oil
- 2 Cups cooked, grated cauliflower or frozen riced cauliflower

Directions:

1 Stir steak with soy sauce and let sit about 15 minutes.

2 Heat oil over medium-high heat and stir fry beef for 3-5 minutes or until browned.

3 Remove from pan.

4 Place broccoli, Splenda and water.

5 Cover and cook 5 minutes or until broccoli start to turn tender, stirring sometimes.

6 Add beef back in and heat up thoroughly.

7 Serve the dish with cauliflower rice

Nutrition:

Fats 16 g Carbohydrates: 9 g Fiber 3 g

51. Bacon and Lemon spiced Muffins

Preparation Time: 10 minutes

Cooking Time: 20 minutes

Servings: 12

Ingredients:

- Lemon thyme, 2 tsps.
- Salt
- Almond flour, 3 cup.
- Melted butter, ½ cup.
- Baking soda, 1 tsp.
- Black pepper
- Medium eggs, 4
- Diced bacon, 1 cup.

Directions:

1. Set a mixing bowl in place and stir in the eggs and baking soda to incorporate well.
2. Whisk in the seasonings, butter, bacon, and lemon thyme
3. Set the mixture in a well-lined muffin pan.
4. Set the oven for 20 minutes at 3500F, allow to bake

5. Allow the muffins to cool before serving

Nutrition:

Calories: 186

Fat: 17.1 Fiber: 0.8

Carbs: 1.8

Protein: 7.4

52. Yogurt Garlic Chicken

Preparation Time: 30 minutes

Cooking Time: 60 min

Servings: 6

Ingredients:

- Pita bread rounds, halved (6 pieces)
- English cucumber, sliced thinly, w/ each slice halved (1 cup)

Chicken & vegetables:

- Olive oil (3 tablespoons)
- Black pepper, freshly ground (1/2 teaspoon)
- Chicken thighs, skinless, boneless (20 ounces)
- Bell pepper, red, sliced into half-inch portions (1 piece)
- Garlic cloves, chopped finely (4 pieces)
- Cumin, ground (1/2 teaspoon)
- Red onion, medium, sliced into half-inch wedges (1 piece)
- Yogurt, plain, fat free (1/2 cup)
- Lemon juice (2 tablespoons)
- Salt (1 ½ teaspoons)
- Red pepper flakes, crushed (1/2 teaspoon)
- Allspice, ground (1/2 teaspoon)
- Bell pepper, yellow, sliced into half-inch portions (1 piece)

Yogurt sauce:

- Olive oil (2 tablespoons)
- Salt (1/4 teaspoon)
- Parsley, flat leaf, chopped finely (1 tablespoon)
- Yogurt, plain, fat free (1 cup)
- Lemon juice, fresh (1 tablespoon)
- Garlic clove, chopped finely (1 piece)

Directions:

1. Mix the yogurt (1/2 cup), garlic cloves (4 pieces), olive oil (1 tablespoon), salt (1 teaspoon), lemon juice (2 tablespoons), pepper (1/4 teaspoon), allspice, cumin, and pepper flakes. Stir in the chicken and coat well. Cover and marinate in the fridge for two hours.
2. Preheat the air fryer at 400 degrees Fahrenheit.
3. Grease a rimmed baking sheet (18x13-inch) with cooking spray.
4. Toss the bell peppers and onion with remaining olive oil (2 tablespoons), pepper (1/4 teaspoon), and salt (1/2 teaspoon).
5. Arrange veggies on the baking sheet's left side and the marinated chicken thighs (drain first) on the right side. Cook in the air fryer for twenty-five to thirty minutes.
6. Mix the yogurt sauce ingredients.
7. Slice air-fried chicken into half-inch strips.
8. Top each pita round with chicken strips, roasted veggies, cucumbers, and yogurt sauce.

Nutrition:

Calories 380 Fat 10 g

Protein 20 g

Carbohydrates 30 g

53. Lemony Parmesan Salmon

Preparation Time: 10 minutes

Cooking Time: 25 minutes

Servings: 4

Ingredients:

- Butter, melted (2 tablespoons)
- Green onions, sliced thinly (2 tablespoons)
- Breadcrumbs, white, fresh (3/4 cup)
- Thyme leaves, dried (1/4 teaspoon)
- Salmon fillet, 1 ¼-pound (1 piece)
- Salt (1/4 teaspoon)
- Parmesan cheese, grated (1/4 cup)
- Lemon peel, grated (2 teaspoons)

Directions:

1. Preheat the oven at 350 degrees Fahrenheit.
2. Mist cooking spray onto a baking pan (shallow). Fill with pat-dried salmon. Brush salmon with butter (1 tablespoon) before sprinkling with salt.
3. Combine the breadcrumbs with onions, thyme, lemon peel, cheese, and remaining butter (1 tablespoon).
4. Cover salmon with the breadcrumb mixture. Air-fry for fifteen to twenty-five minutes.

Nutrition:

Calories 290 Fat 10 g

Protein 30 g Carbohydrates 0 g

54. Easiest Tuna Cobbler Ever

Preparation Time: 15 minutes

Cooking Time: 25 minutes

Servings: 4

Ingredients:

- Water, cold (1/3 cup)
- Tuna, canned, drained (10 ounces)
- Sweet pickle relish (2 tablespoons)
- Mixed vegetables, frozen (1 ½ cups)
- Soup, cream of chicken, condensed (10 ¾ ounces)
- Pimientos, sliced, drained (2 ounces)
- Lemon juice (1 teaspoon)
- Paprika

Directions:

1. Preheat the air fryer at 375 degrees Fahrenheit.
2. Mist cooking spray into a round casserole (1 ½ quarts).
3. Mix the frozen vegetables with milk, soup, lemon juice, relish, pimientos, and tuna in a saucepan. Cook for 8 minutes over medium heat.
4. Fill the casserole with the tuna mixture.
5. Mix the biscuit mix with cold water to form a soft dough. Beat for half a minute before dropping by four spoonsful into the casserole.
6. Dust the dish with paprika before air-frying for twenty to twenty-five minutes.

Nutrition:

Calories 320 Fat 10 g

Protein 20 g Carbohydrates 30 g

55. Deliciously Homemade Pork Buns

Preparation Time: 20 minutes

Cooking Time: 25 minutes

Servings: 8

Ingredients:

- Green onions, sliced thinly (3 pieces)
- Egg, beaten (1 piece)

- Pulled pork, diced, w/ barbecue sauce (1 cup)
- Buttermilk biscuits, refrigerated (16 1/3 ounces)
- Soy sauce (1 teaspoon)

Directions:

1. Preheat the air fryer at 325 degrees Fahrenheit.
2. Use parchment paper to line your baking sheet.
3. Combine pork with green onions.
4. Separate and press the dough to form 8 four-inch rounds.
5. Fill each biscuit round's center with two tablespoons of pork mixture. Cover with the dough edges and seal by pinching. Arrange the buns on the sheet and brush with a mixture of soy sauce and egg.
6. Cook in the air fryer for twenty to twenty-five minutes.

Nutrition:

Calories 240

Fat 0 g

Protein 0 g

Carbohydrates 20 g

56. Mouthwatering Tuna Melts

Preparation Time: 15 minutes

Cooking Time: 20 minutes

Servings: 8

Ingredients:

- Salt (1/8 teaspoon)
- Onion, chopped (1/3 cup)
- Biscuits, refrigerated, flaky layers (16 1/3 ounces)
- Tuna, water packed, drained (10 ounces)
- Mayonnaise (1/3 cup)

- Pepper (1/8 teaspoon)
- Cheddar cheese, shredded (4 ounces)
- Tomato, chopped
- Sour cream
- Lettuce, shredded

Directions:

1. Preheat the air fryer at 325 degrees Fahrenheit.
2. Mist cooking spray onto a cookie sheet.
3. Mix tuna with mayonnaise, pepper, salt, and onion.
4. Separate dough so you have 8 biscuits; press each into 5-inch rounds.
5. Arrange 4 biscuit rounds on the sheet. Fill at the center with tuna mixture before topping with cheese. Cover with the remaining biscuit rounds and press to seal.
6. Air-fry for fifteen to twenty minutes. Slice each sandwich into halves. Serve each piece topped with lettuce, tomato, and sour cream.

Nutrition:

Calories 320 Fat 10 g

Protein 10 g

Carbohydrates 20 g

57. Bacon Wings

Preparation Time: 15 minutes

Cooking Time: 1 hour 15 minutes

Servings: 12

Ingredients:

- Bacon strips (12 pieces)
- Paprika (1 teaspoon)
- Black pepper (1 tablespoon)
- Oregano (1 teaspoon)
- Chicken wings (12 pieces)

- Kosher salt (1 tablespoon)
- Brown sugar (1 tablespoon)
- Chili powder (1 teaspoon)
- Celery sticks
- Blue cheese dressing

Directions:

1. Preheat the air fryer at 325 degrees Fahrenheit.
2. Mix sugar, salt, chili powder, oregano, pepper, and paprika. Coat chicken wings with this dry rub.
3. Wrap a bacon strip around each wing. Arrange wrapped wings in the air fryer basket.
4. Cook for thirty minutes on each side in the air fryer. Let cool for five minutes.
5. Serve and enjoy with celery and blue cheese.

Nutrition:

Calories 100

Fat 0 g

Protein 0 g

Carbohydrates 0 g

58. Pepper Pesto Lamb

Preparation Time: 15 minutes

Cooking Time: 1 hour 15 minutes

Servings: 12

Ingredients:

Pesto:

- Rosemary leaves, fresh (1/4 cup)
- Garlic cloves (3 pieces)
- Parsley, fresh, packed firmly (3/4 cup)
- Mint leaves, fresh (1/4 cup)
- Olive oil (2 tablespoons)

Lamb:

- Red bell peppers, roasted, drained (7 ½ ounces)
- Leg of lamb, boneless, rolled (5 pounds)
- Seasoning, lemon pepper (2 teaspoons)

Directions:

1. Preheat the oven at 325 degrees Fahrenheit.
2. Mix the pesto ingredients in the food processor.
3. Unroll the lamb and cover the cut side with pesto. Top with roasted peppers before rolling up the lamb and tying with kitchen twine.
4. Coat lamb with seasoning (lemon pepper) and air-fry for one hour.

Nutrition:

Calories 310

Fat 10 g

Protein 40.0 g

Carbohydrates 0 g

59. Tuna Spinach Casserole

Preparation Time: 30 minutes

Cooking Time: 25 minutes

Servings: 8

Ingredients:

- Mushroom soup, creamy (18 ounces)
- Milk (1/2 cup)
- White tuna, solid, in-water, drained (12 ounces)
- Crescent dinner rolls, refrigerated (8 ounces)
- Egg noodles, wide, uncooked (8 ounces)
- Cheddar cheese, shredded (8 ounces)

- Spinach, chopped, frozen, thawed, drained (9 ounces)
- Lemon peel grated (2 teaspoons)

Directions:
1. Preheat the oven at 350 degrees Fahrenheit.
2. Mist cooking spray onto a glass baking dish (11x7-inch).
3. Follow package directions in cooking and draining the noodles.
4. Stir the cheese (1 ½ cups) and soup together in a skillet heated on medium. Once cheese melts, stir in your noodles, milk, spinach, tuna, and lemon peel. Once bubbling, pour into the prepped dish.
5. Unroll the dough and sprinkle with remaining cheese (1/2 cup). Roll up dough and pinch at the seams to seal. Slice into 8 portions and place over the tuna mixture.
6. Air-fry for twenty to twenty-five minutes.

Nutrition:
Calories 400
Fat 10 g
Protein 20 g
Carbohydrates 30 g

60. Greek Style Mini Burger Pies

Preparation Time: 15 minutes
Cooking Time: 40 minutes
Servings: 6
Ingredients:
Burger mixture:

- Onion, large, chopped (1 piece)
- Red bell peppers, roasted, diced (1/2 cup)

- Ground lamb, 80% lean (1 pound)
- Red pepper flakes (1/4 teaspoon)
- Feta cheese, crumbled (2 ounces)

Baking mixture:

- Milk (1/2 cup)
- Biscuit mix, classic (1/2 cup)
- Eggs (2 pieces)

Directions:
1. Preheat oven at 350 degrees Fahrenheit.
2. Grease 12 muffin cups using cooking spray.
3. Cook the onion and beef in a skillet heated on medium-high. Once beef is browned and cooked through, drain and let cool for five minutes. Stir together with feta cheese, roasted red peppers, and red pepper flakes.
4. Whisk the baking mixture ingredients together. Fill each muffin cup with baking mixture (1 tablespoon).
5. Air-fry for twenty-five to thirty minutes. Let cool before serving.

Nutrition:
Calories 270
Fat 10 g
Protein 10 g
Carbohydrates 10 g

61. Family Fun Pizza

Preparation Time: 30 minutes
Cooking Time: 25 minutes
Servings: 16
Ingredients:
Pizza crust:

- Water, warm (1 cup)
- Salt (1/2 teaspoon)
- Flour, whole wheat (1 cup)

- Olive oil (2 tablespoons)
- Dry yeast, quick active (1 package)
- Flour, all purpose (1 ½ cups)
- Cornmeal
- Olive oil

Filling:

- Onion, chopped (1 cup)
- Mushrooms, sliced, drained (4 ounces)
- Garlic cloves, chopped finely (2 pieces)
- Parmesan cheese, grated (1/4 cup)
- Ground lamb, 80% lean (1 pound)
- Italian seasoning (1 teaspoon)
- Pizza sauce (8 ounces)
- Mozzarella cheese, shredded (2 cups)

Directions:

1. Mix yeast with warm water. Combine with flours, oil (2 tablespoons), and salt by stirring and then beating vigorously for half a minute. Let the dough sit for twenty minutes.
2. Preheat oven at 350 degrees Fahrenheit.
3. Prep 2 square pans (8-inch) by greasing with oil before sprinkling with cornmeal.
4. Cut the rested dough in half; place each half inside each pan. Set aside, covered, for thirty to forty-five minutes. Cook in the air fryer for twenty to twenty-two minutes.
5. Sauté the onion, beef, garlic, and Italian seasoning until beef is completely cooked. Drain and set aside.
6. Cover the air-fried crusts with pizza sauce before topping with beef mixture, cheeses, and mushrooms.

7. Return to oven and cook for twenty minutes.

Nutrition:

Calories 215

Fat 0 g

Protein 10 g

Carbohydrates 20.0 g

62. Buffalo Chicken Sliders

Preparation Time: **10 minutes**

Cooking Time: **15 minutes**

Servings: **12**

Ingredients:

- Chicken breasts (2 lb., cooked, shredded)
- Wing sauce (1 cup)
- Ranch dressing mix (1 pack)
- Blue cheese dressing (1/4 cup, low fat)
- Lettuce (for topping)
- Buns (12, slider)

Directions:

1. Add the chicken breasts (shredded, cooked) in a large bowl along with the ranch dressing and wing sauce.
2. Stir well to incorporate, then place a piece of lettuce onto each slider roll.
3. Top off using the chicken mixture.
4. Drizzle blue cheese dressing over chicken then top off using top buns of slider rolls
5. Serve.

Nutrition:

Calories: 300 Cal

Fat: 14 g

Cholesterol: 25 mg

63. High Protein Chicken Meatballs

Preparation Time: **5 minutes**

Cooking Time: **25 minutes**

Servings: **2**

Ingredients:

- Chicken (1 lbs., lean, ground)
- Oats (3/4 cup, rolled)
- Onions (2, grated)
- Allspice (2 tsp. ground)
- Salt and black pepper (dash)

Directions:

1. Heat a skillet (large) over medium heat then grease using cooking spray.
2. Add in the onions (grated), chicken (lean, ground), oats (rolled), allspice (earth), and a dash of salt and black pepper in a large-sized bowl, stir well to incorporate.
3. Shape mixture into meatballs (small).
4. Place into the skillet (greased). Cook for roughly 5 minutes until golden brown on all sides.
5. Remove meatballs from heat then serve immediately.

Nutrition:

Calories: 519 Cal Protein: 57g

Carbohydrates: 32 g Fat: 15 g

64. Maple Lemon Tempeh Cubes

Preparation Time: **10 minutes**

Cooking Time: 30 to 40 minutes

Servings: **4**

Ingredients:

- Tempeh: 1 packet
- Coconut oil: 2 to 3 teaspoons
- Lemon juice: 3 tablespoons
- Maple syrup; 2 teaspoons
- Bragg's Liquid Aminos or low-sodium tamari or (optional): 1 to 2 teaspoons
- Water: 2 teaspoons
- Dried basil: 1/4 teaspoon
- Powdered garlic: 1/4 teaspoon
- Black pepper (freshly grounded): to taste

Directions:

1. Heat your oven to 400 ° C.
2. Cut your tempeh block into squares in bite form.
3. Heat coconut oil over medium to high heat in a non-stick skillet.
4. When melted and heated, add the tempeh and cook on one side for 2-4 minutes, or until the tempeh turns down into a golden-brown color.
5. Flip the tempeh bits, and cook for 2-4 minutes.
6. Mix the lemon juice, tamari, maple syrup, basil, water, garlic, and black pepper while the tempeh is browning.
7. Drop the mixture over tempeh, then swirl to cover the tempeh.
8. Sauté for 2-3 minutes, then turn the tempeh and sauté 1-2 minutes more.

9. The tempeh, on both sides, should be soft and orange.

Nutrition:

Carbohydrates: 22 Cal

Fats: 17 g Sugar: 5 g

Protein: 21 g Fiber: 9 g

65. Bok Choy with Tofu Stir Fry

Preparation Time: **15 minutes**

Cooking Time: **15 minutes**

Servings: 4

Ingredients:

- Super-firm tofu: 1 lb. (drained and pressed)
- Coconut oil: one tablespoon
- Clove of garlic: 1 (minced)
- Baby bok choy: 3 heads (chopped)
- Low-sodium vegetable broth;
- Maple syrup: 2 teaspoons
- Braggs liquid aminos
- Sambal oelek: 1 to 2 teaspoons (similar chili sauce)
- Scallion or green onion: 1 (chopped)
- Freshly grated ginger: 1 teaspoon
- Quinoa/rice, for serving

Directions:

1. With paper towels, pat the tofu dry and cut into tiny pieces of bite-size around 1/2 inch wide.

2. Heat coconut oil in a wide skillet over medium heat.

3. Remove tofu and stir-fry until painted softly.

4. Stir-fry for 1-2 minutes, before the choy of the Bok starts to wilt.

5. When this occurs, you'll want to apply the vegetable broth and all the remaining ingredients to the skillet.

6. Hold the mixture stir-frying until all components are well coated, and the bulk of the liquid evaporates, around 5-6 min.

7. Serve over brown rice or quinoa.

Nutrition:

Calories: 263.7 Cal

Fat 4.2 g

Cholesterol: 0.3 mg

Sodium: 683.6 mg

Potassium: 313.7 mg

Carbohydrate: 35.7 g

66. Three-Bean Medley

Preparation Time: **15 minutes**

Cooking Time: **6 to 8 hours**

Servings: 8

Ingredients:

- 11/4 cups dried kidney beans, rinsed and drained
- 11/4 cups dried black beans, rinsed and drained

- 11/4 cups dried black-eyed peas, rinsed and drained
- 1 onion, chopped
- 1 leek, chopped
- 2 garlic cloves, minced
- 2 carrots, peeled and chopped
- 6 cups low-sodium vegetable broth
- 11/2 cups water
- 1/2 teaspoon dried thyme leaves

Directions:

1. In a 6-quart slow cooker, mix all of the ingredients.

2. Cover and cook on low for 6 to 8 hours, or until the beans are tender and the liquid is absorbed.

Nutrition:

Calories: 284 Cal Carbohydrates: 56 g

Sugar: 6 g Fiber: 19 g

Fat: 0 g

Saturated Fat: 0 g

Protein: 19 g

Sodium: 131 mg

67. Zucchini Fritters

Preparation Time: **15 minutes**

Cooking Time: **10 minutes**

Servings: **4**

Ingredients:

- 1 1/2 pound of grated zucchini
- 1 tsp. of salt
- 1/4 cup of grated Parmesan

- 1/4 cup of flour
- 2 cloves of minced garlic
- 2 tbsp. of olive oil
- 1 large egg
- Freshly ground black pepper and kosher salt to taste

Directions:

1. Put the grated zucchini into a colander over the sink

2. Add your salt and toss it to mix properly, then leave it to settle for about 10 minutes.

3. Next, use a clean cheesecloth to drain the zucchini completely.

4. Combine drained zucchini, Parmesan, garlic, flour, and the beaten egg in a large bowl, mix, and season with pepper and salt.

5. Next, heat the olive oil in a skillet applying medium-high heat.

6. Use a tablespoon to scoop batter for each cake, put in the oil, and flatten using a spatula.

7. Allow to cook until the underside is richly golden brown, then flip over to the other side and cook.

8. Your delicious zucchini fritters are ready to be served.

Nutrition:

Total Fat: 12.0 g

Cholesterol: 101.9 mg

Sodium: 728.9 mg

Total Carbohydrate: 11.9 g

Dietary Fiber: 1.9 g

Sugars: 4.6 g

Protein: 8.6 g

68. Barley Risotto

Preparation Time: 15 Minutes

Cooking Time: 7 To 8 Hours

Servings: 8

Ingredients:

- 2¼ cups hulled barley, rinsed
- 1 onion, finely chopped
- 4 garlic cloves, minced
- 1 (8-ounce) package button mushrooms, chopped
- 6 cups low-sodium vegetable broth
- ½ teaspoon dried marjoram leaves
- 1/8 teaspoon freshly ground black pepper
- 2/3 cup grated Parmesan cheese

Directions:

1. In a 6-quart slow cooker, mix the barley, onion, garlic, mushrooms, broth, marjoram, and pepper. Cover and cook on low for 7 to 8 hours, or until the barley has absorbed most of the liquid and is tender, and the vegetables are tender.
2. Stir in the Parmesan cheese and serve.

Nutrition:

Calories: 288 Carbohydrates: 45g

Sugar: 2g Fiber: 9g

Fat: 6g

Saturated Fat: 3g

Protein: 13g

Sodium: 495mg

69. Risotto with Green Beans, Sweet Potatoes, And Peas

Preparation Time: 20 Minutes

Cooking Time: 4 To 5 Hours

Servings: 8

Ingredients:

- 1 large sweet potato, peeled and chopped
- 1 onion, chopped
- 5 garlic cloves, minced
- 2 cups short-grain brown rice
- 1 teaspoon dried thyme leaves
- 7 cups low-sodium vegetable broth
- 2 cups green beans, cut in half crosswise
- 2 cups frozen baby peas
- 3 tablespoons unsalted butter
- ½ cup grated Parmesan cheese

Directions:

1. In a 6-quart slow cooker, mix the sweet potato, onion, garlic, rice, thyme, and broth. Cover and cook on low for 3 to 4 hours, or until the rice is tender.
2. Stir in the green beans and frozen peas. Cover and cook on low for 30 to 40 minutes or until the vegetables are tender.
3. Stir in the butter and cheese. Cover and cook on low for 20 minutes, then stir and serve.

Nutrition:

Calories: 385 Carbohydrates: 52g

Sugar: 4g Fiber: 6g

Fat: 10g

Saturated Fat: 5g

Protein: 10g

Sodium: 426mg

70. Herbed Garlic Black Beans

Preparation Time: 10 Minutes
Cooking Time: 7 To 9 Hours
Servings: 8
Ingredients:

- 3 cups dried black beans, rinsed and drained
- 2 onions, chopped
- 8 garlic cloves, minced
- 6 cups low-sodium vegetable broth
- ½ teaspoon salt
- 1 teaspoon dried basil leaves
- ½ teaspoon dried thyme leaves
- ½ teaspoon dried oregano leaves

Directions:

1. In a 6-quart slow cooker, mix all the ingredients. Cover and cook on low for 7 to 9 hours, or until the beans have absorbed the liquid and are tender.
2. Remove and discard the bay leaf.

Nutrition:
Calories: 250
Carbohydrates: 47g
Sugar: 3g
Fiber: 17g
Fat: 0g
Saturated Fat: 0g
Protein: 15g
Sodium: 253mg

71. Quinoa with Vegetables

Preparation Time: 10 Minutes
Cooking Time: 5 To 6 Hours
Servings: 8
Ingredients:

- 2 cups quinoa, rinsed and drained
- 2 onions, chopped
- 2 carrots, peeled and sliced
- 1 cup sliced cremini mushrooms
- 3 garlic cloves, minced
- 4 cups low-sodium vegetable broth
- ½ teaspoon salt
- 1 teaspoon dried marjoram leaves
- 1/8 teaspoon freshly ground black pepper

Directions:

1. In a 6-quart slow cooker, mix all of the ingredients. Cover and cook on low for 5 to 6 hours, or until the quinoa and vegetables are tender.
2. Stir the mixture and serve.

Nutrition:
Calories: 204
Carbohydrates: 35g
Sugar: 4g
Fiber: 4g
Fat: 3g Saturated Fat: 0g
Protein: 7g
Sodium: 229mg

72. Herbed Wild Rice

Preparation Time: 10 Minutes
Cooking Time: 4 To 6 Hours
Servings: 8
Ingredients:

- 3 cups wild rice, rinsed and drained
- 6 cups Roasted Vegetable Broth (here)
- 1 onion, chopped
- ½ teaspoon salt
- ½ teaspoon dried thyme leaves
- ½ teaspoon dried basil leaves
- 1 bay leaf
- 1/3 cup chopped fresh flat-leaf parsley

Directions:

1. In a 6-quart slow cooker, mix the wild rice, vegetable broth, onion, salt, thyme, basil, and bay leaf. Cover and cook on low for 4 to 6 hours, or until the wild rice is tender but still firm. You can cook this dish longer until the wild rice pops; that will take about 7 to 8 hours.
2. Remove and discard the bay leaf.
3. Stir in the parsley and serve.

Nutrition:

Calories: 258

Carbohydrates: 54g

Sugar: 3g

Fiber: 5g

Fat: 2g

Saturated Fat: 0g

Protein: 6g

Sodium: 257mg

CHAPTER 6:

Salad Recipes

73. Loaded Caesar Salad with Crunchy Chickpeas

Preparation Time: 5 minutes

Cooking Time: 20 minutes

Servings: 6

Ingredients:

For the chickpeas:

- 2 (15-ounce) cans chickpeas, drained and rinsed
- 2 tablespoons extra-virgin olive oil
- 1 teaspoon kosher salt
- 1 teaspoon garlic powder
- 1 teaspoon onion powder
- 1 teaspoon dried oregano

For the dressing:

- ½ cup mayonnaise
- 2 tablespoons grated Parmesan cheese
- 2 tablespoons freshly squeezed lemon juice
- 1 clove garlic, peeled and smashed
- 1 teaspoon Dijon mustard
- ½ tablespoon Worcestershire sauce
- ½ tablespoon anchovy paste

For the salad:

- 3 heads romaine lettuce, cut into bite-size pieces

Directions:

To make the chickpeas:

1. Preheat the oven to 450°F. Line a baking sheet with parchment paper.
2. In a medium bowl, toss together the chickpeas, oil, salt, garlic powder, onion powder, and oregano. Scatter the coated chickpeas on the prepared baking sheet.

3. Roast for about 20 minutes, tossing occasionally, until the chickpeas are golden and have a bit of crunch.

To make the dressing:

1. In a small bowl, whisk the mayonnaise, Parmesan, lemon juice, garlic, mustard, Worcestershire sauce, and anchovy paste until combined.

To make the salad:

2. In a large bowl, combine the lettuce and dressing. Toss to coat. Top with the roasted chickpeas and serve.

Nutrition:

Calories: 367;

Total fat: 22g;

Total carbs: 35g;

Cholesterol: 9mg;

Fiber: 13g;

Protein: 12g;

Sodium: 407mg

74. Coleslaw worth a Second Helping

Preparation Time: 20 minutes

Cooking Time: 10 minutes

Servings: 6

Ingredients:

- 5 cups shredded cabbage
- 2 carrots, shredded
- 1/3 cup chopped fresh flat-leaf parsley
- ½ cup mayonnaise
- ½ cup sour cream
- 3 tablespoons apple cider vinegar
- 1 teaspoon kosher salt
- ½ teaspoon celery seed

Directions:

1. In a large bowl, combine the cabbage, carrots, and parsley.
2. In a small bowl, whisk the mayonnaise, sour cream, vinegar, salt, and celery seed until smooth. Pour the dressing over the vegetables and toss until coated. Transfer to a serving bowl and chill until ready to serve.

Nutrition:

Calories: 192; Total fat: 18g;

Total carbs: 7g; Cholesterol: 18mg;

Fiber: 3g;Protein: 2g;

Sodium: 543mg

75. Romaine Lettuce and Radicchios Mix

Preparation Time: 6 minutes

Cooking Time: 0 minutes

Servings: 4

Ingredients:

- 2 tablespoons olive oil
- A pinch of salt and black pepper
- 2 spring onions, chopped
- 3 tablespoons Dijon mustard
- Juice of 1 lime
- ½ cup basil, chopped
- 4 cups romaine lettuce heads, chopped
- 3 radicchios, sliced

Directions:

1. In a salad bowl, mix the lettuce with the spring onions and the other ingredients, toss and serve.

Nutrition:

Calories: 87, Fats: 2 g, Fiber: 1 g,

Carbs: 1 g, Protein: 2 g

76. Greek Salad

Preparation Time: 15 Minutes

Cooking Time: 15 Minutes

Servings: 5

Ingredients:

For Dressing:

- ½ teaspoon black pepper
- ¼ teaspoon salt
- ½ teaspoon oregano
- 1 tablespoon garlic powder
- 2 tablespoons Balsamic
- 1/3 cup olive oil

For Salad:

- ½ cup sliced black olives
- ½ cup chopped parsley, fresh
- 1 small red onion, thin-sliced
- 1 cup cherry tomatoes, sliced
- 1 bell pepper, yellow, chunked
- 1 cucumber, peeled, quarter and slice
- 4 cups chopped romaine lettuce
- ½ teaspoon salt
- 2 tablespoons olive oil

Directions:

1. In a small bowl, blend all of the ingredients for the dressing and let this set in the refrigerator while you make the salad.
2. To assemble the salad, mix together all the ingredients in a large-sized bowl and toss the veggies gently but thoroughly to mix.
3. Serve the salad with the dressing in amounts as desired

Nutrition:

Calories: 234, Fat: 16.1 g,

Protein: 5 g,

Carbs: 48 g

77. Asparagus and Smoked Salmon Salad

Preparation Time: 15 minutes

Cooking Time: 10 minutes

Servings: 8

Ingredients:

- 1 lb. fresh asparagus, trimmed and cut into 1 inch pieces
- 1/2 cup pecans,
- 2 heads red leaf lettuce, rinsed and torn
- 1/2 cup frozen green peas, thawed
- 1/4 lb. smoked salmon, cut into 1 inch chunks
- 1/4 cup olive oil
- 2 tablespoons. lemon juice
- 1 teaspoon Dijon mustard
- 1/2 teaspoon salt
- 1/4 teaspoon pepper

Dircctions:

1. Boil a pot of water. Stir in asparagus and cook for 5 minutes until tender. Let it drain; set aside.
2. In a skillet, cook the pecans over medium heat for 5 minutes, stirring constantly until lightly toasted.
3. Combine the asparagus, toasted pecans, salmon, peas, and red leaf lettuce and toss in a large bowl.
4. In another bowl, combine lemon juice, pepper, Dijon mustard, salt, and olive oil. You can coat the salad with the dressing or serve it on its side.

Nutrition:

Calories: 159 Total Carbohydrate: 7 g

Cholesterol: 3 mg Total Fat: 12.9 g

Protein: 6 g Sodium: 304 mg

78. Shrimp Cobb Salad

Preparation Time: 25 minutes

Cooking Time: 10 minutes

Servings: 2

Ingredients:

- 4 slices center-cut bacon
- 1 lb. large shrimp, peeled and deveined
- 1/2 teaspoon ground paprika
- 1/4 teaspoon ground black pepper
- 1/4 teaspoon salt, divided
- 2 1/2 tablespoons. Fresh lemon juice
- 1 1/2 tablespoons. Extra-virgin olive oil
- 1/2 teaspoon whole grain Dijon mustard
- 1 (10 oz.) package romaine lettuce hearts, chopped
- 2 cups cherry tomatoes, quartered
- 1 ripe avocado, cut into wedges
- 1 cup shredded carrots

Directions:

1. In a large skillet over medium heat, cook the bacon for 4 minutes on each side till crispy.
2. Take away from the skillet and place on paper towels; let cool for 5 minutes. Break the bacon into bits. Pour out most of the bacon fat, leaving behind only 1 tablespoon. in the skillet. Bring the skillet back to medium-high heat. Add black pepper and paprika to the shrimp for seasoning. Cook the shrimp around 2 minutes each side until it is opaque. Sprinkle with 1/8 teaspoon of salt for seasoning.
3. Combine the remaining 1/8 teaspoon of salt, mustard, olive oil

and lemon juice together in a small bowl. Stir in the romaine hearts.

4. On each serving plate, place on 1 and 1/2 cups of romaine lettuce. Add on top the same amounts of avocado, carrots, tomatoes, shrimp and bacon.

Nutrition:

Calories: 528

Total Carbohydrate: 22.7 g

Cholesterol: 365 mg

Total Fat: 28.7 g

Protein: 48.9 g

Sodium: 1166 mg

79. Toast with Smoked Salmon, Herbed Cream Cheese, and Greens

Preparation Time: 10 minutes

Cooking Time: 5 minutes

Servings: 2

Ingredients:

For the herbed cream cheese:

- ¼ cup cream cheese, at room temperature
- 2 tablespoons chopped fresh flat-leaf parsley
- 2 tablespoons chopped fresh chives or sliced scallion
- ½ teaspoon garlic powder
- ¼ teaspoon kosher salt

For the toast:

- 2 slices bread
- 4 ounces smoked salmon
- Small handful microgreens or sprouts
- 1 tablespoon capers, drained and rinsed
- ¼ small red onion, very thinly sliced

Directions:

1. To make the herbed cream cheese
2. In a medium bowl, combine the cream cheese, parsley, chives, garlic powder, and salt. Using a fork, mix until combined. Chill until ready to use.
3. To make the toast
4. Toast the bread until golden. Spread the herbed cream cheese over each piece of toast, then top with the smoked salmon.
5. Garnish with the microgreens, capers, and red onion.

Nutrition: Calories: 194; Total fat: 8g; Cholesterol: 26mg; Fiber: 2g; Protein: 12g; Sodium: 227mg

80. Crab Melt with Avocado and Egg

Preparation Time: 15 minutes

Cooking Time: 15 minutes

Servings: 2

Ingredients:

- 2 English muffins, split
- 3 tablespoons butter, divided
- 2 tomatoes, cut into slices
- 1 (4-ounce) can lump crabmeat
- 6 ounces sliced or shredded cheddar cheese
- 4 large eggs
- Kosher salt
- 2 large avocados, halved, pitted, and cut into slices
- Microgreens, for garnish

Directions:

1. Preheat the broiler.

2. Toast the English muffin halves. Place the toasted halves, cut-side up, on a baking sheet.
3. Spread 1½ teaspoons of butter evenly over each half, allowing the butter to melt into the crevices. Top each with tomato slices, then divide the crab over each, and finish with the cheese.
4. Broil for about 4 minutes until the cheese melts.
5. Meanwhile, in a medium skillet over medium heat, melt the remaining 1 tablespoon of butter, swirling to coat the bottom of the skillet. Crack the eggs into the skillet, giving ample space for each. Sprinkle with salt. Cook for about 3 minutes. Flip the eggs and cook the other side until the yolks are set to your liking. Place 1 egg on each English muffin half.
6. Top with avocado slices and microgreens.

Nutrition:
Calories: 1221;
Total fat: 84g;
Cholesterol: 94mg;
Fiber: 2g;
Protein: 12g;
Sodium: 888mg

81. Tomato Cucumber Avocado Salad
Preparation Time: 15 minutes
Cooking Time: 0 minutes
Servings: 4
Ingredients:

- 12 oz cherry tomatoes, cut in half
- 5 small cucumbers, chopped
- 3 small avocados, chopped
- ½ tsp ground black pepper
- 2 tbsp olive oil
- 2 tbsp fresh lemon juice
- ¼ cup fresh cilantro, chopped
- 1 tsp sea salt

Directions:
1. Add cherry tomatoes, cucumbers, avocados, and cilantro into the large mixing bowl and mix well.
2. Mix together olive oil, lemon juice, black pepper, and salt and pour over salad.
3. Toss well and serve immediately.

Nutrition:
Calories 442   Fat 31 g
Carbs 30.3 g   Sugar 4 g
Protein 2 g   Cholesterol 0 mg

82. Healthy Broccoli Salad
Preparation Time: 25 minutes
Cooking Time: 0 minutes
Servings: 6
Ingredients:

- 3 cups broccoli, chopped
- 1 tbsp apple cider vinegar
- ½ cup Greek yogurt
- 2 tbsp sunflower seeds
- 3 bacon slices, cooked and chopped
- 1/3 cup onion, sliced
- ¼ tsp stevia

Directions:
1. In a mixing bowl, mix together broccoli, onion, and bacon.

2. In a small bowl, mix together yogurt, vinegar, and stevia and pour over broccoli mixture. Stir to combine.

3. Sprinkle sunflower seeds on top of the salad.

4. Store salad in the refrigerator for 30 minutes.

5. Serve and enjoy.

Nutrition:

Calories 90   Fat 9 g   Carbs 4 g

Sugar 5 g   Protein 2 g

Cholesterol 12 mg

83. Avocado Lime Shrimp Salad

Preparation Time: 15 minutes

Cooking Time: 0 minutes

Servings: 2

Ingredients:

- 14 ounces of jumbo cooked shrimp, peeled and deveined; chopped
- 4 ½ ounces of avocado, diced
- 1 ½ cup of tomato, diced
- ¼ cup of chopped green onion
- ¼ cup of jalapeno with the seeds removed, diced fine
- 1 teaspoon of olive oil
- 2 tablespoons of lime juice
- 1/8 teaspoon of salt
- 1 tablespoon of chopped cilantro

Directions:

1. Get a small bowl and combine green onion, olive oil, lime juice, pepper, a pinch of salt. Wait for about 5 minutes for all of them to marinate and mellow the flavor of the onion.

2. Get a large bowl and combined chopped shrimp, tomato, avocado, jalapeno. Combine all of the ingredients, add cilantro, and gently toss.

3. Add pepper and salt as desired.

Nutrition:

Calories: 314

Protein: 26g

Carbs: 15g

Fiber: 9g

84. Grilled Mahi Mahi with Jicama Slaw

Preparation Time: 20 minutes

Cooking Time: 10 minutes

Servings: 4

Ingredients:

- 1 teaspoon each for pepper and salt, divided
- 1 tablespoon of lime juice, divided
- 2 tablespoon + 2 teaspoons of extra virgin olive oil
- 4 raw mahi-mahi fillets, which should be about 8 oz. each
- ½ cucumber which should be thinly cut into long strips like matchsticks (it should yield about 1 cup)
- 1 jicama, which should be thinly cut into long strips like matchsticks (it should yield about 3 cups)
- 1 cup of alfalfa sprouts
- 2 cups of coarsely chopped watercress

Directions:

1. Combine ½ teaspoon of both pepper and salt, 1 teaspoon of lime juice, and 2 teaspoons of oil in a small bowl. Then brush the mahi-mahi fillets all through with the olive oil mixture.

2. Grill the mahi-mahi on medium-high heat until it becomes done in about 5 minutes, turn it to the other side, and let it be done for about 5 minutes. (You will have an internal temperature of about 1450F).

3. For the slaw, combine the watercress, cucumber, jicama, and alfalfa sprouts in a bowl. Now combine ½ teaspoon of both pepper and salt, 2 teaspoons of lime juice, and 2 tablespoons of extra virgin oil in a small bowl. Drizzle it over slaw and toss together to combine.

Nutrition:
Calories: 320
Protein: 44g
Carbohydrate: 10g
Fat: 11 g

85. Mediterranean Chicken Salad

Preparation Time: 5 minutes
Cooking Time: 25 minutes
Servings: 4
Ingredients:
For Chicken:

- 1 ¾ lb. boneless, skinless chicken breast
- ¼ teaspoon each of pepper and salt (or as desired)
- 1 ½ tablespoon of butter, melted

For Mediterranean salad:

- 1 cup of sliced cucumber
- 6 cups of romaine lettuce, that is torn or roughly chopped
- 10 pitted Kalamata olives
- 1 pint of cherry tomatoes
- 1/3 cup of reduced-fat feta cheese
- ¼ teaspoon each of pepper and salt (or lesser)
- 1 small lemon juice (it should be about 2 tablespoons)

Directions:
1. Preheat your oven or grill to about 3500F.
2. Season the chicken with salt, butter, and black pepper
3. Roast or grill chicken until it reaches an internal temperature of 1650F in about 25 minutes. Once your chicken breasts are cooked, remove and keep aside to rest for about 5 minutes before you slice it.
4. Combine all the salad ingredients you have and toss everything together very well
5. Serve the chicken with Mediterranean salad

Nutrition:
Calories: 340 Protein: 45g
Carbohydrate: 9g
Fat: 4 g

86. Rosemary Cauliflower Rolls

Preparation Time: 10 minutes
Cooking Time: 30 minutes
Servings: 3
Ingredients:

- 1/3 cup of almond flour
- 4 cups of riced cauliflower
- 1/3 cup of reduced-fat, shredded mozzarella or cheddar cheese
- 2 eggs

- 2 tablespoon of fresh rosemary, finely chopped
- ½ teaspoon of salt

Directions:

1. Preheat your oven to 4000F
2. Combine all the listed ingredients in a medium-sized bowl
3. Scoop cauliflower mixture into 12 evenly-sized rolls/biscuits onto a lightly-greased and foil-lined baking sheet.
4. Bake until it turns golden brown, which should be achieved in about 30 minutes.
5. Note: if you want to have the outside of the rolls/biscuits crisp, then broil for some minutes before serving.

Nutrition: Calories: 254 Protein: 24g Carbohydrate: 7g Fat: 8 g

87. Broccoli Cheddar Breakfast Bake

Preparation Time: 10 minutes
Cooking Time: 45 minutes
Servings: 4
Ingredients:

- 9 eggs
- 6 cups of small broccoli florets
- ¼ teaspoon of salt
- 1 cup of unsweetened almond milk
- ¼ teaspoon of cayenne pepper
- ¼ teaspoon of ground pepper
- Cooking spray
- 4 oz. of shredded, reduced-fat cheddar

Directions:

1. Preheat your oven to about 375 degrees
2. In your large microwave-safe, add broccoli and 2 to 3 tablespoon of water. Microwave on high heat for 4 minutes or until it becomes tender. Now transfer the broccoli to a colander to drain excess liquid
3. Get a medium-sized bowl and whisk the milk, eggs, and seasonings together.
4. Set the broccoli neatly on the bottom of a lightly greased 13 x 9-inch baking dish. Sprinkle the cheese gently on the broccoli and pour the egg mixture on top of it.
5. Bake for about 45 minutes or until the center is set and the top forms a light brown crust.

Nutrition:
Calories: 290 Protein: 25g
Carbohydrate: 8g Fat: 18 g

88. Tomato Braised Cauliflower with Chicken

Preparation Time: 10 minutes
Cooking Time: 30 minutes
Servings: 4
Ingredients:

- 4 garlic cloves, sliced
- 3 scallions, to be trimmed and cut into 1-inch pieces
- ¼ teaspoon of dried oregano
- ¼ teaspoon of crushed red pepper flakes
- 4 ½ cups of cauliflower
- 1 ½ cups of diced canned tomatoes

- 1 cup of fresh basil, gently torn
- ½ teaspoon each of pepper and salt, divided
- 1 ½ teaspoon of olive oil
- 1 ½ lb. of boneless, skinless chicken breasts

Directions:

1. Get a saucepan and combine the garlic, scallions, oregano, crushed red pepper, cauliflower, and tomato, and add ¼ cup of water. Get everything boil together and add ¼ teaspoon of pepper and salt for seasoning, then cover the pot with a lid. Let it simmer for 10 minutes and stir as often as possible until you observe that the cauliflower is tender. Now, wrap up the seasoning with the remaining ¼ teaspoon of pepper and salt.

2. Toss the chicken breast with oil, olive preferably and let it roast in the oven with the heat of 4500F for 20 minutes and an internal temperature of 1650F. Allow the chicken to rest for like 10 minutes.

3. Now slice the chicken, and serve on a bed of tomato braised cauliflower.

Nutrition: Calories: 290 Fat: 10 g
Carbohydrate: 13 g Protein: 38 g

89. Braised Collard Greens in Peanut Sauce with Pork Tenderloin

Preparation Time: 20 minutes
Cooking Time: 1 hour 12 minutes
Servings: 4
Ingredients:

- 2 cups of chicken stock
- 12 cups of chopped collard greens
- 5 tablespoon of powdered peanut butter
- 3 cloves of garlic, crushed
- 1 teaspoon of salt
- ½ teaspoon of allspice
- ½ teaspoon of black pepper
- 2 teaspoon of lemon juice
- ¾ teaspoon of hot sauce
- 1 ½ lb. of pork tenderloin

Directions:

1. Get a pot with a tight-fitting lid and combine the collards with the garlic, chicken stock, hot sauce, and half of the pepper and salt. Cook on low heat for about 1 hour or until the collards become tender.

2. Once the collards are tender, stir in the allspice, lemon juice. And powdered peanut butter. Keep warm.

3. Season the pork tenderloin with the remaining pepper and salt, and broil in a toaster oven for 10 minutes when you have an internal temperature of 1450F. Make sure to turn the tenderloin every 2 minutes to achieve an even browning all over. After that, you can take away the pork from the oven and allow it to rest for like 5 minutes.

4. Slice the pork as you will

Nutrition:
Calories: 320 Fat: 10 g
Carbohydrate: 15 g Protein: 45 g

90. Tomatillo and Green Chili Pork Stew

Preparation Time: 10 minutes
Cooking Time: 20 minutes
Servings: 4
Ingredients:

- 2 scallions, chopped
- 2 cloves of garlic
- 1 lb. tomatillos, trimmed and chopped
- 8 large romaine or green lettuce leaves, divided
- 2 serrano chilies, seeds, and membranes
- ½ tsp of dried Mexican oregano (or you can use regular oregano)
- 1 ½ lb. of boneless pork loin, to be cut into bite-sized cubes
- ¼ cup of cilantro, chopped
- ¼ tablespoon (each) salt and paper
- 1 jalapeno, seeds and membranes to be removed and thinly sliced
- 1 cup of sliced radishes
- 4 lime wedges

Directions:

1. Combine scallions, garlic, tomatillos, 4 lettuce leaves, serrano chilies, and oregano in a blender. Then puree until smooth
2. Put pork and tomatillo mixture in a medium pot. 1-inch of puree should cover the pork; if not, add water until it covers it. Season with pepper & salt, and cover it simmers. Simmer on heat for approximately 20 minutes.
3. Now, finely shred the remaining lettuce leaves.

4. When the stew is done cooking, garnish with cilantro, radishes, finely shredded lettuce, sliced jalapenos, and lime wedges.

Nutrition:
Calories: 370 Protein: 36g
Carbohydrate: 14g Fat: 19 g

91. Optavia Cloud Bread

Preparation Time: 25 minutes
Cooking Time: 35 minutes
Servings: 3
Ingredients:

- ½ cup of Fat-free 0% Plain Greek Yogurt (4.4 0z)
- 3 Eggs, Separated
- 16 teaspoon Cream of Tartar
- 1 Packet sweetener (a granulated sweetener just like stevia)

Directions:

1. For about 30 minutes before making this meal, place the Kitchen Aid Bowl and the whisk attachment in the freezer.
2. Preheat your oven to 30 degrees
3. Remove the mixing bowl and whisk attachment from the freezer
4. Separate the eggs. Now put the egg whites in the Kitchen Aid Bowl, and they should be in a different medium-sized bowl.
5. In the medium-sized bowl containing the yolks, mix in the sweetener and yogurt.
6. In the bowl containing the egg white, add in the cream of tartar. Beat this mixture until the egg whites turn to stiff peaks.

7. Now, take the egg yolk mixture and carefully fold it into the egg whites. Be cautious and avoid over-stirring.

8. Place baking paper on a baking tray and spray with cooking spray.

9. Scoop out 6 equally-sized "blobs" of the "dough" onto the parchment paper.

10. Bake for about 25-35 minutes (make sure you check when it is 25 minutes, in some ovens, they are done at this timestamp). You will know they are done as they will get brownish at the top and have some crack.

11. Most people like them cold against being warm

12. Most people like to re-heat in a toast oven or toaster to get them a little bit crispy.

13. Your serving size should be about 2 pieces.

Nutrition:

Calories: 234 Protein: 23g

Carbs: 5g Fiber: 8g Sodium: 223g

92. Shrimp Salad Cocktails

Preparation Time: 35 minutes

Cooking Time: 35 minutes

Servings: 8 servings

Ingredients:

- 2 cups mayonnaise
  - 6 plum tomatoes, seeded and finely chopped
  - 1/4 cup ketchup
  - 1/4 cup lemon juice
  - 2 cups seedless red and green grapes, halved
- 1 tablespoon. Worcestershire sauce
- 2 lbs. peeled and deveined cooked large shrimp
- 2 celery ribs, finely chopped
- 3 tablespoons. minced fresh tarragon or 3 teaspoon dried tarragon
- salt and 1/4 teaspoon pepper
- shredded 2 of cups romaine
- papaya or 1/2 cup peeled chopped mango
- parsley or minced chives

Directions:

1. Combine Worcestershire sauce, lemon juice, ketchup and mayonnaise together in a small bowl. Combine pepper, salt, tarragon, celery and shrimp together in a large bowl. Put in 1 cup of dressing toss well to coat.

2. Scoop 1 tablespoon. of the dressing into 8 cocktail glasses. Layer each glass with 1/4 cup of lettuce, followed by 1/2 cup of the shrimp mixture, 1/4 cup of grapes, 1/3 cup of tomatoes and finally 1 tablespoon. of mango.

3. Spread the remaining dressing over top; sprinkle chives on top. Serve immediately.

Nutrition: Calories: 580 Total Carbohydrate: 16 g Cholesterol: 192 mg Total Fat: 46 g Fiber: 2 g Protein: 24 g

93. Garlic Chive Cauliflower Mash

Preparation Time: 20 minutes

Cooking Time: 18 minutes

Servings: 5

Ingredients:

- 4 cups cauliflower
    - 1/3 cup vegetarian mayonnaise
    - 1 garlic clove
    - 1/2 teaspoon. kosher salt
    - 1 tablespoon. water
    - 1/8 teaspoon. pepper
    - 1/4 teaspoon. lemon juice
    - 1/2 teaspoon lemon zest
    - 1 tablespoon Chives, minced

Directions:

1. In a bowl that is save to microwave, add the cauliflower, mayo, garlic, water, and salt/pepper and mix until the cauliflower is well coated. Cook on high for 15-18 minutes, until the cauliflower is almost mushy.
2. Blend the mixture in a strong blender until completely smooth, adding a little more water if the mixture is too chunky. Season with the remaining ingredients and serve.

Nutrition: Calories: 178 Total Carbohydrate: 14 g Cholesterol: 18 mg Total Fat: 18 g Fiber: 4 g Protein: 2 g

94. Beet Greens with Pine Nuts Goat Cheese

Preparation Time: 25 minutes

Cooking Time: 15 minutes

Servings: 3

Ingredients:

- 4 cups beet tops, washed and chopped roughly
    - 1 teaspoon. EVOO
    - 1 tablespoon. no sugar added balsamic vinegar
    - 2 oz. crumbled dry goat cheese
    - 2 tablespoons. Toasted pine nuts

Directions:

1. Warm the oil in a pan, then cook the beet greens on medium high heat until they release their moisture. Let it cook until almost tender. Flavor with salt and pepper and remove from heat.
2. Toss the greens in a mixture of balsamic vinegar and olive oil, then top with the nuts and cheese. Serve warm.

Nutrition: Calories: 215 Total Carbohydrate: 4 g Cholesterol: 12 mg Total Fat: 18 g Fiber: 2 g Protein: 10 g

95. Shrimp with Dipping Sauce

Preparation Time: 5 minutes

Cooking Time: 15 minutes

Servings: 6

Ingredients:

- 1 tablespoon. reduced-sodium soy sauce
    - 2 teaspoons. Hot pepper sauce
    - 1 teaspoon. canola oil
    - 1/4 teaspoon. garlic powder

- 1/8 to 1/4 teaspoon. cayenne pepper
- 1 lb. uncooked medium shrimp, peeled and deveined
- 2 tablespoons. Chopped green onions
- Dipping Sauce:
- 3 tablespoons Reduced-sodium soy sauce
- 1 teaspoon. rice vinegar
- 1 tablespoon. orange juice
- 2 teaspoons. Sesame oil
- 2 teaspoons. Honey
- 1 garlic clove, minced
- 1-1/2 teaspoons. Minced fresh gingerroot

Directions:

1. Heat the initial 5 ingredients in a big nonstick frying pan for 30 seconds, then mix continuously. Add onions and shrimp and stir fry for 4-5 minutes or until the shrimp turns pink. Mix together the sauce and serve it with the shrimp.

Nutrition: Calories: 97 Total Carbohydrate: 4 g Cholesterol: 112 mg Total Fat: 3 g Fiber: 0 g Protein: 13 g

96. Celeriac Cauliflower Mash

Preparation Time: 20 minutes

Cooking Time: 12 minutes

Servings: 6

Ingredients:

- 1 head cauliflower
  - 1 small celery root
  - 1/4 cup butter

- 1 tablespoon. chopped rosemary
- 1 tablespoon. chopped thyme
- 1 cup cream cheese

Directions:

1. Skin the celery root and cut into small pieces. Cut the cauliflower into similar sized pieces and combine.
2. Toast the herbs in the butter in a large pan, until they become fragrant. Add the cauliflower and celery root and stir to combine. Season and cook at medium high until whatever moisture are in the vegetables releases itself, then covers and cook on low for 10-12 minutes.
3. Once the vegetables are soft, remove from the heat and place them in the blender. Make it smooth, then put the cream cheese and puree again. Season and serve.

Nutrition: Calories: 225 Total Carbohydrate: 4 g Cholesterol: 1 mg Total Fat: 20 g Fiber: 0 g Protein: 5 g

97. Roasted Cauliflower with Pepper Jack Cheese

Preparation Time: 4 minutes

Cooking Time: 21 minutes

Servings: 2

Ingredients:

- 1/3 teaspoon shallot powder
- 1 teaspoon ground black pepper
- 1 ½ large-sized heads of cauliflower, broken into florets

- 1/4 teaspoon cumin powder
- ½ teaspoon garlic salt
- 1/4 cup Pepper Jack cheese, grated
- 1 ½ tablespoons vegetable oil
- 1/3 teaspoon paprika

Directions:

1. Boil cauliflower in a large pan of salted water approximately 5 minutes. After that, drain the cauliflower florets; now, transfer them to a baking dish. Toss the cauliflower florets with the rest of the above ingredients. Roast at 395 degrees F for 16 minutes, turn them halfway through the process. Enjoy!

Nutrition: Calories: 271Fat: 23g

Carbs: 8.9g Protein: 9.8g Sugars: 2.8g

Fiber: 4.5g

98. Kale Slaw and Strawberry Salad + Poppyseed Dressing

Preparation Time: **10 minutes**

Cooking Time: **20 minutes**

Servings: **2**

Ingredients:

- Chicken breast; 8 ounces; sliced and baked
- Kale; 1 cup; chopped
- Slaw mix; 1 cup (cabbage, broccoli slaw, carrots mixed)
- Slivered almonds; 1/4 cup
- Strawberries; 1 cup; sliced

For the dressing:

- Light mayonnaise; 1 tablespoon
- Dijon mustard
- Olive oil; 1 tablespoon

- Apple cider vinegar; 1 tablespoon
- Lemon juice; 1/2 teaspoon
- 1 tablespoon of honey
- Onion powder; 1/4 teaspoon
- Garlic powder; 1/4 teaspoon
- Poppyseeds

Directions:

1. Whisk the dressing ingredients together until well mixed, then leave to cool in the fridge.
2. Slice the chicken breasts.
3. Divide 2 bowls of spinach, slaw, and strawberries.
4. Cover with a sliced breast of chicken (4 oz. each), then scatter with almonds.
5. Divide the dressing between the two bowls and drizzle.

Nutrition:

Calories: 340 Cal Fats: 13.6 g

Saturated Fat: 6.2 g

99. Green Beans

Preparation time: **5 minutes**

Cooking time: 13 minutes

Servings: 4

Ingredients:

- 1-pound green beans
- ¾ teaspoon garlic powder
- ¾ teaspoon ground black pepper
- 1 ¼ teaspoon salt
- ½ teaspoon paprika

Directions:

1. Turn on the fryer, insert the basket, grease with olive oil, close the lid, set the fryer at 400 degrees F, and preheat for 5 minutes.

2. Meanwhile, put the beans in a bowl, sprinkle generously with olive oil, sprinkle with garlic powder, black pepper, salt, and paprika and stir until well coated.

3. Open the air fryer, add the green beans, close with the lid and cook for 8 minutes until golden and crisp, stirring halfway through the frying process.

4. When the fryer beeps, open the lid, transfer the green beans to a serving plate and serve.

Nutrition:

Calories: 45 Carbs: 2 g

Fat: 11 g

Protein: 4 g

Fiber: 3 g

100. Grilled Eggplants

Preparation Time: **10 minutes**

Cooking Time: **10 minutes**

Servings: 4

Ingredients:

- 1 large eggplant, cut into thick circles
- Salt and pepper to taste
- 1 tsp. smoked paprika
- 1 tbsp. coconut flour
- 1 tsp. lime juice
- 1 tbsp. olive oil

Directions:

1. Coat the eggplants in smoked paprika, salt, pepper, lime juice, coconut flour, and let it sit for 10 minutes.

2. In a grilling pan, add the olive oil.

3. Grill the eggplants for 3 minutes on each side.

4. Serve.

Nutrition:

Fat: 0.1 g Sodium: 1.6 mg

Carbohydrates: 4.8 g

Fiber: 2.4 g Sugars: 2.9 g Protein: 0.8 g

101. Fried Zucchini

Preparation time: **10 minutes**

Cooking time: **8 minutes**

Servings: 4

Ingredients:

- 2 medium zucchinis, cut into strips 19 mm. thick
- 60 g all-purpose flour
- 12 g of salt
- 2 g black pepper
- 2 beaten eggs
- 15 ml. of milk
- 84 g Italian seasoned breadcrumbs
- 25 g grated Parmesan cheese
- Nonstick spray oil
- Ranch sauce, to serve

Directions:

1. Cut the zucchini into strips 19 mm thick.
2. Mix the flour, salt, and pepper on a plate.
3. Mix the eggs and milk in a separate dish.
4. Put breadcrumbs and Parmesan cheese in another dish.
5. Cover each piece of zucchini with flour, then dip them in egg and milk mixture, and pass them through the crumbs. Leave aside.
6. Preheat the air fryer, set it to 175°C.
7. Place the covered zucchini in the preheated air fryer and spray with oil spray. Set the timer to 8 minutes and press Start / Pause.
8. Be sure to shake the baskets in the middle of cooking.
9. Serve with tomato sauce or ranch sauce.

Nutrition:

Calories: 68 Carbs: 2 g Fat: 11 g
Protein: 4 g Fiber: 143 g

102. Fried Avocado

Preparation time: **15 minutes**

Cooking time: **10 minutes**

Servings: 2

Ingredients:

- 2 avocados cut into wedges 25 mm. thick
- 50 g breadcrumbs
- 2 g garlic powder
- 2 g onion powder
- 1 g smoked paprika
- 1 g cayenne pepper
- Salt and pepper to taste
- 60 g all-purpose flour
- 2 eggs, beaten
- Nonstick spray oil
- Tomato sauce or ranch sauce, to serve

Directions:

1. Cut the avocados into 25 mm. thick pieces.
2. Combine the crumbs, garlic powder, onion powder, smoked paprika, cayenne pepper, and salt in a bowl.
3. Separate each wedge of avocado in the flour, then dip the beaten eggs and stir in the breadcrumb mixture.
4. Preheat the air fryer.
5. Place the avocados in the preheated air fryer baskets, spray with oil spray, and cook at 205°C for 10 minutes. Turn the fried avocado halfway through cooking and sprinkle with cooking oil.
6. Serve with tomato sauce or ranch sauce.

Nutrition:

Calories: 123

Carbs: 2 g

Fat: 11 g

Protein: 4 g

Fiber: 0 g

103. Fried Squash Croquettes

Preparation Time: 5 minutes

Cooking Time: 17 minutes

Servings: 4

Ingredients:

- 1/3 cup all-purpose flour
- 1/3 teaspoon freshly ground black pepper, or more to taste
- 1/3 teaspoon dried sage
- 4 cloves garlic, minced
- 1 ½ tablespoons olive oil
- 1/3 butternut squash, peeled and grated
- 2 eggs, well whisked
- 1 teaspoon fine sea salt
- A pinch of ground allspice

Directions:

1. Thoroughly combine all ingredients in a mixing bowl.
2. Preheat your Air Fryer to 345 degrees and set the timer for 17 minutes; cook until your fritters are browned; serve right away.

Nutrition: Calories: 152 Fat: 10.02g

Carbs: 9.4g Protein: 5.8g

Sugars: 0.3g Fiber: 0.4g

104. Tamarind Glazed Sweet Potatoes

Preparation Time: 2 minutes

Cooking Time: 22 minutes

Servings: 4

Ingredients:

- 1/3 teaspoon white pepper
- 1 tablespoon butter, melted
- 1/2 teaspoon turmeric powder
- 5 garnet sweet potatoes, peeled and diced

- A few drops liquid Stevia
- 2 teaspoons tamarind paste
- 1 1/2 tablespoons fresh lime juice
- 1 1/2 teaspoon ground allspice

Directions:

1. In a mixing bowl, toss all ingredients until sweet potatoes are well coated.
2. Air-fry them at 335 degrees F for 12 minutes.
3. Pause the Air Fryer and toss again. Increase the temperature to 390 degrees F and cook for an additional 10 minutes. Eat warm.

Nutrition: Calories: 103 Fat: 9.1g Carbs: 4.9g Protein: 1.9g Sugars: 1.2g Fiber: 0.3g

105. Creamed Coconut Curry Spinach

Preparation Time: 30 minutes

Cooking Time: 30 seconds

Servings: 6

Ingredients:

- 1-pound frozen spinach, thawed and drained of moisture
  - 1 small can whole fat coconut milk
  - 2 teaspoons yellow curry paste
  - 1 teaspoon lemon zest
  - Cashews for garnish

Directions:

1. Heat a medium sized pan to medium high heat, then add the curry paste and cook for 30 seconds. Add a small amount of the coconut milk and stir to combine, and then cook until the paste is aromatic.

2. Add the spinach, and then season. Separate the rest of the ingredients, from the cashews, and allow the sauce to reduce slightly.

3. Keep the sauce creamy, but reduce it to coat the spinach well. Serve with chopped cashews.

Nutrition: Calories: 191 Total Carbohydrate: 9 g Cholesterol: 2 mg Total Fat: 14 g Fiber: 1 g Protein: 4 g

106. Crispy-Topped Baked Vegetables

Preparation Time: **10 minutes**

Cooking Time: **40 minutes**

Servings: **4**

Ingredients:

- 2 tbsp. olive oil
- 1 onion, chopped
- 1 celery stalk, chopped
- 2 carrots, grated
- 1/2-pound turnips, sliced
- 1 cup vegetable broth
- 1 tsp. turmeric
- Sea salt and black pepper, to taste
- 1/2 tsp. liquid smoke
- 1 cup Parmesan cheese, shredded
- 2 tbsp fresh chives, chopped

Directions:

1. Set oven to 360ºF and grease a baking dish with olive oil.

2. Set a skillet over medium heat and warm olive oil.

3. Sweat the onion until soft, and place in the turnips, carrots, and celery; and cook for 4 minutes.

4. Remove the vegetable mixture to the baking dish.

5. Combine vegetable broth with turmeric, pepper, liquid smoke, and salt.

6. Spread this mixture over the vegetables.

7. Sprinkle with Parmesan cheese and bake for about 30 minutes.

8. Garnish with chives to serve.

Nutrition:

Calories: 242 Cal Fats: 16.3 g

Carbohydrates: 8.6 g Protein: 16.3 g

107. Roasted Root Vegetables

Preparation Time: **20 minutes**

Cooking Time: **6 to 8 hours**

Servings: **8**

Ingredients:

- 6 carrots, cut into 1-inch chunks
- 2 yellow onions, each cut into 8 wedges
- 2 sweet potatoes, peeled and cut into chunks
- 6 Yukon Gold potatoes, cut into chunks
- 8 whole garlic cloves, peeled
- 4 parsnips, peeled and cut into chunks
- 3 tablespoons olive oil

- 1 teaspoon dried thyme leaves
- 1/2 teaspoon salt
- 1/8 teaspoon freshly ground black pepper

Directions:

1. In a 6-quart slow cooker, mix all of the ingredients.
2. Cover and cook on low for 6 to 8 hours, or until the vegetables are tender.
3. Serve and enjoy!

Nutrition:

Calories: 214 Cal Carbohydrates: 40 g

Sugar: 7 g Fiber: 6 g

Fat: 5 g Saturated Fat: 1 g

Protein: 4 g Sodium: 201 mg

108. Vegan Edamame Quinoa Collard Wraps

Preparation Time: **5 minutes**

Cooking Time: **15 minutes**

Servings: **4**

Ingredients:

For the wrap:

- Collard leaves; 2 to 3
- Grated carrot; 1/4 cup
- Sliced cucumber; 1/4 cup
- Red bell pepper; 1/4; thin strips
- Orange bell pepper; 1/4; thin strips
- Cooked quinoa; 1/3 cup
- Shelled defrosted edamame; 1/3 cup

For the dressing:

- Fresh ginger root; 3 tablespoons; peeled and chopped
- Cooked chickpeas; 1 cup
- Clove of garlic; 1
- Rice vinegar; 4 tablespoons
- Low sodium tamari/coconut aminos; 2 tablespoons
- Lime juice; 2 tablespoons
- Water; 1/4 cup
- Few pinches of chili flakes
- Stevia; 1 pack

Directions:

1. For the dressing, combine all the ingredients and purée in a food processor until smooth.
2. Load into a little jar or tub, and set aside.
3. Place the collar leaves on a flat surface, covering one another to create a tighter tie.
4. Take one tablespoon of ginger dressing and blend it up with the prepared quinoa.
5. Spoon the prepared quinoa onto the leaves and shape a simple horizontal line at the closest end.
6. Supplement the edamame with all the veggie fillings left over.
7. Drizzle around one tablespoon of the ginger dressing on top, then fold the cover's sides inwards.

8.   Pullover the fillings, the side of the cover closest to you, then turn the whole body away to seal it up.

Nutrition:
Calories: 295 Cal
Sugar: 3 g
Sodium: 200 mg
Fat: 13 g

CHAPTER 7:

Snack recipes

109. Cucumber Sandwich Bites

Preparation Time: 5 minutes

Cooking Time: 0 minutes

Servings: 12

Ingredients:

- 1 cucumber, sliced
- 8 slices whole wheat bread
- 2 tablespoons cream cheese, soft
- 1 tablespoon chives, chopped
- ¼ cup avocado, peeled, pitted and mashed
- 1 teaspoon mustard
- Salt and black pepper to the taste

Directions:

1. Spread the mashed avocado on each bread slice, also spread the rest of the ingredients except the cucumber slices.
2. Divide the cucumber slices on the bread slices, cut each slice in thirds, arrange on a platter and serve as an appetizer.

Nutrition:

Calories 187;

Fat 12.4 g;

Fiber 2.1 g;

Carbs 4.5 g;

Protein 8.2 g

110. Cucumber Rolls

Preparation Time: 5 minutes

Cooking Time: 0 minutes

Servings: 6

Ingredients:

- 1 big cucumber, sliced lengthwise
- 1 tablespoon parsley, chopped
- 8 ounces canned tuna, drained and mashed
- Salt and black pepper to the taste
- 1 teaspoon lime juice

Directions:

1. Arrange cucumber slices on a working surface, divide the rest of the ingredients, and roll.
2. Arrange all the rolls on a platter and serve as an appetizer.

Nutrition: Calories 200 Fat 6 g

Fiber 3.4 g Carbs 7.6 g Protein 3.5 g

111. Olives and Cheese Stuffed Tomatoes

Preparation Time: 10 minutes

Cooking Time: 0 minutes

Servings: 24

Ingredients:

- 24 cherry tomatoes, top cut off and insides scooped out
- 2 tablespoons olive oil
- ¼ teaspoon red pepper flakes

- ½ cup feta cheese, crumbled
- 2 tablespoons black olive paste
- ¼ cup mint, torn

Directions:

1. In a bowl, mix the olives paste with the rest of the ingredients except the cherry tomatoes and whisk well.
2. Stuff the cherry tomatoes with this mix, arrange them all on a platter and serve as an appetizer.

Nutrition:

Calories 136; Fat 8.6 g;

Fiber 4.8 g; Carbs 5.6 g; Protein 5.1 g

112. Tomato Salsa

Preparation Time: 5 minutes

Cooking Time: 0 minutes

Servings: 6

Ingredients:

- 1 garlic clove, minced
- 4 tablespoons olive oil
- 5 tomatoes, cubed
- 1 tablespoon balsamic vinegar
- ¼ cup basil, chopped
- 1 tablespoon parsley, chopped
- 1 tablespoon chives, chopped
- Salt and black pepper to the taste
- Pita chips for serving

Directions:

1. In a bowl, mix the tomatoes with the garlic and the rest of the ingredients except the pita chips, stir, divide into small cups and serve with the pita chips on the side.

Nutrition:

Calories 160; Fat 13.7 g;

Fiber 5.5 g; Carbs 10.1 g;

Protein 2.2

113. Chili Mango and Watermelon Salsa

Preparation Time: 5 minutes

Cooking Time: 0 minutes

Servings: 12

Ingredients:

- 1 red tomato, chopped
- Salt and black pepper to the taste
- 1 cup watermelon, seedless, peeled and cubed
- 1 red onion, chopped
- 2 mangos, peeled and chopped
- 2 chili peppers, chopped
- ¼ cup cilantro, chopped
- 3 tablespoons lime juice
- Pita chips for serving

Directions:

1. In a bowl, mix the tomato with the watermelon, the onion and the rest of the ingredients except the pita chips and toss well.
2. Divide the mix into small cups and serve with pita chips on the side.

Nutrition:

Calories 62;

Fat 4g;

Fiber 1.3 g;

Carbs 3.9 g;

Protein 2.3 g

114. Creamy Spinach and Shallots Dip

Preparation Time: 10 minutes

Cooking Time: 0 minutes

Servings: 4

Ingredients:

- 1 pound spinach, roughly chopped

- 2 shallots, chopped
- 2 tablespoons mint, chopped
- ¾ cup cream cheese, soft
- Salt and black pepper to the taste

Directions:

1. In a blender, combine the spinach with the shallots and the rest of the ingredients, and pulse well.
2. Divide into small bowls and serve as a party dip.

Nutrition:

Calories 204; Fat 11.5 g;

Fiber 3.1 g; Carbs 4.2 g;

Protein 5.9 g

115. Feta Artichoke Dip

Preparation Time: 10 minutes

Cooking Time: 30 minutes

Servings: 8

Ingredients:

- 8 ounces artichoke hearts, drained and quartered
- ¾ cup basil, chopped
- ¾ cup green olives, pitted and chopped
- 1 cup parmesan cheese, grated
- 5 ounces feta cheese, crumbled

Directions:

1. In your food processor, mix the artichokes with the basil and the rest of the ingredients, pulse well, and transfer to a baking dish.
2. Introduce in the oven, bake at 375° F for 30 minutes and serve as a party dip.

Nutrition:

Calories 186; Fat 12.4 g; Fiber 0.9 g;

Carbs 2.6 g; Protein 1.5 g

116. Avocado Dip

Preparation Time: 5 minutes

Cooking Time: 0 minutes

Servings: 8

Ingredients:

- ½ cup heavy cream
- 1 green chili pepper, chopped
- Salt and pepper to the taste
- 4 avocados, pitted, peeled and chopped
- 1 cup cilantro, chopped
- ¼ cup lime juice

Directions:

1. In a blender, combine the cream with the avocados and the rest of the ingredients and pulse well.
2. Divide the mix into bowls and serve cold as a party dip.

Nutrition:

Calories 200;

Fat 14.5 g;

Fiber 3.8 g;

Carbs 8.1 g;

Protein 7.6 g

117. Goat Cheese and Chives Spread

Preparation Time: 10 minutes

Cooking Time: 0 minute

Servings: 4

Ingredients:

- 2 ounces goat cheese, crumbled
- ¾ cup sour cream
- 2 tablespoons chives, chopped
- 1 tablespoon lemon juice
- Salt and black pepper to the taste
- 2 tablespoons extra virgin olive oil

Directions:

1. In a bowl, mix the goat cheese with the cream and the rest of the ingredients and whisk really well.
2. Keep in the fridge for 10 minutes and serve as a party spread.

Nutrition:

Calories 220;

Fat 11.5 g;

Fiber 4.8 g;

Carbs 8.9 g;

Protein 5.6 g

118. Veggie Fritters

Preparation Time: 10 minutes

Cooking Time: 10 minutes

Servings: 4

Ingredients:

- 2 garlic cloves, minced
- 2 yellow onions, chopped
- 4 scallions, chopped
- 2 carrots, grated
- 2 teaspoons cumin, ground
- ½ teaspoon turmeric powder
- Salt and black pepper to the taste
- ¼ teaspoon coriander, ground
- 2 tablespoons parsley, chopped
- ¼ teaspoon lemon juice
- ½ cup almond flour
- 2 beets, peeled and grated
- 2 eggs, whisked
- ¼ cup tapioca flour
- 3 tablespoons olive oil

Directions:

1. In a bowl, combine the garlic with the onions, scallions and the rest of the ingredients except the oil, stir well and shape medium fritters out of this mix.
2. Heat up a pan with the oil over medium-high heat, add the fritters, cook for 5 minutes on each side, arrange on a platter and serve.

Nutrition:

Calories 209; Fat 11.2 g;

Fiber 3 g; Carbs 4.4 g; Protein 4.8 g

119. White Bean Dip

Preparation Time: 10 minutes

Cooking Time: 0 minute

Servings: 4

Ingredients:

- 15 ounces canned white beans, drained and rinsed
- 6 ounces canned artichoke hearts, drained and quartered
- 4 garlic cloves, minced
- 1 tablespoon basil, chopped
- 2 tablespoons olive oil
- Juice of ½ lemon
- Zest of ½ lemon, grated
- Salt and black pepper to the taste

Directions:

1. In your food processor, combine the beans with the artichokes and the rest of the ingredients except the oil and pulse well.
2. Add the oil gradually, pulse the mix again, divide into cups and serve as a party dip.

Nutrition:

Calories 274; Fat 11.7 g;

Fiber 6.5 g;

Carbs 18.5 g;

Protein 16.5 g

120. Eggplant Dip

Preparation Time: 10 minutes

Cooking Time: 40 minutes

Servings: 4

Ingredients:

- 1 eggplant, poked with a fork
- 2 tablespoons tahini paste
- 2 tablespoons lemon juice
- 2 garlic cloves, minced
- 1 tablespoon olive oil
- Salt and black pepper to the taste
- 1 tablespoon parsley, chopped

Directions:

1. Put the eggplant in a roasting pan, bake at 400° F for 40 minutes, cool down, peel and transfer to your food processor.
2. Add the rest of the ingredients except the parsley, pulse well, divide into small bowls and serve as an appetizer with the parsley sprinkled on top.

Nutrition:

Calories 121; Fat 4.3 g;

Fiber 1 g; Carbs 1.4 g;

Protein 4.3 g

121. Bulgur Lamb Meatballs

Preparation Time: 10 minutes

Cooking Time: 15 minute

Servings: 6

Ingredients:

- 1 and ½ cups Greek yogurt
- ½ teaspoon cumin, ground
- 1 cup cucumber, shredded
- ½ teaspoon garlic, minced
- A pinch of salt and black pepper
- 1 cup bulgur

- 2 cups water
- 1 pound lamb, ground
- ¼ cup parsley, chopped
- ¼ cup shallots, chopped
- ½ teaspoon allspice, ground
- ½ teaspoon cinnamon powder
- 1 tablespoon olive oil

Directions:

1. In a bowl, combine the bulgur with the water, cover the bowl, leave aside for 10 minutes, drain and transfer to a bowl.
2. Add the meat, the yogurt and the rest of the ingredients except the oil, stir well and shape medium meatballs out of this mix.
3. Heat up a pan with the oil over medium-high heat, add the meatballs, cook them for 7 minutes on each side, arrange them all on a platter and serve as an appetizer.

Nutrition:

Calories 300; Fat 9.6 g;

Fiber 4.6 g;

Carbs 22.6 g;

Protein 6.6 g

122. Cucumber Bites

Preparation Time: 10 minutes

Cooking Time: 0 minutes

Servings: 12

Ingredients:

- 1 English cucumber, sliced into 32 rounds
- 10 ounces hummus
- 16 cherry tomatoes, halved
- 1 tablespoon parsley, chopped
- 1 ounce feta cheese, crumbled

Directions:

1. Spread the hummus on each cucumber round, divide the tomato halves on each, sprinkle the cheese and parsley on to and serve as an appetizer.

Nutrition:

Calories 162; Fat 3.4 g;

Fiber 2 g; Carbs 6.4 g; Protein 2.4 g

123. Stuffed Avocado

Preparation Time: 10 minutes

Cooking Time: 0 minute

Servings: 2

Ingredients:

- 1 avocado, halved and pitted
- 10 ounces canned tuna, drained
- 2 tablespoons sun-dried tomatoes, chopped
- 1 and ½ tablespoon basil pesto
- 2 tablespoons black olives, pitted and chopped
- Salt and black pepper to the taste
- 2 teaspoons pine nuts, toasted and chopped
- 1 tablespoon basil, chopped

Directions:

1. In a bowl, combine the tuna with the sun-dried tomatoes and the rest of the ingredients except the avocado and stir.
2. Stuff the avocado halves with the tuna mix and serve as an appetizer.

Nutrition:

Calories 233; Fat 9 g;

Fiber 3.5 g;

Carbs 11.4 g;

Protein 5.6 g

124. Hummus with Ground Lamb

Preparation Time: 10 minutes

Cooking Time: 15 minute

Servings: 8

Ingredients:

- 10 ounces hummus
- 12 ounces lamb meat, ground
- ½ cup pomegranate seeds
- ¼ cup parsley, chopped
- 1 tablespoon olive oil
- Pita chips for serving

Directions:

1. Heat up a pan with the oil over medium-high heat, add the meat, and brown for 15 minutes stirring often.
2. Spread the hummus on a platter, spread the ground lamb all over, also spread the pomegranate seeds and the parsley and serve with pita chips as a snack.

Nutrition:

Calories 133; Fat 9.7 g;

Fiber 1.7 g; Carbs 6.4 g; Protein 5

125. Wrapped Plums

Preparation Time: 5 minutes

Cooking Time: 0 minutes

Servings: 8

Ingredients:

- 2 ounces prosciutto, cut into 16 pieces
- 4 plums, quartered
- 1 tablespoon chives, chopped
- A pinch of red pepper flakes, crushed

Directions:

3. Wrap each plum quarter in a prosciutto slice, arrange them all on a platter, sprinkle the chives and pepper flakes all over and serve.

Nutrition:

Calories 30; Fat 1 g;

Fiber 0 g;

Carbs 4 g;

Protein 2 g

126. Fluffy Bites

Preparation Time: **20 minutes**

Cooking Time: **60 minutes**

Servings: **12**

Ingredients:

- 2 teaspoons cinnamon
- 2/3 cup sour cream
- 2 cups heavy cream
- 1 teaspoon scraped vanilla bean
- ¼ teaspoon cardamom
- 4 egg yolks
- Stevia to taste

Directions:

1. Start by whisking your egg yolks until creamy and smooth.

2. Get out a double boiler, and add your eggs with the rest of your ingredients. Mix well.

3. Remove from heat, allowing it to cool until it reaches room temperature.

4. Refrigerate for an hour before whisking well.

5. Pour into molds, and freeze for at least an hour before serving.

Nutrition:

Calories: 363

Protein: 2 g

Fat: 40 g

Carbohydrates: 1 g

127. Coconut Fudge

Preparation Time: **20 minutes**

Cooking Time: **60 minutes**

Servings: **12**

Ingredients:

- 2 cups coconut oil
- ½ cup dark cocoa powder
- ½ cup coconut cream
- ¼ cup almonds, chopped
- ¼ cup coconut, shredded
- 1 teaspoon almond extract
- Pinch of salt
- Stevia to taste

Directions:

1. Pour your coconut oil and coconut cream in a bowl, whisking with an electric beater until smooth. Once the mixture becomes smooth and glossy, do not continue.

2. Begin to add in your cocoa powder while mixing slowly, making sure that there aren't any lumps.

3. Add in the rest of your ingredients, and mix well.

4. Line a pan with parchment paper, and freeze until it sets.

5. Slice into squares before serving.

Nutrition:

Calories: 172 Fat: 20 g

Carbohydrates: 3 g

128. Nutmeg Nougat

Preparation Time: **30 minutes**

Cooking Time: **60 minutes**

Servings: **12**

Ingredients:

- 1 cup heavy cream
- 1 cup cashew butter
- 1 cup coconut, shredded
- ½ teaspoon nutmeg
- 1 teaspoon vanilla extract, pure
- Stevia to taste

Directions:

1. Melt your cashew butter using a double boiler, and then stir in your vanilla extract, dairy cream, nutmeg, and stevia. Make sure it's mixed well.

2. Remove from heat, allowing it to cool down before refrigerating it for half an hour.

3. Shape into balls, and coat with shredded coconut. Chill for at least two hours before serving.

Nutrition:

Calories: 341 Fat: 34 g

Carbohydrates: 5 g

129. Sweet Almond Bites

Preparation Time: **30 minutes**

Cooking Time: **90 minutes**

Servings: **12**

Ingredients:

- 18 ounces butter, grass fed
- 2 ounces heavy cream
- ½ cup Stevia
- 2/3 cup cocoa powder
- 1 teaspoon vanilla extract, pure
- 4 tablespoons almond butter

Direction:

1. Use a double boiler to melt your butter before adding in all of your remaining ingredients.

2. Place the mixture into molds, freezing for two hours before serving.

Nutrition:

Calories: 350

Protein: 2 g Fat: 38 g

130. Strawberry Cheesecake Minis

Preparation Time: **30 minutes**

Cooking Time: **120 minutes**

Servings: 12

Ingredients:

- 1 cup coconut oil
- 1 cup coconut butter
- ½ cup strawberries, sliced
- ½ teaspoon lime juice
- 2 tablespoons cream cheese, full fat
- Stevia to taste

Directions:

1. Blend your strawberries together.

2. Soften your cream cheese, and then add in your coconut butter.

3. Combine all ingredients together, and then pour your mixture into silicone molds.

4. Freeze for at least two hours before serving.

Nutrition:

Calories: 372

Protein: 1 g

Fat: 41 g

Carbohydrates: 2 g

131. Cocoa Brownies

Preparation Time: 10 minutes

Cooking Time: 30 minutes

Servings: 12

Ingredients:

- 1 egg
- 2 tablespoons butter, grass-fed
- 2 teaspoons vanilla extract, pure
- ¼ teaspoon baking powder
- ¼ cup cocoa powder
- 1/3 cup heavy cream
- ¾ cup almond butter
- Pinch sea salt

Directions:

1. Break your egg into a bowl, whisking until smooth.

2. Add in all of your wet ingredients, mixing well.

3. Mix all dry ingredients into a bowl.

4. Sift your dry ingredients into your wet ingredients, mixing to form a batter.

5. Get out a baking pan, greasing it before pouring in your mixture.

6. Heat your oven to 350 and bake for twenty-five minutes.

7. Allow it to cool before slicing and serve at room temperature or warm.

Nutrition:

Calories: 184

Protein: 1 g

Fat: 20 g

Carbohydrates: 1 g

132. Chocolate Orange Bites

Preparation Time: **20 minutes**

Cooking Time: **120 minutes**

Servings: **6**

Ingredients:

- 10 ounces coconut oil
- 4 tablespoons cocoa powder
- ¼ teaspoon orange extract
- Stevia to taste

Directions:

1. Melt half of your coconut oil using a double boiler, and then add in your stevia and orange extract.

2. Get out candy molds, pouring the mixture into it. Fill

each mold halfway, and then place in the fridge until they set.

3. Melt the other half of your coconut oil, stirring in your cocoa powder and stevia, making sure that the mixture is smooth with no lumps.

4. Pour into your molds, filling them up all the way, and then allow it to set in the fridge before serving.

Nutrition:

Calories: 188 g

Protein: 1 g

Fat: 21g

Carbohydrates: 5 g

133. Caramel Cones

Preparation Time: 25 minutes

Cooking Time: 120 minutes

Servings: 6

Ingredients:

- 2 tablespoons heavy whipping cream
- 2 tablespoons sour cream
- 1 tablespoon caramel sugar
- 1 teaspoon sea salt, fine
- 1/3 cup butter, grass-fed
- 1/3 cup coconut oil
- Stevia to taste

Directions:

1. Soften your coconut oil and butter, mixing together.

2. Mix all ingredients to form a batter, and then place them in molds.

3. Top with a little salt, and keep refrigerated until serving.

Nutrition:

Calories: 100

Fat: 12 g

Carbohydrates: 1 g

134. Cinnamon Bites

Preparation Time: **20 minutes**

Cooking Time: **95 minutes**

Servings: **6**

Ingredients:

- 1/8 teaspoon nutmeg
- 1 teaspoon vanilla extract
- ¼ teaspoon cinnamon
- 4 tablespoons coconut oil
- ½ cup butter, grass-fed
- 8 ounces cream cheese
- Stevia to taste

Directions:

1. Soften your coconut oil and butter, mixing in your cream cheese.

2. Add all of your remaining ingredients, and mix well.

3. Pour into molds, and freeze until set.

Nutrition:

Calories: 178

Protein: 1g

Fat: 19 g

135. Sweet Chai Bites

Preparation Time: 20 minutes

Cooking Time: 45 minutes

Servings: 6

Ingredients:

- 1 cup cream cheese
- 1 cup coconut oil
- 2 ounces butter, grass-fed
- 2 teaspoons ginger
- 2 teaspoons cardamom
- 1 teaspoon nutmeg
- 1 teaspoon cloves
- 1 teaspoon vanilla extract, pure
- 1 teaspoon Darjeeling black tea
- Stevia to taste

Directions:

1. Melt your coconut oil and butter before adding in your black tea. Allow it to set for one to two minutes.

2. Add in your cream cheese, removing your mixture from heat.

3. Add in all of your spices, and stir to combine.

4. Pour into molds, and freeze before serving.

Nutrition: Calories: 178 Protein: 1 g

Fat: 19 g

136. Easy Vanilla Bombs

Preparation Time: 20 minutes

Cooking Time: 45 minutes

Servings: 14

Ingredients:

- 1 cup macadamia nuts, unsalted

- ¼ cup coconut oil / ¼ cup butter
- 2 teaspoons vanilla extract, sugar-free
- 20 drops liquid Stevia
- 2 tablespoons erythritol, powdered

Directions:

1. Pulse your macadamia nuts in a blender, and then combine all of your ingredients together. Mix well.

2. Get out mini muffin tins with a tablespoon and a half of the mixture.

3. Refrigerate it for a half hour before serving.

Nutrition:

Calories: 125

Fat: 5 g

Carbohydrates: 5 g

137. Jalapeno Lentil Burgers

Preparation Time: *15 minutes*

Cooking Time: *10 minutes*

Servings: *5*

Ingredients:

- Dried red lentils; half cup; rinsed
- Chickpeas; 1 to 12 ounces can; rinsed
- Ground cumin; one teaspoon
- Chili powder; one teaspoon
- Sea salt; one teaspoon
- Packed cilantro; half cup
- Garlic cloves minced
- Jalapeno finely chopped

- Red onion; half, small; minced
- Red bell pepper
- Carrot; shredded
- Oat bran/oat flour; 1/4 cup (gluten-free)
- Lettuce/hamburger buns
  For Pico:
- Ripe mango (1) diced
- Ripe avocado (1) diced
- Red onion; half, small; finely diced
- Chopped cilantro; half cup
- Fresh lime juice; half teaspoon
- Sea salt

Directions:

1. Put all ingredients in a large bowl and mix.
2. Stir in the salt to compare.
3. Put a medium saucepan on medium heat, add lentils plus 1 1/2 cups of water, then bring water to a boil, cover it afterward, lower the heat to low, and then simmer lentils until the water is absorbed.
4. Drain, and set aside some extra water.
5. In a food processor, put the cooked lentils, chickpeas, garlic, sea salt, cilantro, chili powder and cumin, and blend until the beans and lentils are smooth.
6. Add tomato, red pepper, jalapeno, and carrot to compare.
7. Divide into 6 equal parts and use your hands to create dense patties.

8. Heat skillet over a medium-high flame; apply 1/2 tablespoon of olive oil
9. Place a few burgers in at a time and cook on either side for a couple of minutes, just until crisp and golden brown.
10. Repeat with remaining patties and add olive oil whenever desired.
11. Place the patties in a bun or lettuce and finish with mango avocado pico.

Nutrition:
Carbohydrates: 34.9 g
Calories: 225 Cal
Sugar: 7.7 g
Fats: 6.1 g

138. Grandma's Rice

Preparation Time: **15 minutes**
Cooking Time: **2 hours**
Servings: **4**
Ingredients:

- 40 g butter
- 1/2 cup brown sugar
- 1/2 cup arborio rice
- 3 cups milk
- 1/2 tbsp. ground cinnamon
- 1/8 tbsp. ground nutmeg
- 1 tbsp. vanilla paste
- 1/2 cup raisins
- 300 ml. cream

Directions:

1. Preheat oven to 300F.
2. Grease a 1-liter ability oven-safe plate.

3. Heat butter in a saucepan and add sugar and rice.

4. Stir for 1 minute to thoroughly coat the rice.

5. Remove from heat and wish in milk, spices, and vanilla.

6. Stir through raisins then pour into prepared dish.

7. Bake for 30 minutes, then remove from the oven and stir well.

8. Drizzle over the cream and return to the oven for an additional hour.

9. Check that the rice is cooked through.

10. Return to the oven for 15-30 minutes if required.

11. Serve with extra cream and nutmeg.

Nutrition:
Fat: 20 g
Protein: 23 g
Cholesterol: 25 mg
Carbohydrates: 30 g
Sodium: 1000 mg

139. Baked Beef Zucchini

Preparation Time: **10 minutes**

Cooking Time: **40 minutes**

Servings: **4**

Ingredients:

- 2 large zucchinis
- 1 cup minced beef
- 1 cup mushroom, chopped
- 1 tomato, chopped
- 1/2 cup spinach, chopped
- 1 tbsp. chives, minced
- 2 tbsp. olive oil
- Salt and pepper to taste
- 1 tbsp. almond butter
- 1 tsp. garlic powder
- 1 cup cheddar cheese, grated
- 1/3 tsp. ginger powder

Directions:

1. Preheat the oven to 400 degrees F.

2. Add aluminum foil on a baking sheet.

3. Cut the zucchini in half. Scoop out the seeds and make pockets to stuff it later.

4. In a pan, add the olive oil.

5. Toss the beef until brown.

6. Add the mushroom, tomato, chives, salt, pepper, garlic, ginger, and spinach.

7. Cook for 2 minutes. Take off the heat.

8. Stuff the zucchinis using the mix.

9. Add them onto the baking sheet. Sprinkle the cheese on top.

10. Add the butter on top. Bake for 30 minutes. Serve warm.

Nutrition:
Fat: 12.8 g
Cholesterol: 79.7 mg Sodium: 615.4 mg
Potassium: 925.8 mg Carbohydrate: 26.8 g

140. Baked Tuna with Asparagus

Preparation Time: **10 minutes**

Cooking Time: **10 minutes**

Servings: **2**

Ingredients:

- 2 tuna steak
- 1 cup asparagus, trimmed
- 1 tsp. almond butter
- 1 tsp. rosemary
- 1/2 tsp. oregano
- 1/2 tsp. garlic powder
- 1tsp. lemon juice
- 1/2 tsp. ginger powder
- 1 tbsp. olive oil
- 1 tsp. red chili powder
- Salt and pepper to taste

Directions:

1. Marinate the tuna using oregano, lemon juice, salt, pepper, red chili powder, garlic, ginger, and let it sit for 10 minutes.
2. In a pan, add the olive oil.
3. Fry the tuna steaks 2 minutes per side.
4. In another pan, melt the almond butter.
5. Toss the asparagus with salt, pepper, and rosemary for 3 minutes.
6. Serve.

Nutrition:

Fat: 4.7 g Cholesterol: 0.0 mg
Sodium: 98.5 mg Potassium: 171.6 mg
Carbohydrate: 3.2 g

141. Lamb Stuffed Avocado

Preparation Time: **10 minutes**

Cooking Time: **40 minutes**

Servings: **4**

Ingredients:

- 2 avocados
- 1 1/2 cup minced lamb
- 1/2 cup cheddar cheese, grated
- 1/2 cup parmesan cheese, grated
- 2 tbsp. almond, chopped
- 1 tbsp. coriander, chopped
- 2 tbsp. olive oil
- 1 tomato, chopped
- 1 jalapeno, chopped
- Salt and pepper to taste
- 1 tsp. garlic, chopped
- 1-inch ginger, chopped

Directions:

1. Cut the avocados in half. Remove the pit and scoop out some flesh to stuff it later.
2. In a skillet, add half of the oil.
3. Toss the ginger, garlic for 1 minute.
4. Add the lamb and toss for 3 minutes.
5. Add the tomato, coriander, parmesan, jalapeno, salt, pepper, and cook for 2 minutes.
6. Take off the heat. Stuff the avocados.
7. Sprinkle the almonds, cheddar cheese, and add olive oil on top.

8. Add to a baking sheet and bake for 30 minutes. Serve.

Nutrition:

Fat: 19.5 g

Cholesterol: 167.5 mg

Sodium: 410.7 mg

Potassium: 617.1 mg

Carbohydrate: 13.1 g

142. Mozzarella Sticks

Preparation Time: **8 minutes**

Cooking Time: **2 minutes**

Servings: **2**

Ingredients:

- 1 large whole egg
- 3 sticks mozzarella cheese in half (frozen overnight)
- 2 tablespoon grated parmesan cheese
- 1/2 cup almond flour
- 1/4 cup coconut oil
- 2 1/2 teaspoons Italian seasoning blend
- 1 tablespoon chopped parsley
- 1/2 teaspoon salt

Directions:

1. Heat the coconut oil in a cast-iron skillet of medium size over low-medium heat.

2. Crack the egg in a small bowl in the meantime and beat it well.

3. Take another bowl of medium size and add parmesan cheese, almond flour, and seasonings to it. Whisk together the ingredients until a smooth mixture is prepared.

4. Take the overnight frozen mozzarella stick and dip in the beaten egg, then coat it well with the dry mixture. Do the same with all the remaining cheese sticks.

5. Place all the coated sticks in the preheated skillet and cook them for 2 minutes or until they start giving a golden-brown look from all sides.

6. Remove from the skillet once cooked properly and place over a paper towel so that any extra oil gets absorbed.

7. Sprinkle parsley over the sticks if you desire and serve with keto marinara sauce.

Nutrition:

Calories: 430

Fat: 39 g

Carbohydrates: 10 g

Protein: 20 g

143. Avocado Taco Boats

Preparation Time: **5 minutes**

Cooking Time: **20 minutes**

Servings: **4**

Ingredients:

- 4 grape tomatocs
- 2 large avocados
- 1 lbs. ground beef
- 4 tablespoon taco seasoning
- 3/4 cup shredded sharp cheddar cheese
- 4 slices pickled jalapeño

- 1/4 cup salsa
- 3 shredded romaine leaves
- 1/4 cup sour cream
- 2/3 cup water

Directions:

1. Take a skillet of large size, grease it with oil, and heat it over medium-high heat. Cook the ground beef in it for 10-15 minutes or until it gives a brownish look.

2. Once the beef gets brown, drain the grease from the skillet and add the water and the taco seasoning.

3. Reduce the heat once the taco seasoning gets mixed well and simmer for 8-10 minutes.

4. Take both avocados and prepare their halves using a sharp knife.

5. Take each avocado shell and fill it with ¼ of the shredded romaine leaves.

6. Fill each shell with ¼ of the cooked ground beef.

7. Do the topping with sour cream, cheese, jalapeno, salsa, and tomato before you serve the delicious avocado taco boats.

Nutrition: Calories: 430 Fat: 35 g Carbohydrates: 5 g Protein: 32 g

144. Cauliflower Crust Pizza

Preparation Time: **20 minutes**
Cooking Time: **45 minutes**
Servings: **4**

- *Ingredients:*
- I cauliflower (it should be cut into smaller portions)
- 1/4 grated parmesan cheese
- 1 egg
- 1 tsp. Italian seasoning
- 1/4 tsp. kosher salt
- 2 cups of freshly grated mozzarella
- 1/4 cup of spicy pizza sauce
- Basil leaves, for garnishing

Directions:

1. Begin by preheating your oven while using the parchment paper to rim the baking sheet.

2. Process the cauliflower into a fine powder, and then transfer to a bowl before putting it into the microwave.

3. Leave for about 5-6 minutes to get it soft.

4. Transfer the microwaved cauliflower to a clean and dry kitchen towel.

5. Leave it to cool off.

6. When cold, use the kitchen towel to wrap the cauliflower and then get rid of all the moisture by wringing the towel.

7. Continue squeezing until water is gone completely.

8. Put the cauliflower, Italian seasoning, Parmesan, egg, salt, and mozzarella (1 cup).

9. Stir very well until well combined.

10. Transfer the combined mixture to the baking sheet previously prepared, pressing it into a 10-inch round shape.

11. Bake for 10-15 minutes until it becomes golden in color.

12. Take the baked crust out of the oven and use the spicy pizza sauce and mozzarella (the leftover 1 cup) to top it.

13. Bake again for 10 more minutes until the cheese melts and looks bubbly.

14. Garnish using fresh basil leaves.

15. You can also enjoy this with salad.

Nutrition:

Calories: 74 Cal

Carbohydrates: 4 g

Protein: 6 g

Fat: 4 g

Fiber: 2 g

MEDITERRANEAN DIET COOKBOOK FOR BEGINNERS

CHAPTER 8:

Dinner Recipes

145. Balsamic Beef and Mushrooms Mix

Preparation Time: 5 minutes

Cooking Time: 8 hours

Servings: 4

Ingredients:

- 2 pounds' beef, cut into strips
- ¼ cup balsamic vinegar
- 2 cups beef stock
- 1 tablespoon ginger, grated
- Juice of ½ lemon
- 1 cup brown mushrooms, sliced
- A pinch of salt and black pepper
- 1 teaspoon ground cinnamon

Directions:

1. Mix all the ingredients in your slow cooker, cover and cook on low for 8 hours.
2. Divide everything between plates and serve.

Nutrition:

Calories 446, Fat 14,

Fiber 0.6, Carbs 2.9, Protein 70,8

146. Oregano Pork Mix

Preparation Time: 5 minutes

Cooking Time: 7 hours and 6 minutes

Servings: 4

Ingredients:

- 2 pounds' pork roast

- 7 ounces' tomato paste
- 1 yellow onion, chopped
- 1 cup beef stock
- 2 tablespoons ground cumin
- 2 tablespoons olive oil
- 2 tablespoons fresh oregano, chopped
- 1 tablespoon garlic, minced
- ½ cup fresh thyme, chopped

Directions:

1. Heat up a sauté pan with the oil over medium-high heat, add the roast, brown it for 3 minutes on each side and then transfer to your slow cooker.
2. Add the rest of the ingredients, toss a bit, cover and cook on low for 7 hours.
3. Slice the roast, divide it between plates and serve.

Nutrition:

Calories 623, Fat 30.1, Fiber 6.2,

Carbs 19.3, Protein 69,2

147. Simple Beef Roast

Preparation Time: 10 minutes

Cooking Time: 8 hours

Servings: 8

Ingredients:

- 5 pounds' beef roast
- 2 tablespoons Italian seasoning

- 1 cup beef stock
- 1 tablespoon sweet paprika
- 3 tablespoons olive oil

Directions:

1. In your slow cooker, mix all the ingredients, cover and cook on low for 8 hours.
2. Carve the roast, divide it between plates and serve.

Nutrition:

Calories 587, Fat 24.1, Fiber 0.3, Carbs 0.9, Protein 86.5

148. Chicken Breast Soup

Preparation Time: 5 minutes

Cooking Time: 4 hours

Servings: 4

Ingredients:

- 3 chicken breasts, skinless, boneless, cubed
- 2 celery stalks, chopped
- 2 carrots, chopped
- 2 tablespoons olive oil
- 1 red onion, chopped
- 3 garlic cloves, minced
- 4 cups chicken stock
- 1 tablespoon parsley, chopped

Directions:

1. In your slow cooker, mix all the ingredients except the parsley, cover and cook on High for 4 hours.
2. Add the parsley, stir, ladle the soup into bowls and serve.

Nutrition:

Calories 445, Fat 21.1, Fiber 1.6, Carbs 7.4, Protein 54,3

149. Cauliflower Curry

Preparation Time: 5 minutes

Cooking Time: 5 hours

Servings: 4

Ingredients:

- 1 cauliflower head, florets separated
- 2 carrots, sliced
- 1 red onion, chopped
- ¾ cup coconut milk
- 2 garlic cloves, minced
- 2 tablespoons curry powder
- A pinch of salt and black pepper
- 1 tablespoon red pepper flakes
- 1 teaspoon garam masala

Directions:

1. In your slow cooker, mix all the ingredients.
2. Cover, cook on high for 5 hours, divide into bowls and serve.

Nutrition:

Calories 160, Fat 11.5, Fiber 5.4, Carbs 14.7, Protein 3,6

150. Pork and Peppers Chili

Preparation Time: 5 minutes

Cooking Time: 8 hours 5 minutes

Servings: 4

Ingredients:

- 1 red onion, chopped
- 2 pounds' pork, ground
- 4 garlic cloves, minced
- 2 red bell peppers, chopped
- 1 celery stalk, chopped
- 25 ounces' fresh tomatoes, peeled, crushed

- ¼ cup green chilies, chopped
- 2 tablespoons fresh oregano, chopped
- 2 tablespoons chili powder
- A pinch of salt and black pepper
- A drizzle of olive oil

Directions:

1. Heat up a sauté pan with the oil over medium-high heat and add the onion, garlic and the meat. Mix and brown for 5 minutes then transfer to your slow cooker.
2. Add the rest of the ingredients, toss, cover and cook on low for 8 hours.
3. Divide everything into bowls and serve.

Nutrition: Calories 448 Fat 13 Fiber 6.6 Carbs 20.2 Protein 63g

151. Greek Style Quesadillas

Preparation Time: 10 minutes

Cooking Time: 10 minutes

Servings: 4

Ingredients:

- 4 whole wheat tortillas
- 1 cup Mozzarella cheese, shredded
- 1 cup fresh spinach, chopped
- 2 tablespoon Greek yogurt
- 1 egg, beaten
- ¼ cup green olives, sliced
- 1 tablespoon olive oil
- 1/3 cup fresh cilantro, chopped

Directions:

1. In the bowl, combine together Mozzarella cheese, spinach, yogurt, egg, olives, and cilantro.
2. Then pour olive oil in the skillet.
3. Place one tortilla in the skillet and spread it with Mozzarella mixture.

4. Top it with the second tortilla and spread it with cheese mixture again.
5. Then place the third tortilla and spread it with all remaining cheese mixture.
6. Cover it with the last tortilla and fry it for 5 minutes from each side over the medium heat.

Nutrition:

Calories 193

Fat 7.7

Fiber 3.2

Carbs 23.6

Protein 8.3

152. Creamy Penne

Preparation Time: 10 minutes

Cooking Time: 25 minutes

Servings: 4

Ingredients:

- ½ cup penne, dried
- 9 oz. chicken fillet
- 1 teaspoon Italian seasoning
- 1 tablespoon olive oil
- 1 tomato, chopped
- 1 cup heavy cream
- 1 tablespoon fresh basil, chopped
- ½ teaspoon salt
- 2 oz. Parmesan, grated
- 1 cup water, for cooking

Directions:

1. Pour water in the pan, add penne, and boil it for 15 minutes. Then drain water.
2. Pour olive oil in the skillet and heat it up.
3. Slice the chicken fillet and put it in the hot oil.

4. Sprinkle chicken with Italian seasoning and roast for 2 minutes from each side.
5. Then add fresh basil, salt, tomato, and grated cheese.
6. Stir well.
7. Add heavy cream and cooked penne.
8. Cook the meal for 5 minutes more over the medium heat. Stir it from time to time.

Nutrition:
Calories 388 Fat 23.4
Fiber 0.2
Carbs 17.6
Protein 17.6

153. Light Paprika Moussaka
Preparation Time: 15 minutes
Cooking Time: 45 minutes
Servings: 3
Ingredients:
- 1 eggplant, trimmed
- 1 cup ground chicken
- 1/3 cup white onion, diced
- 3 oz. Cheddar cheese, shredded
- 1 potato, sliced
- 1 teaspoon olive oil
- 1 teaspoon salt
- ½ cup milk
- 1 tablespoon butter
- 1 tablespoon ground paprika
- 1 tablespoon Italian seasoning
- 1 teaspoon tomato paste

Directions:
1. Slice the eggplant lengthwise and sprinkle with salt.
2. Pour olive oil in the skillet and add sliced potato.

3. Roast potato for 2 minutes from each side.
4. Then transfer it in the plate.
5. Put eggplant in the skillet and roast it for 2 minutes from each side too.
6. Pour milk in the pan and bring it to boil.
7. Add tomato paste, Italian seasoning, paprika, butter, and Cheddar cheese.
8. Then mix up together onion with ground chicken.
9. Arrange the sliced potato in the casserole in one layer.
10. Then add ½ part of all sliced eggplants.
11. Spread the eggplants with ½ part of chicken mixture.
12. Then add remaining eggplants.
13. Pour the milk mixture over the eggplants.
14. Bake moussaka for 30 minutes at 355F.

Nutrition:
Calories 387, Fat 21.2,
Fiber 8.9, Carbs 26.3,
Protein 25.4

154. Cucumber Bowl with Spices and Greek Yogurt
Preparation Time: 10 minutes
Cooking Time: 20 minutes
Servings: 3
Ingredients:
- 4 cucumbers
- ½ teaspoon chili pepper
- ¼ cup fresh parsley, chopped
- ¾ cup fresh dill, chopped
- 2 tablespoons lemon juice
- ½ teaspoon salt

- ½ teaspoon ground black pepper
- ¼ teaspoon sage
- ½ teaspoon dried oregano
- 1/3 cup Greek yogurt

Directions:

1. Make the cucumber dressing: blend the dill and parsley until you get green mash.
2. Then combine together green mash with lemon juice, salt, ground black pepper, sage, dried oregano, Greek yogurt, and chili pepper.
3. Churn the mixture well.
4. Chop the cucumbers roughly and combine them with cucumber dressing. Mix up well.
5. Refrigerate the cucumber for 20 minutes.

Nutrition:

Calories 114

Fat 1.6

Fiber 4.1

Carbs 23.2

Protein 7.6

155. Stuffed Bell Peppers with Quinoa

Preparation Time: 10 minutes

Cooking Time: 35 minutes

Servings: 2

Ingredients:

- 2 bell peppers
- 1/3 cup quinoa
- 3 oz. chicken stock
- ¼ cup onion, diced
- ½ teaspoon salt
- ¼ teaspoon tomato paste
- ½ teaspoon dried oregano

- 1/3 cup sour cream
- 1 teaspoon paprika

Directions:

1. Trim the bell peppers and remove the seeds.
2. Then combine together chicken stock and quinoa in the pan.
3. Add salt and boil the ingredients for 10 minutes or until quinoa will soak all liquid.
4. Then combine together cooked quinoa with dried oregano, tomato paste, and onion.
5. Fill the bell peppers with the quinoa mixture and arrange in the casserole mold.
6. Add sour cream and bake the peppers for 25 minutes at 365F.
7. Serve the cooked peppers with sour cream sauce from the casserole mold.

Nutrition:

Calories 237 Fat 10.3

Fiber 4.5

Carbs 31.3

Protein 6.9

156. Mediterranean Burrito

Preparation Time: 10 minutes

Cooking Time: 0 minutes

Servings: 2

Ingredients:

- 2 wheat tortillas
- 2 oz. red kidney beans, canned, drained
- 2 tablespoons hummus
- 2 teaspoons tahini sauce
- 1 cucumber
- 2 lettuce leaves
- 1 tablespoon lime juice

- 1 teaspoon olive oil
- ½ teaspoon dried oregano

Directions:

1. Mash the red kidney beans until you get a puree.
2. Then spread the wheat tortillas with beans mash from one side.
3. Add hummus and tahini sauce.
4. Cut the cucumber into the wedges and place them over tahini sauce.
5. Then add lettuce leaves.
6. Make the dressing: mix up together olive oil, dried oregano, and lime juice.
7. Drizzle the lettuce leaves with the dressing and wrap the wheat tortillas in the shape of burritos.

Nutrition:

Calories 288

Fat 10.2

Fiber 14.6

Carbs 38.2

Protein 12.5

157. Sweet Potato Bacon Mash

Preparation Time: 10 minutes

Cooking Time: 20 minutes

Servings: 4

Ingredients:

- 3 sweet potatoes, peeled
- 4 oz. bacon, chopped
- 1 cup chicken stock
- 1 tablespoon butter
- 1 teaspoon salt
- 2 oz. Parmesan, grated

Directions:

1. Chop sweet potato and put it in the pan.
2. Add chicken stock and close the lid.

3. Boil the vegetables for 15 minutes or until they are soft.
4. After this, drain the chicken stock.
5. Mash the sweet potato with the help of the potato masher. Add grated cheese and butter.
6. Mix up together salt and chopped bacon. Fry the mixture until it is crunchy (10-15 minutes).
7. Add cooked bacon in the mashed sweet potato and mix up with the help of the spoon.
8. It is recommended to serve the meal warm or hot.

Nutrition:

Calories 304

Fat 18.1

Fiber 2.9

Carbs 18.8

Protein 17

158. Prosciutto Wrapped Mozzarella Balls

Preparation Time: 10 minutes

Cooking Time: 10 minutes

Servings: 4

Ingredients:

- 8 Mozzarella balls, cherry size
- 4 oz. bacon, sliced
- ¼ teaspoon ground black pepper
- ¾ teaspoon dried rosemary
- 1 teaspoon butter

Directions:

1. Sprinkle the sliced bacon with ground black pepper and dried rosemary.
2. Wrap every Mozzarella ball in the sliced bacon and secure them with toothpicks.

3. Melt butter.
4. Brush wrapped Mozzarella balls with butter.
5. Line the tray with the baking paper and arrange Mozzarella balls in it.
6. Bake the meal for 10 minutes at 365F.

Nutrition:

Calories 323 Fat 26.8

Fiber 0.1

Carbs 0.6

Protein 20.6

159. Garlic Chicken Balls

Preparation Time: 15 minutes

Cooking Time: 10 minutes

Servings: 4

Ingredients:

- 2 cups ground chicken
- 1 teaspoon minced garlic
- 1 teaspoon dried dill
- 1/3 carrot, grated
- 1 egg, beaten
- 1 tablespoon olive oil
- ¼ cup coconut flakes
- ½ teaspoon salt

Directions:

1. In the mixing bowl mix up together ground chicken, minced garlic, dried dill, carrot, egg, and salt.
2. Stir the chicken mixture with the help of the fingertips until homogenous.
3. Then make medium balls from the mixture.
4. Coat every chicken ball in coconut flakes.
5. Heat up olive oil in the skillet.

6. Add chicken balls and cook them for 3 minutes from each side. The cooked chicken balls will have a golden-brown color.

Nutrition:

Calories 200

Fat 11.5

Fiber 0.6

Carbs 1.7

Protein 21.9

160. Zucchini Salmon Salad

Preparation Time: 5 minutes

Cooking Time: 10 minutes

Servings: 3

Ingredients:

- 2 salmon fillets
- 2 tablespoons soy sauce
- 2 zucchinis, sliced
- Salt and pepper to taste
- 2 tablespoons extra virgin olive oil
- 2 tablespoons sesame seeds
- Salt and pepper to taste

Directions:

1. Drizzle the salmon with soy sauce.
2. Heat a grill pan over medium flame. Cook salmon on the grill on each side for 2-3 minutes.
3. Season the zucchini with salt and pepper and place it on the grill as well. Cook on each side until golden.
4. Place the zucchini, salmon and the rest of the ingredients in a bowl.
5. Serve the salad fresh.

Nutrition:

Calories: 224 Fat: 19g

Protein: 18g

Carbohydrates: 0g

161. Pan Fried Salmon

Preparation Time: 5 minutes
Cooking Time: 20 minutes
Servings: 4
Ingredients:

- 4 salmon fillets
- Salt and pepper to taste
- 1 teaspoon dried oregano
- 1 teaspoon dried basil
- 3 tablespoons extra virgin olive oil

Directions:

1. Season the fish with salt, pepper, oregano and basil.
2. Heat the oil in a pan and place the salmon in the hot oil, with the skin facing down.
3. Fry on each side for 2 minutes until golden brown and fragrant.
4. Serve the salmon warm and fresh.

Nutrition:
Calories: 327
Fat: 25g
Protein: 36g
Carbohydrates: 0.3g

162. Grilled Salmon with Pineapple Salsa

Preparation Time: 5 minutes
Cooking Time: 30 minutes
Servings: 4
Ingredients:

- 4 salmon fillets
- Salt and pepper to taste
- 2 tablespoons Cajun seasoning
- 1 fresh pineapple, peeled and diced
- 1 cup cherry tomatoes, quartered
- 2 tablespoons chopped cilantro
- 2 tablespoons chopped parsley
- 1 teaspoon dried mint
- 2 tablespoons lemon juice
- 2 tablespoons extra virgin olive oil
- 1 teaspoon honey
- Salt and pepper to taste

Directions:

1. Add salt, pepper and Cajun seasoning to the fish.
2. Heat a grill pan over medium flame. Cook fish on the grill on each side for 3-4 minutes.
3. For the salsa, mix the pineapple, tomatoes, cilantro, parsley, mint, lemon juice and honey in a bowl. Season with salt and pepper.
4. Serve the grilled salmon with the pineapple salsa.

Nutrition:
Calories: 332
Fat: 12g
Protein: 34g
Carbohydrates: 0g

163. Mediterranean Chickpea Salad

Preparation Time: 5 minutes
Cooking Time: 20 minutes
Servings: 6
Ingredients:

- 1 can chickpeas, drained
- 1 fennel bulb, sliced
- 1 red onion, sliced
- 1 teaspoon dried basil
- 1 teaspoon dried oregano
- 2 tablespoons chopped parsley
- 4 garlic cloves, minced
- 2 tablespoons lemon juice
- 2 tablespoons extra virgin olive oil

- Salt and pepper to taste

Directions:

1. Combine the chickpeas, fennel, red onion, herbs, garlic, lemon juice and oil in a salad bowl.
2. Add salt and pepper and serve the salad fresh.

Nutrition:

Calories: 200

Fat: 9g

Protein: 4g

Carbohydrates: 28g

164. Warm Chorizo Chickpea Salad

Preparation Time: 5 minutes

Cooking Time: 20 minutes

Servings: 6

Ingredients:

- 1 tablespoon extra-virgin olive oil
- 4 chorizo links, sliced
- 1 red onion, sliced
- 4 roasted red bell peppers, chopped
- 1 can chickpeas, drained
- 2 cups cherry tomatoes
- 2 tablespoons balsamic vinegar
- Salt and pepper to taste

Directions:

1. Heat the oil in a skillet and add the chorizo. Cook briefly just until fragrant then add the onion, bell peppers and chickpeas and cook for 2 additional minutes.
2. Transfer the mixture in a salad bowl then add the tomatoes, vinegar, salt and pepper.
3. Mix well and serve the salad right away.

Nutrition:

Calories: 359

Fat: 18g

Protein: 15g

Carbohydrates: 21g

165. Greek Roasted Fish

Preparation Time: 5 minutes

Cooking Time: 30 minutes

Servings: 4

Ingredients:

- 4 salmon fillets
- 1 tablespoon chopped oregano
- 1 teaspoon dried basil
- 1 zucchini, sliced
- 1 red onion, sliced
- 1 carrot, sliced
- 1 lemon, sliced
- 2 tablespoons extra virgin olive oil
- Salt and pepper to taste

Directions:

1. add all the ingredients in a deep dish baking pan.
2. Season with salt and pepper and cook in the preheated oven at 350F for 20 minutes.
3. Serve the fish and vegetables warm.

Nutrition:

Calories: 328 Fat: 13g

Protein: 38g Carbohydrates: 8g

166. Tomato Fish Bake

Preparation Time: 5 minutes

Cooking Time: 30 minutes

Servings: 4

Ingredients:

- 4 cod fillets

- 4 tomatoes, sliced
- 4 garlic cloves, minced
- 1 shallot, sliced
- 1 celery stalk, sliced
- 1 teaspoon fennel seeds
- 1 cup vegetable stock
- Salt and pepper to taste

Directions:

1. Layer the cod fillets and tomatoes in a deep dish baking pan.
2. Add the rest of the ingredients and add salt and pepper.
3. Cook in the preheated oven at 350F for 20 minutes.
4. Serve the dish warm or chilled.

Nutrition:

Calories: 299 Fat: 3g

Protein: 64g Carbohydrates: 2g

167. Garlicky Tomato Chicken Casserole

Preparation Time: 5 minutes

Cooking Time: 50 minutes

Servings: 4

Ingredients:

- 4 chicken breasts
- 2 tomatoes, sliced
- 1 can diced tomatoes
- 2 garlic cloves, chopped
- 1 shallot, chopped
- 1 bay leaf
- 1 thyme sprig
- ½ cup dry white wine
- ½ cup chicken stock
- Salt and pepper to taste

Directions:

1. Combine the chicken and the remaining ingredients in a deep dish baking pan.
2. Adjust the taste with salt and pepper and cover the pot with a lid or aluminum foil.
3. Cook in the preheated oven at 330F for 40 minutes.
4. Serve the casserole warm.

Nutrition:

Calories: 313 Fat: 8g Protein: 47g

Carbohydrates: 6g

168. Chicken Cacciatore

Preparation Time: 5 minutes

Cooking Time: 45 minutes

Servings: 6

Ingredients:

- 2 tablespoons extra virgin olive oil
- 6 chicken thighs
- 1 sweet onion, chopped
- 2 garlic cloves, minced
- 2 red bell peppers, cored and diced
- 2 carrots, diced
- 1 rosemary sprig
- 1 thyme sprig
- 4 tomatoes, peeled and diced
- ½ cup tomato juice
- ¼ cup dry white wine
- 1 cup chicken stock
- 1 bay leaf
- Salt and pepper to taste

Directions:

1. Heat the oil in a heavy saucepan.
2. Cook chicken on all sides until golden.

3. Stir in the onion and garlic and cook for 2 minutes.
4. Stir in the rest of the ingredients and season with salt and pepper.
5. Cook on low heat for 30 minutes.
6. Serve the chicken cacciatore warm and fresh.

Nutrition:

Calories: 363

Fat: 14g

Protein: 42g

Carbohydrates: 9g

169. Fennel Wild Rice Risotto

Preparation Time: 5 minutes

Cooking Time: 35 minutes

Servings: 6

Ingredients:

- 2 tablespoons extra virgin olive oil
- 1 shallot, chopped
- 2 garlic cloves, minced
- 1 fennel bulb, chopped
- 1 cup wild rice
- ¼ cup dry white wine
- 2 cups chicken stock
- 1 teaspoon grated orange zest
- Salt and pepper to taste

Directions:

1. Heat the oil in a heavy saucepan.
2. Add the garlic, shallot and fennel and cook for a few minutes until softened.
3. Stir in the rice and cook for 2 additional minutes then add the wine, stock and orange zest, with salt and pepper to taste.
4. Cook on low heat for 20 minutes.
5. Serve the risotto warm and fresh.

Nutrition:

Calories: 162 Fat: 2g

Protein: 8g

Carbohydrates: 20g

170. Wild Rice Prawn Salad

Preparation Time: 5 minutes

Cooking Time: 35 minutes

Servings: 6

Ingredients:

- ¾ cup wild rice
- 1¾ cups chicken stock
- 1 pound prawns
- Salt and pepper to taste
- 2 tablespoons lemon juice
- 2 tablespoons extra virgin olive oil
- 2 cups arugula

Directions:

1. Combine the rice and chicken stock in a saucepan and cook until the liquid has been absorbed entirely.
2. Transfer the rice in a salad bowl.
3. Season the prawns with salt and pepper and drizzle them with lemon juice and oil.
4. Heat a grill pan over medium flame.
5. Place the prawns on the hot pan and cook on each side for 2-3 minutes.
6. For the salad, combine the rice with arugula and prawns and mix well.
7. Serve the salad fresh.

Nutrition:

Calories: 207 Fat: 4g

Protein: 20.6g

Carbohydrates: 17g

171. Chicken Broccoli Salad with Avocado Dressing

Preparation Time: 5 minutes
Cooking Time: 40 minutes
Servings: 6
Ingredients:

- 2 chicken breasts
- 1 pound broccoli, cut into florets
- 1 avocado, peeled and pitted
- ½ lemon, juiced
- 2 garlic cloves
- ¼ teaspoon chili powder
- ¼ teaspoon cumin powder
- Salt and pepper to taste

Directions:

1. Cook the chicken in a large pot of salty water.
2. Drain and cut the chicken into small cubes. Place in a salad bowl.
3. Add the broccoli and mix well.
4. Combine the avocado, lemon juice, garlic, chili powder, cumin powder, salt and pepper in a blender. Pulse until smooth.
5. Spoon the dressing over the salad and mix well.
6. Serve the salad fresh.

Nutrition:

Calories: 195 Fat: 11g

Protein: 14g

Carbohydrates: 3g

172. Seafood Paella

Preparation Time: 5 minutes
Cooking Time: 45 minutes
Servings: 8
Ingredients:

- 2 tablespoons extra virgin olive oil
- 1 shallot, chopped
- 2 garlic cloves, chopped
- 1 red bell pepper, cored and diced
- 1 carrot, diced
- 2 tomatoes, peeled and diced
- 1 cup wild rice
- 1 cup tomato juice
- 2 cups chicken stock
- 1 chicken breast, cubed
- Salt and pepper to taste
- 2 monkfish fillets, cubed
- ½ pound fresh shrimps, peeled and deveined
- ½ pound prawns
- 1 thyme sprig
- 1 rosemary sprig

Directions:

1. Heat the oil in a skillet and stir in the shallot, garlic, bell pepper, carrot and tomatoes. Cook for a few minutes until softened.
2. Stir in the rice, tomato juice, stock, chicken, salt and pepper and cook on low heat for 20 minutes.
3. Add the rest of the ingredients and cook for 10 additional minutes.
4. Serve the paella warm and fresh.

Nutrition:

Calories: 245 Fat: 8g Protein: 27g

Carbohydrates: 20.6g

173. Herbed Roasted Chicken Breasts

Preparation Time: 5 minutes
Cooking Time: 50 minutes
Servings: 4
Ingredients:

- 2 tablespoons extra virgin olive oil

- 2 tablespoons chopped parsley
- 2 tablespoons chopped cilantro
- 1 teaspoon dried oregano
- 1 teaspoon dried basil
- 2 tablespoons lemon juice
- Salt and pepper to taste
- 4 chicken breasts

Directions:

1. Combine the oil, parsley, cilantro, oregano, basil, lemon juice, salt and pepper in a bowl.
2. Spread this mixture over the chicken and rub it well into the meat.
3. Place in a deep dish baking pan and cover with aluminum foil.
4. Cook in the preheated oven at 350F for 20 minutes then remove the foil and cook for 25 additional minutes.
5. Serve the chicken warm and fresh with your favorite side dish.

Nutrition:

Calories: 330

Fat: 15g

Protein: 40.7g

Carbohydrates: 1g

174. Marinated Chicken Breasts

Preparation Time: 5 minutes

Cooking Time: 2 hours

Servings: 4

Ingredients:

- 4 chicken breasts
- Salt and pepper to taste
- 1 lemon, juiced
- 1 rosemary sprig
- 1 thyme sprig
- 2 garlic cloves, crushed
- 2 sage leaves

- 3 tablespoons extra virgin olive oil
- ½ cup buttermilk

Directions:

1. 1. Boil the chicken with salt and pepper and place it in a resealable bag.
2. 2. Add remaining ingredients and seal bag.
3. 3. Refrigerate for at least 1 hour.
4. 4. After 1 hour, heat a roasting pan over medium heat, then place the chicken on the grill.
5. 5. Cook on each side for 8-10 minutes or until juices are gone.
6. Serve the chicken warm with your favorite side dish.

Nutrition:

Calories: 371

Fat: 21g

Protein: 46g

Carbohydrates: 2g

175. Buffalo Cauliflower

Preparation Time: 5 minutes

Cooking Time: 15 minutes

Servings: 1

Ingredients:

- Cauliflower
- 1 cup of panko breadcrumbs
- 1 tsp. salt
- 2 cup of cauliflower florets
- Buffalo coating
- 1/4 cup of Vegan Buffalo sauce
- 1/4 cup of melted vegan butter

Directions:

1. Melt butter in microwave and whisk in buffalo sauce.
2. Dip each cauliflower floret into buffalo mixture, ensuring it gets coated well. Holdover a bowl till floret is done dripping.
3. Mix breadcrumbs with salt.
4. Immerse dipped florets into breadcrumbs and place them into Instant Crisp Air Fryer. Lock the air fryer lid. Set temperature to 350°F and set time to 15 minutes. When slightly browned, they are ready to eat!
5. Serve with your favorite Keto dipping sauce!

Nutrition:

Calories: 194

Fat: 17 g

Protein: 10 g

176. Instant Pot Chipotle Chicken & Cauliflower Rice Bowls

Preparation Time: **10 minutes**

Cooking Time: **20 minutes**

Servings: 4

Ingredients:

- 1/3 cup of salsa
- 1 quantity of 14.5 oz. of can fire-roasted diced tomatoes
- 1 canned chipotle pepper + 1 teaspoon sauce
- ½ teaspoon of dried oregano
- 1 teaspoon of cumin
- 1 ½ lb. of boneless, skinless chicken breast

- ¼ teaspoon of salt
- 1 cup of reduced-fat shredded Mexican cheese blend
- 4 cups of frozen riced cauliflower
- ½ medium-sized avocado, sliced

Directions:

1. Combine the first ingredients in a blender and blend until they become smooth
2. Place chicken inside your instant pot, and pour the sauce over it. Cover the lid and close the pressure valve.
3. Set it to 20 minutes at high temperature. Let the pressure release on its own before opening.
4. Remove the piece and the chicken and then add it back to the sauce.
5. Microwave the riced cauliflower according to the directions on the package.
6. Before you serve, divide the riced cauliflower, cheese, avocado, and chicken equally among the four bowls.

Nutrition:

Calories: 287 Protein: 35 g

Carbohydrate: 19 g

Fat: 12 g

177. Courgette Risotto

Preparation Time: **10 minutes**

Cooking Time: **5 minutes**

Servings: 8

Ingredients:

- 2 tablespoons olive oil

- 4 cloves garlic, finely chopped
- 1.5 pounds Arborio rice
- 6 tomatoes, chopped
- 2 teaspoons chopped rosemary
- 6 courgettes, finely diced
- 1 ¼ cups peas, fresh or frozen
- 12 cups hot vegetable stock
- Salt to taste
- Freshly ground pepper

Directions:

1. Place a large, heavy-bottomed pan over medium heat. Add oil. When the oil is heated, add onion and sauté until translucent.
2. Stir in the tomatoes and cook until soft.
3. Stir in the rice and rosemary. Mix well.
4. Add half the stock and cook until dry. Stir frequently.
5. Add remaining stock and cook for 3-4 minutes.
6. Add courgette and peas and cook until rice is tender. Add salt and pepper to taste.
7. Stir in the basil. Let it sit for 5 minutes.

Nutrition:

Calories 406

Fats 5 g

Carbohydrates 82 g

Proteins 14 g

178. Homemade Chicken Broth

Preparation Time: 5 minutes

Cooking Time: 30 minutes

Servings: 4

Ingredients:

- 1 tablespoon olive oil
- 1 chopped onion
- 2 chopped stalks celery
- 2 chopped carrots
- 1 whole chicken
- 2+ quarts of water
- 1 tablespoon salt
- ½ teaspoon pepper
- 1 teaspoon fresh sage

Directions:

1. Sauté vegetables in oil.
2. Add chicken and water and simmer for 2+ hours until the chicken falls off the bone. Keep adding water as needed.
3. Remove the chicken carcass from the broth, place on a platter, and let it cool. Pull chicken off the carcass and put it into the broth.
4. Pour broth mixture into pint and quart mason jars. Be sure to add meat to each jar.
5. Leave one full inch of space from the top of the jar or it will crack when it freezes as liquids expand. Place jars in freezer for up to a year.
6. Take out and use whenever you make a soup.

Nutrition:

Calories: 213 Fat: 6g

Fiber: 13g Carbs: 16g

Protein: 22g

179. Homemade Vegetable Broth

Preparation Time: 5 minutes
Cooking Time: 30 minutes
Servings: 4
Ingredients:

- 1 tablespoon olive oil
- 1 chopped onion
- 2 chopped stalks celery
- 2 chopped carrots
- 1 head bok choy
- 6 cups or 1 package fresh spinach
- 2+ quarts of water
- 1 tablespoon salt
- ½ teaspoon pepper
- 1 teaspoon fresh sage

Directions:

1. Sauté vegetables in oil. Add water and simmer for 1 hour.
2. Keep adding water as needed.
3. Pour broth mixture into pint and quart mason jars.
4. Leave one full inch of space from the top of the jar or it will crack when it freezes as liquids expand. Place jars in freezer for up to a year.
5. Take out and use whenever you make a soup.

Nutrition: Calories: 140 Fat: 2g
Fiber: 23g Carbs: 22g
Protein: 47g

180. Fish Stew

Preparation Time: 5 minutes
Cooking Time: 30 minutes
Servings: 4
Ingredients:

- 1 tablespoon olive oil
- 1 chopped onion or leek
- 2 chopped stalks celery
- 2 chopped carrots
- 1 clove minced garlic
- 1 tablespoon parsley
- 1 bay leaf
- 1 clove
- 1/8 teaspoon kelp or dulse (seaweed)
- ¼ teaspoon salt
- Fish—leftover, cooked, diced
- 2–3 cups chicken or vegetable broth

Directions:

1. Add all of ingredients and simmer on the stove for 20 minutes.

Nutrition:
Calories: 342
Fat: 15g
Fiber: 11g
Carbs: 8g
Protein: 10g

CHAPTER 9:

Side Dish Recipes

181. Brussels Sprouts and Rhubarb Mix

Preparation time: 5 minutes

Cooking time: 20 minutes

Servings: 4

Ingredients

- 1 pound Brussels sprouts, trimmed and halved
- ½ pound rhubarb, sliced
- 2 tablespoons avocado oil
- Juice of 1 lemon
- A pinch of salt and black pepper
- 1 tablespoon chives, chopped
- 1 teaspoon chili paste

Directions

1. In a pan that fits the air fryer, mix the sprouts with the rhubarb and the other ingredients, toss, put the pan in the fryer and cook at 390 degrees F for 20 minutes.
2. Divide between plates and serve as a side dish.

Nutrition: Calories 200, Fat 9, Fiber 2, Carbs 6, Protein 9

182. Creamy Cauliflower

Preparation time: 5 minutes

Cooking time: 20 minutes

Servings: 4

Ingredients

- 1 pound cauliflower florets
- 1 cup cream cheese, soft
- ½ cup mozzarella, shredded
- ½ cup coconut cream
- 4 bacon strips, cooked and chopped
- Salt and black pepper to the taste

Directions

1. In the air fryer's pan, mix the cauliflower with the cream cheese and the other ingredients, toss, introduce the pan in the machine and cook at 400 degrees F for 20 minutes.
2. Divide between plates and serve as a side dish.

Nutrition: Calories 203, Fat 13, Fiber 2, Carbs 5, Protein 9

183. Cumin Cauliflower

Preparation time: 5 minutes

Cooking time: 20 minutes

Servings: 4

Ingredients

- 1 pound cauliflower florets
- 1 teaspoon cumin, ground
- Juice of 1 lime
- 1 tablespoon butter, melted
- A pinch of salt and black pepper
- 1 tablespoon chives, chopped
- ¼ teaspoon cloves, ground

Directions

1. In the air fryer, mix the cauliflower with the cumin, lime juice and the other ingredients, toss and cook at 390 degrees F for 20 minutes.
2. Divide between plates and serve as a side dish.

Nutrition: Calories 182, Fat 8, Fiber 2, Carbs 4, Protein 8

184. Kale Mash

Preparation time: 5 minutes

Cooking time: 20 minutes

Servings: 4

Ingredients 2 tablespoons butter, melted

- 1 pound kale, torn
- 1 cup heavy cream
- 4 garlic cloves, minced
- 2 spring onions, chopped
- A pinch of salt and black pepper
- 1 tablespoon chives, chopped

Directions

1. In a pan that fits the air fryer, mix the kale with the butter, cream and the other ingredients, stir, introduce the pan in the machine and cook at 380 degrees F for 20 minutes.
2. Blend the mix using an immersion blender, divide between plates and serve.

Nutrition: Calories 198, Fat 9, Fiber 2, Carbs 6, Protein 8

185. Avocado and Cauliflower Mix

Preparation time: 5 minutes

Cooking time: 20 minutes

Servings: 4

Ingredients 2 pounds cauliflower florets

- 1 cup avocado, peeled, pitted and cubed
- Juice of 1 lime
- ½ teaspoon chili powder
- 1 tablespoon olive oil
- Salt and black pepper to the taste
- 2 garlic cloves, minced
- 1 red chili pepper, chopped

Directions

1. In a pan that fits the air fryer, mix the cauliflower with the avocado, lime juice and the other ingredients, toss, introduce the pan in the machine and cook at 380 degrees F for 20 minutes.
2. Divide between plates and serve as a side dish.

Nutrition: Calories 187, Fat 8, Fiber 2, Carbs 5, Protein 7

186. Creamy Broccoli Quinoa

Preparation time: 5 minutes

Cooking time: 20 minutes

Servings: 4

Ingredients

- 1 cup quinoa
- 1 cup veggie stock
- ½ cup broccoli florets
- 2 tablespoons butter, melted
- 1 tablespoon cilantro, chopped
- 2 tablespoons parmesan, grated

Directions

1. In a pan that fits your air fryer, mix the quinoa with the stock, broccoli and the other ingredients, stir, introduce in the fryer and cook at 360 degrees F for 20 minutes.
2. Divide between plates and serve as a side dish.

Nutrition: Calories 193, Fat 4, Fiber 3, Carbs 5, Protein 6

187. Tomato Quinoa

Preparation time: 5 minutes

Cooking time: 20 minutes

Servings: 4

Ingredients

- 2 tablespoons butter, melted
- 1 cup quinoa
- 1 cup chicken stock
- 1 cup tomatoes, cubed
- 1 tablespoon chives, chopped

Directions

1. In the air fryer's pan, mix the quinoa with the stock and the other ingredients, toss, introduce the pan in the fryer and cook at 360 degrees F for 20 minutes.
2. Divide between plates and serve as a side dish.

Nutrition: Calories 193, Fat 8, Fiber 2, Carbs 5, Protein 9

188. Lemon Leeks and Broccoli

Preparation time: 5 minutes

Cooking time: 20 minutes

Servings: 4

Ingredients

- 1 pound broccoli florets
- 2 leeks, sliced
- 2 tablespoons olive oil
- Juice of 1 lemon
- ½ teaspoon cumin, ground
- ½ teaspoon coriander, ground
- Salt and black pepper to the taste
- 2 garlic cloves, minced

Directions

1. In a pan that fits your air fryer, mix the broccoli with the leeks, oil and the other ingredients, toss, introduce the pan in the machine and cook at 360 degrees F for 20 minutes.
2. Divide between plates and serve as a side dish.

Nutrition: Calories 201, Fat 9, Fiber 2, Carbs 6, Protein 9

189. Balsamic Sweet Potatoes

Preparation time: 5 minutes

Cooking time: 20 minutes

Servings: 4

Ingredients

- 2 pounds sweet potatoes, peeled and cut into wedges
- 2 tablespoons balsamic vinegar
- 2 tablespoons olive oil
- 1 tablespoon parsley, chopped
- A pinch of salt and black pepper

Directions

1. In the air fryer's basket, mix the sweet potatoes with the vinegar and the other ingredients, toss and cook at 400 degrees F for 20 minutes.
2. Divide between plates and serve as a side dish.

Nutrition: Calories 203, Fat 9, Fiber 3, Carbs 6, Protein 5

190. Creamy Zucchini Noodles

Preparation time: 5 minutes

Cooking time: 15 minutes

Servings: 4

Ingredients

- 1 pound zucchinis, cut with a spiralizer
- 1 tablespoon olive oil
- 1 cup heavy cream
- ½ teaspoon turmeric powder
- 1 tablespoon chives, chopped
- Salt and black pepper to the taste
- 1 tablespoon basil, chopped

Directions

1. In a pan that fits your air fryer, mix the zucchini noodles with the oil, cream and the other ingredients, toss, introduce in the fryer and cook at 380 degrees F for 15 minutes. Divide between plates and serve as a side dish.

Nutrition: Calories 194, Fat 7, Fiber 2, Carbs 4, Protein 9

191. Zucchini and Cucumber Mix

Preparation time: 5 minutes

Cooking time: 15 minutes

Servings: 4

Ingredients

- 1 pound zucchinis, roughly cubed
- 1 cup cucumber, sliced
- 1 cup mozzarella, shredded
- 1 tablespoon olive oil
- Juice of 1 lime
- 1 tablespoon dill, chopped

Directions

1. In the air fryer's pan, mix the zucchinis with the cucumber and the other ingredients, toss, introduce in the air fryer and cook at 370 degrees F for 15

minutes. Divide between plates and serve as a side dish.

Nutrition: Calories 220, Fat 14, Fiber 2, Carbs 5, Protein 9

192. Coconut Artichokes

Preparation time: 5 minutes

Cooking time: 20 minutes

Servings: 4

Ingredients 1 tablespoon butter, melted

- 2 cups canned artichoke hearts, drained
- ½ cup heavy cream
- 1 tablespoon parmesan, grated - 1 tablespoon dill, chopped
- Salt and black pepper to the taste

Directions

1. In a pan that fits your air fryer, combine the artichokes with the butter, cream and the other ingredients, toss, introduce the pan in the air fryer and cook at 380 degrees F for 20 minutes.
2. Divide between plates and serve as a side dish.

Nutrition: Calories 195, Fat 6, Fiber 2, Carbs 4, Protein 8

193. Basil Squash

Preparation time: 5 minutes

Cooking time: 20 minutes

Servings: 4

Ingredients

- 1 pound butternut squash, peeled and cut into wedges
- 2 tablespoons olive oil

- 1 tablespoon basil, chopped
- ¼ cup lemon juice
- ½ teaspoon sweet paprika
- Salt and black pepper to the taste

Directions

1. In a pan that fits your air fryer, mix the squash with the oil, basil and the other ingredients, toss, introduce the pan in the air fryer and cook at 370 degrees F for 20 minutes.
2. Divide between plates and serve as a side dish.

Nutrition: Calories 201, Fat 7, Fiber 2, Carbs 4, Protein 9

194. Cheddar Green Beans

Preparation time: 5 minutes

Cooking time: 20 minutes

Servings: 4

Ingredients

- 2 pounds green beans, trimmed and halved
- 1 cup cheddar cheese, shredded
- 1 cup heavy cream
- 2 teaspoons turmeric powder
- 1 teaspoon turmeric powder
- A pinch of salt and black pepper

Directions

1. In the air fryer's pan, mix the green beans with the cheese, cream and the other ingredients, toss, put the pan in the machine and cook at 370 degrees F for 20 minutes.

2. Divide between plates and serve as a side dish.

Nutrition: Calories 120, Fat 5, Fiber 1, Carbs 4, Protein 2

195. Garlic Sprouts

Preparation time: 5 minutes

Cooking time: 20 minutes

Servings: 4

Ingredients **1** pound Brussels sprouts, trimmed and halved

- 3 garlic cloves, minced
- 1 tablespoon avocado oil
- Salt and black pepper to the taste
- Juice of ½ lemon

Directions

1. In the air fryer's pan, mix the sprouts with the garlic, oil and the other ingredients, toss, put the pan in the machine and cook at 400 degrees F for 20 minutes.
2. Divide between plates and serve.

Nutrition: Calories 173, Fat 12, Fiber 2, Carbs 5, Protein 7

196. Asparagus and Pineapple Mix

Preparation time: 5 minutes

Cooking time: 20 minutes

Servings: 4

Ingredients **1** pound asparagus stalks

- 1 cup pineapple, peeled and cubed
- 2 tablespoons avocado oil
- 1 tablespoon balsamic vinegar

- Salt and black pepper to the taste
- 1 teaspoon sweet paprika

Directions

1. In the air fryer's pan, mix the asparagus with the pineapple, oil and the other ingredients, toss, put the pan in the machine and cook at 370 degrees F for 20 minutes.
2. Divide between plates and serve.

Nutrition: Calories 187, Fat 6, Fiber 2, Carbs 4, Protein 9

197. Mustard Greens and Corn Mix

Preparation time: 5 minutes

Cooking time: 15 minutes

Servings: 4

Ingredients

- 1 pound mustard greens
- 1 cup corn
- 1 tablespoon olive oil
- 1 tablespoon balsamic vinegar
- A pinch of salt and black pepper
- 1 tablespoon chives, chopped

Directions

1. In a pan that fits your air fryer, mix the mustard greens with the corn, oil and the other ingredients, toss, introduce in the air fryer and cook at 360 degrees F for 15 minutes.

2. Divide between plates and serve as a side dish.

Nutrition: Calories 121, Fat 3, Fiber 4, Carbs 6, Protein 5

198. Hot Zucchini Rice

Preparation time: 5 minutes

Cooking time: 20 minutes

Servings: 4

Ingredients

- 1 cup wild rice
- 2 cups veggie stock
- ½ cup zucchinis, cubed
- 1 red onion, chopped
- ½ teaspoon chili powder
- 2 teaspoons olive oil
- Salt and black pepper to the taste
- ¼ cup parsley, chopped

Directions

1. In a pan that fits your air fryer, combine the rice with the stock, zucchinis and the other ingredients, introduce in the fryer and cook at 370 degrees F for 20 minutes.
2. Divide between plates and serve as a side dish.

Nutrition: Calories 200, Fat 6, Fiber 3, Carbs 4, Protein 5

199. Pesto Sweet Potatoes

Preparation time: 5 minutes

Cooking time: 25 minutes

Servings: 4

Ingredients

- 1 pound sweet potatoes, peeled and cut into wedges
- 2 tablespoons avocado oil
- 2 tablespoons basil pesto

- Juice of 1 lime
- 1 tablespoon cilantro, chopped
- Salt and black pepper to the taste

Directions

1. In the air fryer's basket, combine the sweet potatoes with the oil, pesto and the other ingredients, toss and cook at 370 degrees F for 25 minutes.
2. Divide between plates and serve as a side dish.

Nutrition: Calories 200, Fat 8, Fiber 2, Carbs 4, Protein 10

200. Sauteed Asparagus

Preparation time: 10 minutes

Cooking time: 8 minutes

Servings: 2

Ingredients

- 1 onion, chopped
- 1/2 lemon
- 14 oz asparagus
- 1 teaspoon ghee
- 1 teaspoon salt

Directions

1. Place the onion, salt, and ghee in the air fryer basket.
2. Cook it at 400 F for 2 minutes.
3. Meanwhile, chop the asparagus roughly.
4. Place the chopped asparagus in the air fryer basket.
5. Squeeze the lemon juice over the asparagus and stir it.
6. Cook the side dish for 6 minutes at 395 F. Stir it every 3 minutes of cooking.

7. Let the cooked asparagus chill little.
8. Enjoy!

Nutrition: Calories 86, Fat 2.5, Fiber 5.9, Carbs 14.8, Protein 5.2

201. Roasted Apple with Bacon

Preparation time: 20 minutes
Cooking time: 10 minutes
Servings: 8
Ingredients

- 6 apples
- 7 oz bacon, chopped
- ½ teaspoon salt
- ½ teaspoon paprika
- ½ teaspoon ground black pepper
- 1 tablespoon avocado oil

Directions

1. Make the medium holes in the apples.
2. Combine together the chopped bacon, salt, paprika, ground black pepper, and avocado oil.
3. Stir the mixture. Fill the apple holes with the bacon mixture. Put the apples in the air fryer basket.
4. Cook the apples for 10 minutes at 380 F. When the time is over and the apples are cooked – chill them for 6 minutes and serve!

Nutrition: Calories 224, Fat 10.9, Fiber 4.2, Carbs 23.7, Protein 9.7

202. Fennel Slices

Preparation time: 10 minutes
Cooking time: 10 minutes
Servings: 2
Ingredients

- 12 oz fennel bulb
- 1 teaspoon paprika
- ½ teaspoon chili flakes
- 1 tablespoon olive oil
- 1 teaspoon cilantro, dried

Directions

1. Slice the fennel bulb and sprinkle it with the paprika, chili flakes, and dried cilantro on each side.
2. Then sprinkle the fennel with the olive oil and transfer the vegetables to the air fryer basket.
3. Cook the fennel slices for 10 minutes at 380 F. Flip the fennel slices into another side after 5 minutes of cooking.
4. Enjoy the cooked side dish!

Nutrition: Calories 116, Fat 7.5, Fiber 5.7, Carbs 13, Protein 2.3

203. Butternut Squash Rice

Preparation time: 10 minutes
Cooking time: 20 minutes
Servings: 4
Ingredients

- 1-pound butternut squash
- 1 tablespoon ghee
- 1 onion, diced
- 1 teaspoon salt
- 1 oz fresh parsley, chopped
- 1 tablespoon olive oil

Directions

1. Chop the butternut squash into the rice pieces.
2. Put the ghee in the air fryer basket and add diced onion.
3. Sprinkle the onion with the salt and olive oil.
4. Cook it at 400 F for 2 minutes.

5. Then stir the onion and add the butternut squash rice. Stir it and cook the meal for 18 minutes at 380 F. Stir the squash every 4 minutes.
6. When the meal is cooked – sprinkle it with the chopped parsley and stir.
7. Serve it immediately!

Nutrition: Calories 123, Fat 6.9, Fiber 3.1, Carbs 16.3, Protein 1.7

204. Eggplant Lasagna

Preparation time: 20 minutes

Cooking time: 30 minutes

Servings: 3

Ingredients

- 1 eggplant
- 2 tomatoes
- 1 tablespoon olive oil
- 1 onion, diced
- 1 garlic clove, chopped
- 1 teaspoon dried basil
- 1 teaspoon ground black pepper
- ½ teaspoon turmeric
- 1 teaspoon cumin
- ½ cup chicken stock
- 1 tablespoon fresh dill, chopped
- 4 oz mushrooms, chopped

Directions

1. Slice the eggplants.
2. Slice the tomatoes.
3. Combine together the diced onion, olive oil, chopped garlic, dried basil, ground black pepper, turmeric, cumin, and fresh dill in the bowl.
4. Stir the mixture.
5. Then make the layer of the sliced eggplants in the air fryer basket.

6. Sprinkle it with the spice mixture.
7. Put the tomatoes over the eggplants and add mushrooms.
8. Sprinkle the vegetables with the spice mixture and repeat all the steps till you finish all the ingredients.
9. Add chicken stock and cook lasagna for 30 minutes at 365 F. Let the cooked lasagna chill little and serve it!

Nutrition: Calories 127, Fat 5.6, Fiber 8, Carbs 18.9, Protein 4.4

205. Stuffed Eggplants with Cherry Tomatoes

Preparation time: 15 minutes

Cooking time: 25 minutes

Servings: 2

Ingredients

- 1 eggplant
- 5 oz cherry tomatoes
- 1 shallot, chopped
- ½ teaspoon salt
- ¾ teaspoon nutmeg
- ¾ teaspoon chili pepper
- 1 tablespoon olive oil

Directions

1. Cut the eggplant into the halves.
2. Remove the meat from the eggplants.
3. Chop the cherry tomatoes and combine them together with the salt, shallot, nutmeg, chili pepper, and olive oil. Stir the mixture.
4. Fill the eggplants with the vegetables.
5. Put the stuffed vegetables in the air fryer basket and cook for 25 minutes at 370 F. Then chill the cooked eggplants little. Serve!

Nutrition: Calories 136, Fat 7.9, Fiber 9.2, Carbs 16.9, Protein 3

206. Eggplant Satay

Preparation time: 15 minutes

Cooking time: 18 minutes

Servings: 3

Ingredients *3 eggplants*

- 1 tablespoon vinegar
- 1 tablespoon olive oil
- 1 teaspoon sesame seeds
- 1 teaspoon dried dill
- ½ teaspoon dried parsley
- ½ teaspoon ground nutmeg

Directions

1. Cut the eggplants into the cubes.
2. Then skew the eggplant onto the skewers.
3. Sprinkle the eggplants with the olive oil, vinegar, sesame seeds, dried dill, dried parsley, and ground nutmeg.
4. Place the eggplant satay in the air fryer basket and cook it for 18 minutes at 375 F.
5. When the eggplants are soft – the meal is cooked.
6. Let it chill little and serve!

Nutrition: Calories 187, Fat 6.3, Fiber 19.6, Carbs 32.9, Protein 5.7

207. Chinese Eggplant with Chili and Garlic

Preparation time: 10 minutes

Cooking time: 24 minutes

Servings: 4

Ingredients

- 2 eggplants
- 1 chili pepper, chopped
- 1 garlic clove, chopped
- ¼ teaspoon ground coriander
- 1 tablespoon olive oil
- ¼ teaspoon salt
- 1 tablespoon vinegar
- 3 teaspoon water
- ¼ teaspoon chili flakes

Directions

1. Peel the eggplants and chop them.
2. Put the chopped eggplants in the air fryer basket.
3. Add chopped garlic, chili pepper, ground coriander, salt, and water.
4. Stir the vegetables and cook for 24 minutes at 365 F.
5. When the eggplants are soft – transfer them to the bowl and sprinkle with the chili flakes and vinegar.
6. Stir well and serve immediately!

Nutrition: Calories 101, Fat 4, Fiber 9.7, Carbs 16.5, Protein 2.8

208. Thyme Mushrooms and Carrot Bowl

Preparation time: 10 minutes

Cooking time: 20 minutes

Servings: 4

Ingredients 1 cup baby carrot

- 8 oz mushrooms, sliced
- 1 teaspoon thyme
- 1 teaspoon salt
- 1 cup chicken stock
- 1 teaspoon chili flakes
- 1 teaspoon coconut oil

Directions

1. Place the baby carrot in the air fryer basket.
2. Add thyme, salt, and chili flakes.
3. Cook the baby carrot for 10 minutes at 380 F.
4. Then add the sliced mushrooms and coconut oil.
5. Stir it well and cook the vegetables for 10 minutes more at 370 F.
6. Stir the vegetables after 5 minutes of cooking.
7. Chill the cooked side dish and enjoy!

Nutrition: Calories 25, Fat 1.5, Fiber 0.7, Carbs 2.2, Protein 2

209. Sesame Mushroom Slices

Preparation time: 10 minutes

Cooking time: 6 minutes

Servings: 3

Ingredients

- 1 tablespoon sesame seeds
- 1 tablespoon avocado oil
- 14 oz mushrooms, sliced
- 1 teaspoon chili flakes
- ¼ teaspoon ground paprika

Directions

1. Put the sliced mushrooms in the air fryer basket.
2. Add chili flakes and ground paprika.
3. Then add avocado oil and stir the mushrooms.
4. Cook the mushrooms for 4 minutes at 400 F. Stir the mushrooms after 2 minutes of cooking.
5. Sprinkle the mushrooms with the sesame seeds and stir well.
6. Cook the mushrooms for 2 minutes more at the same temperature.

7. Serve the mushrooms immediately!

Nutrition: Calories 52, Fat 2.5, Fiber 2, Carbs 5.4, Protein 4.8

210. Popcorn Mushrooms

Preparation time: 10 minutes

Cooking time: 10 minutes

Servings: 4

Ingredients

- 16 oz mushrooms
- 2 tablespoons almond flour
- 2 tablespoons water
- ½ teaspoon minced garlic
- 1 tablespoon olive oil
- ¼ teaspoon chili flakes

Directions

1. Mix up together the almond flour, water, minced garlic, and chili flakes in the bowl. Stir the mixture.
2. Coat the mushrooms with the almond flour mixture.
3. Spray the olive oil inside the air fryer basket.
4. Put the mushrooms and cook them for 10 minutes at 365 F.
5. Stir the mushrooms every 2 minutes.
6. Serve the cooked popcorn mushrooms only hot!

Nutrition: Calories 135, Fat 10.8, Fiber 2.6, Carbs 6.9, Protein 6.6

211. Leek Saute

Preparation time: 10 minutes

Cooking time: 15 minutes

Servings: 2

Ingredients

- 10 oz leek, chopped

- 8 oz mushrooms, chopped
- 1 shallot, chopped
- 2 teaspoons olive oil
- ¼ teaspoon salt
- ½ teaspoon chili flakes

Directions

1. Put the chopped mushrooms in the air fryer basket.
2. Add olive oil and salt.
3. Then sprinkle the mushrooms with the chili flakes and stir well.
4. Cook the mushrooms for 5 minutes at 365 F.
5. Stir the mushrooms and add chopped shallot and leek.
6. Stir the vegetables.
7. Continue to cook the vegetables for 10 minutes more at 360 F.
8. Stir the vegetable time to time.
9. When all the ingredients are soft – the meal is cooked.

Nutrition: Calories 151, Fat 5.4, Fiber 3.7, Carbs 23.9, Protein 5.7

212. Sweet Potato Hasselback

Preparation time: 15 minutes

Cooking time: 35 minutes

Servings: 4

Ingredients

- 4 sweet potatoes
- 4 garlic cloves, peeled
- ½ teaspoon thyme
- 1 tablespoon olive oil
- 1 teaspoon dried basil
- ½ teaspoon dried oregano
- 1 teaspoon chili flakes
- 3 tablespoons water

Directions

1. Peel the sweet potatoes and cut them into the shape of the Hasselback.
2. Put the sweet potatoes in the air fryer basket and cook them at 360 F for 20 minutes.
3. Meanwhile, mix up together the thyme, olive oil, dried basil, dried oregano, chili flakes, and water.
4. Chop the garlic and add it to the mixture too.
5. Stir the spices.
6. Brush the Hasselback sweet potatoes with the spice mixture generously.
7. Cook the meal for 15 minutes more.
8. When the meal is cooked – let it chill little.
9. Enjoy!

Nutrition: Calories 36, Fat 3.6, Fiber 0.2, Carbs 1.3, Protein 0.2

213. Stuffed Tomatoes

Preparation time: 20 minutes

Cooking time: 15 minutes

Servings: 2

Ingredients

- 7 oz mushrooms, chopped
- 1 teaspoon minced garlic
- 1 tablespoon fresh dill, chopped
- 1 onion diced
- 2 tomatoes
- 1 tablespoon olive oil
- ½ teaspoon chili flakes

Directions

1. Remove the meat from the tomatoes to make the tomato cups.
2. Combine together the chopped mushrooms, minced garlic, fresh dill, diced onion, olive oil, and chili flakes.

3. Stir the mixture well.
4. Fill the tomato cups with the mushroom mixture and put them in the air fryer.
5. Cook the side dish for 15 minutes at 360 F.
6. When the tomatoes are cooked – let them rest for 5 minutes and serve!

Nutrition: Calories 132, Fat 7.7, Fiber 3.9, Carbs 14.5, Protein 5.2

214. Ratatouille Kebabs

Preparation time: 10 minutes

Cooking time: 20 minutes

Servings: 4

Ingredients

- 1 eggplant
- 1 sweet pepper
- 1 zucchini
- 1 onion, peeled
- 1 tomato
- 1 tablespoon olive oil
- ½ teaspoon chili flakes
- ½ teaspoon ground coriander
- ½ teaspoon salt

Directions

1. Slice the eggplant, zucchini, and onion.
2. Cut the sweet pepper and tomato into the squares.
3. Skew the vegetables on the skewers.
4. Then sprinkle the vegetables with the olive oil, chili flakes, ground coriander, and salt.
5. Put the kebabs in the air fryer basket and cook for 20 minutes at 360 F.
6. Then transfer the cooked kebabs on the serving plate gently.

7. Enjoy!

Nutrition: Calories 90, Fat 3.9, Fiber 5.8, Carbs 13.8, Protein 2.5

215. Caramelized Onion Quesadilla

Preparation Time: 10 minutes

Cooking Time: 25 minutes

Servings: 4

Ingredients:

- A whole grain of tortilla
- 1 big caramelize onion
- 1 cup of fresh spinach
- Black beans
- Cheese (Nonfat)

Directions:

1. Slice the onion
2. On a medium heat, heat the onion, use dry sautéing to caramelize
3. Add a pinch of salt so that it can bring out the moisture out of the onion
4. Cook it until the color changes to brown and translucent, then set it aside.
5. Heat your tortilla in a skillet
6. Then add your beans, spinach and onion mixture in one side of the tortilla
7. Add your cheese and fold over the tortilla

Nutrition:

Protein: 13.9 g Carbohydrates: 40.9 g

Dietary Fiber: 3 g Sugars: 3.2 g

Fat: 26 g Cholesterol: 40 mg

216. Roasted Garlic Potatoes

Preparation Time: 5 minutes

Cooking Time: 1 hour

Servings: 6

Ingredients:

- 1 Teaspoon of dried or fresh chopped rosemary
- 6 cups of potatoes (unpeeled)
- 1 teaspoon of onion powder
- 1teaspoon of pepper (freshly ground)

Directions:

1. Preheat the oven to 425F
2. Toss the potatoes and mix with rosemary, garlic, onion powder, salt and pepper to enable it to coat
3. On an even layer over the already prepared baking sheet, spread the potatoes and bake for 20 minutes
4. Stir potatoes to promote even browning of the potatoes.
5. Continue for about 3 to 10 minutes until the potato becomes browner and more tender.
6. Remove from the oven and serve it warm

Nutrition:

Protein: 2.8 g

Carbohydrates: 23.5 g

Dietary Fiber: 2.2 g

Sugars: 1.7 g

Fat: 7.9 g

Cholesterol: 16.5 mg

CHAPTER 10:

Dessert Recipes

217. Tasty Banana Cake

Preparation Time: 10 minutes

Cooking Time: 30 Minutes

Servings: 4

Ingredients:

- 1 tbsp. butter, soft
- 1 egg
- 1/3 cup brown sugar
- 2 tbsp. honey
- 1 banana
- 1 cup white flour
- 1 tbsp. baking powder
- ½ tbsp. cinnamon powder
- Cooking spray

Directions:

1. Spurt cake pan with cooking spray.
2. Mix in butter with honey, sugar, banana, cinnamon, egg, flour and baking powder in a bowl then beat.
3. Empty mix in cake pan with cooking spray, put into air fryer and cook at 350°F for 30 minutes.
4. Allow for cooling, slice.
5. Serve.

Nutrition:

Calories: 435

Total Fat: 7g

Total carbs: 15g

218. Simple Cheesecake

Preparation Time: 10 minutes

Cooking Time: 15 Minutes

Servings: 15

Ingredients:

- 1 lb. cream cheese
- ½ tbsp. vanilla extract
- 2 eggs
- 4 tbsp. sugar
- 1 cup graham crackers
- 2 tbsp. butter

Directions:

1. Mix in butter with crackers in a bowl.
2. Compress crackers blend to the bottom cake pan, put into air fryer and cook at 350° F for 4 minutes.
3. Mix cream cheese with sugar, vanilla, egg in a bowl and beat properly.
4. Sprinkle filling on crackers crust and cook cheesecake in air fryer at 310° F for 15 minutes.
5. Keep cake in fridge for 3 hours, slice.
6. Serve.

Nutrition: Calories: 257

Total Fat: 18g

Total carbs: 22g

219. Bread Pudding

Preparation Time: 10 minutes

Cooking Time: 10 Minutes

Servings: 4

Ingredients:

- 6 glazed doughnuts
- 1 cup cherries
- 4 egg yolks
- 1 and ½ cups whipping cream
- ½ cup raisins
- ¼ cup sugar
- ½ cup chocolate chips.

Directions:

1. Mix in cherries with whipping cream and egg in a bowl then turn properly.
2. Mix in raisins with chocolate chips, sugar and doughnuts in a bowl then stir.
3. Mix the 2 mixtures, pour into oiled pan then into air fryer and cook at 310° F for 1 hour.
4. Cool pudding before cutting.
5. Serve.

Nutrition:

Calories: 456

Total Fat: 11g

Total carbs: 6g

220. Bread Dough and Amaretto Dessert

Preparation Time: 15 minutes

Cooking Time: 8 Minutes

Servings: 12

Ingredients:

- 1 lb. bread dough
- 1 cup sugar
- ½ cup butter
- 1 cup heavy cream
- 12 oz. chocolate chips
- 2 tbsp. amaretto liqueur

Directions:

1. Turn dough, cut into 20 slices and cut each piece in halves.
2. Sweep dough pieces with spray sugar, butter, put into air fryer's basket and cook them at 350°F for 5 minutes. Turn them, cook for 3 minutes still. Move to a platter.
3. Melt the heavy cream in pan over medium heat, put chocolate chips and turn until they melt.
4. Put in liqueur, turn and move to a bowl.
5. Serve bread dippers with the sauce.

Nutrition:

Calories: 179

Total Fat: 18g

Total carbs: 17g

221. Wrapped Pears

Preparation Time: 10 minutes

Cooking Time: 10 Minutes

Servings: 4

Ingredients:

- 4 puff pastry sheets
- 14 oz. vanilla custard
- 2 pears
- 1 egg
- ½ tbsp. cinnamon powder
- 2 tbsp. sugar

Directions:

1. Put wisp pastry slices on flat surface, add spoonful of vanilla custard at the center of each, add pear halves and wrap.

2. Sweep pears with egg, cinnamon and spray sugar, put into air fryer's basket and cook at 320°F for 15 minutes.
3. Split parcels on plates.
4. Serve.

Nutrition:

Calories: 285

Total Fat: 14g

Total carbs: 30g

222. Air Fried Bananas

Preparation Time: 5 minutes

Cooking Time: 10 Minutes

Servings: 4

Ingredients:

- 3 tbsp. butter
- 2 eggs
- 8 bananas
- ½ cup corn flour
- 3 tbsp. cinnamon sugar
- 1 cup panko

Directions:

1. Warm up pan with the butter over medium heat, put panko, turn and cook for 4 minutes then move to a bowl.
2. Spin each in flour, panko, egg blend, assemble them in air fryer's basket, grime with cinnamon sugar and cook at 280° F for 10 minutes.
3. Serve immediately.

Nutrition:

Calories: 337

Total Fat: 3g

Total carbs: 23g

223. Cocoa Cake

Preparation Time: 5 minutes

Cooking Time: 17 Minutes

Servings: 6

Ingredients:

- oz. butter
- 3 eggs
- 3 oz. sugar
- 1 tbsp. cocoa powder
- 3 oz. flour
- ½ tbsp. lemon juice

Directions:

1. Mix in 1 tablespoon butter with cocoa powder in a bowl and beat.
2. Mix in the rest of the butter with eggs, flour, sugar and lemon juice in another bowl, blend properly and move half into a cake pan
3. Put half of the cocoa blend, spread, add the rest of the butter layer and crest with remaining cocoa.
4. Put into air fryer and cook at 360° F for 17 minutes.
5. Allow to cool before slicing.
6. Serve.

Nutrition:

Calories: 221

Total Fat: 5g

Total carbs: 12g

224. Apple Bread

Preparation Time: 5 minutes

Cooking Time: 40 Minutes

Servings: 6

Ingredients:

- 3 cups apples
- 1 cup sugar
- 1 tbsp. vanilla

- 2 eggs
- 1 tbsp. apple pie spice
- 2 cups white flour
- 1 tbsp. baking powder
- 1 stick butter
- 1 cup water

Directions:

1. Mix in egg with 1 butter stick, sugar, apple pie spice and turn using mixer.
2. Put apples and turn properly.
3. Mix baking powder with flour in another bowl and turn.
4. Blend the 2 mixtures, turn and move it to spring form pan.
5. Get spring form pan into air fryer and cook at 320°F for 40 minutes
6. Slice.
7. Serve.

Nutrition:

Calories: 401 Total Fat: 9g

Total carbs: 29g

225. Banana Bread

Preparation Time: 5 minutes

Cooking Time: 40 Minutes

Servings: 6

Ingredients:

- ¾ cup sugar
- 1/3 cup butter
- 1 tbsp. vanilla extract
- 1 egg
- 2 bananas
- 1 tbsp. baking powder
- 1 and ½ cups flour
- ½ tbsp. baking soda
- 1/3 cup milk
- 1 and ½ tbsp. cream of tartar
- Cooking spray

Directions:

1. Mix in milk with cream of tartar, vanilla, egg, sugar, bananas and butter in a bowl and turn whole.
2. Mix in flour with baking soda and baking powder.
3. Blend the 2 mixtures, turn properly, move into oiled pan with cooking spray, put into air fryer and cook at 320°F for 40 minutes.
4. Remove bread, allow to cool, slice.
5. Serve.

Nutrition:

Calories: 540

Total Fat: 16g

Total carbs: 28g

226. Mini Lava Cakes

Preparation Time: 5 minutes

Cooking Time: 20 Minutes

Servings: 3

Ingredients:

- 1 egg
- 4 tbsp. sugar
- 2 tbsp. olive oil
- 4 tbsp. milk
- 4 tbsp. flour
- 1 tbsp. cocoa powder
- ½ tbsp. baking powder
- ½ tbsp. orange zest

Directions:

1. Mix in egg with sugar, flour, salt, oil, milk, orange zest, baking powder and cocoa powder, turn properly. Move it to oiled ramekins.
2. Put ramekins in air fryer and cook at 320°F for 20 minutes.

3. Serve warm.

Nutrition: Calories: 329

Total Fat: 8.5g Total carbs: 12.4g

227. Crispy Apples
Preparation Time: 10 minutes
Cooking Time: 10 Minutes
Servings: 4
Ingredients:

- 2 tbsp. cinnamon powder
- 5 apples
- ½ tbsp. nutmeg powder
- 1 tbsp. maple syrup
- ½ cup water
- 4 tbsp. butter
- ¼ cup flour
- ¾ cup oats
- ¼ cup brown sugar

Directions:

1. Get the apples in a pan, put in nutmeg, maple syrup, cinnamon and water.
2. Mix in butter with flour, sugar, salt and oat, turn, put spoonful of blend over apples, get into air fryer and cook at 350°F for 10 minutes.
3. Serve while warm.

Nutrition: Calories: 387 Total Fat: 5.6g

Total carbs: 12.4g

228. Ginger Cheesecake
Preparation Time: 20 minutes
Cooking Time: 20 Minutes
Servings: 6
Ingredients:

- 2 tbsp. butter
- ½ cup ginger cookies
- 16 oz. cream cheese

- 2 eggs
- ½ cup sugar
- 1 tbsp. rum
- ½ tbsp. vanilla extract
- ½ tbsp. nutmeg

Directions:

1. Spread pan with the butter and sprinkle cookie crumbs on the bottom.
2. Whisk cream cheese with rum, vanilla, nutmeg and eggs, beat properly and sprinkle the cookie crumbs.
3. Put in air fryer and cook at 340° F for 20 minutes.
4. Allow cheese cake to cool in fridge for 2 hours before slicing.
5. Serve.

Nutrition:

Calories: 312

Total Fat: 9.8g

Total carbs: 18g

229. Cocoa Cookies
Preparation Time: 10 minutes
Cooking Time: 14 Minutes
Servings: 12
Ingredients:

- 6 oz. coconut oil
- 6 eggs
- 3 oz. cocoa powder
- 2 tbsp. vanilla
- ½ tbsp. baking powder
- 4 oz. cream cheese
- 5 tbsp. sugar

Directions:

1. Mix in eggs with coconut oil, baking powder, cocoa powder, cream cheese, vanilla in a blender and sway and turn using a mixer.
2. Get it into a lined baking dish and into the fryer at 320°F and bake for 14 minutes.
3. Split cookie sheet into rectangles.
4. Serve.

Nutrition:

Calories: 149 Total Fat: 2.4g

Total carbs: 27.2g

230. Special Brownies

Preparation Time: 10 minutes

Cooking Time: 22 Minutes

Servings: 4

Ingredients:

- 1 egg
- 1/3 cup cocoa powder
- 1/3 cup sugar
- 7 tbsp. butter
- ½ tbsp. vanilla extract
- ¼ cup white flour
- ¼ cup walnuts
- ½ tbsp. baking powder
- 1 tbsp. peanut butter

Directions:

1. Warm pan with 6 tablespoons butter and the sugar over medium heat, turn, cook for 5 minutes, move to a bowl, put salt, egg, cocoa powder, vanilla extract, walnuts, baking powder and flour, turn mix properly and into a pan.
2. Mix peanut butter with one tablespoon butter in a bowl, heat in microwave for some seconds, turn

properly and sprinkle brownies blend over.

3. Put in air fryer and bake at 320° F and bake for 17 minutes.
4. Allow brownies to cool, cut.
5. Serve.

Nutrition:

Calories: 438 Total Fat: 18g

Total carbs: 16.5g

231. Blueberry Scones

Preparation Time: 10 minutes

Cooking Time: 10 Minutes

Servings: 10

Ingredients:

- 1 cup white flour
- 1 cup blueberries
- 2 eggs
- ½ cup heavy cream
- ½ cup butter
- 5 tbsp. sugar
- 2 tbsp. vanilla extract
- 2 tbsp. baking powder

Directions:

1. Mix in flour, baking powder, salt and blueberries in a bowl and turn.
2. Mix heavy cream with vanilla extract, sugar, butter and eggs and turn properly.
3. Blend the 2 mixtures, squeeze till dough is ready, obtain 10 triangles from mix, put on baking sheet into air fryer and cook them at 320°F for 10 minutes.
4. Serve cold.

Nutrition:

Calories: 525 Total Fat: 21g

Total carbs: 37g

232. Yogurt Mint

Preparation Time: 5 minutes

Cooking Time: 10 minutes

Servings: 2

Ingredients:

- 1 cup of water
- 5 cups of milk
- ¾ cup plain yogurt
- ¼ cup fresh mint
- 1 tbsp. maple syrup

Directions:

1. Add 1 cup water to the Instant Pot Pressure Cooker.
2. Press the STEAM function button and adjust to 1 minute.
3. Once done, add the milk, then press the YOGURT function button and allow boiling.
4. Add yogurt and fresh mint, then stir well.
5. Pour into a glass and add maple syrup.
6. Enjoy.

Nutrition:

Calories: 25

Fat: 0.5 g

Carbs: 5 g

Protein: 2 g

233. Chocolate Fondue

Preparation Time: 5 minutes

Cooking Time: 10 minutes

Servings: 2

Ingredients:

- 1 cup water
- ½ tsp. sugar
- ½ cup coconut cream
- ¾ cup dark chocolate, chopped

Directions:

1. Pour the water into your Instant Pot.
2. To a heatproof bowl, add the chocolate, sugar, and coconut cream.
3. Place in the Instant Pot.
4. Seal the lid, select MANUAL, and cook for 2 minutes. When ready, do a quick release and carefully open the lid. Stir well and serve immediately.

Nutrition:

Calories: 216

Fat: 17 g

Carbs: 11 g

Protein: 2 g

234. Rice Pudding

Preparation Time: 5 minutes

Cooking Time: 12 minutes

Servings: 2

Ingredients:

- ½ cup short grain rice
- ¼ cup of sugar
- 1 cinnamon stick
- 1½ cup milk
- 1 slice lemon peel
- Salt to taste

Directions:

1. Rinse the rice under cold water.
2. Put the milk, cinnamon stick, sugar, salt, and lemon peel inside the Instant Pot Pressure Cooker.
3. Close the lid, lock in place, and make sure to seal the valve. Press the PRESSURE button and cook for 10 minutes on HIGH.
4. When the timer beeps, choose the QUICK PRESSURE release. This will take about 2 minutes.

5. Remove the lid. Open the pressure cooker and discard the lemon peel and cinnamon stick. Spoon in a serving bowl and serve.

Nutrition:
Calories: 111
Fat: 6 g
Carbs: 21 g
Protein: 3 g

235. Braised Apples
Preparation Time: 5 minutes
Cooking Time: 12 minutes
Servings: 2
Ingredients:

- 2 cored apples
- ½ cup of water
- ½ cup red wine
- 3 tbsp. sugar
- ½ tsp. ground cinnamon

Directions:

1. In the bottom of Instant Pot, add the water and place apples.
2. Pour wine on top and sprinkle with sugar and cinnamon. Close the lid carefully and cook for 10 minutes at HIGH PRESSURE.
3. When done, do a quick pressure release.
4. Transfer the apples onto serving plates and top with cooking liquid.
5. Serve immediately.

Nutrition:
Calories: 245
Fat: 0.5 g
Carbs: 53 g
Protein: 1 g

236. Wine Figs
Preparation Time: 5 minutes
Cooking Time: 3 minutes
Servings: 2
Ingredients:

- ½ cup pine nuts
- 1 cup red wine
- 1 lb. figs
- Sugar, as needed

Directions:

1. Slowly pour the wine and sugar into the Instant Pot.
2. Arrange the trivet inside it; place the figs over it. Close the lid and lock. Ensure that you have sealed the valve to avoid leakage.
3. Press MANUAL mode and set timer to 3 minutes.
4. After the timer reads zero, press CANCEL and quick-release pressure.
5. Carefully remove the lid.
6. Divide figs into bowls, and drizzle wine from the pot over them.
7. Top with pine nuts and enjoy.

Nutrition:
Calories: 95
Fat: 3 g
Carbs: 5 g
Protein: 2 g

237. Lemon Curd
Preparation Time: 10 minutes
Cooking Time: 10 minutes
Servings: 2
Ingredients:

- 4 tbsp. butter
- 1 cup sugar
- 2/3 cup lemon juice

- 3 eggs
- 2 tsp. lemon zest
- 1 ½ cups of water

Directions:

1. Whisk the butter and sugar thoroughly until smooth.
2. Add 2 whole eggs and incorporate just the yolk of the other egg.
3. Add the lemon juice.
4. Transfer the mixture into the two jars and tightly seal the tops
5. Pour 1 ½ cups of water into the bottom of the Instant Pot and place in steaming rack. Put the jars on the rack and cook on HIGH PRESSURE for 10 minutes.
6. Natural-release the pressure for 10 minutes before quick releasing the rest.
7. Stir in the zest and put the lids back on the jars.

Nutrition:

Calories: 45

Fat: 1 g

Carbs: 8 g

Protein: 1 g

238. Rhubarb Dessert

Preparation Time: 4 minutes

Cooking Time: 5 minutes

Servings: 2

Ingredients:

- 3 cups rhubarb, chopped
- 1 tbsp. ghee, melted
- 1/3 cup water
- 1 tbsp. stevia
- 1 tsp. vanilla extract

Directions:

1. Put all the listed **Ingredients:** in your Instant Pot, cover, and cook on HIGH for 5 minutes.
2. Divide into small bowls and serve cold.
3. Enjoy!

Nutrition:

Calories: 83

Fat: 2 g

Carbs: 2 g

Protein: 2 g

239. Raspberry Compote

Preparation Time: 11 minutes

Cooking Time: 30 minutes

Servings: 2

Ingredients:

- 1 cup raspberries
- ½ cup Swerve
- 1 tsp freshly grated lemon zest
- 1 tsp vanilla extract
- 2 cups water

Directions:

1. Press the SAUTÉ button on your Instant Pot, then add all the listed Ingredients.
2. Stir well and pour in 1 cup of water.
3. Cook for 5 minutes, continually stirring, then pour in 1 more cup of water and press the CANCEL button.
4. Secure the lid properly, press the MANUAL button, and set the timer to 15 minutes on LOW pressure.
5. When the timer buzzes, press the CANCEL button and release the pressure naturally for 10minutes.

6. Move the pressure handle to the "venting" position to release any remaining pressure and open the lid.
7. Let it cool before serving.

Nutrition:
Calories: 48
Fat: 0.5 g
Carbs: 5 g
Protein: 1 g

240. Poached Pears
Preparation Time: 8 minutes
Cooking Time: 10 minutes
Servings: 2
Ingredients:

- 1 tbsp. lime juice
- 2 tsp. lime zest
- 1 cinnamon stick
- 2 whole pears, peeled
- 1 cup of water
- Fresh mint leaves for garnish

Directions:

1. Add all **Ingredients:** except for the mint leaves to the Instant Pot.
2. Seal the Instant Pot and choose the MANUAL button.
3. Cook on HIGH for 10 minutes.
4. Perform a natural pressure release.
5. Remove the pears from the pot.
6. Serve in bowls and garnish with mint on top.

Nutrition:
Calories: 59
Fat: 0.1 g
Carbs: 14 g
Protein: 0.3 g

241. Apple Crisp
Preparation Time: 10 minutes
Cooking Time: 13 minutes
Servings: 2
Ingredients:

- 2 apples, sliced into chunks
- 1 tsp. cinnamon
- ¼ cup rolled oats
- 1/4 cup brown sugar
- ½ cup of water

Directions:

1. Put all the listed Ingredients: in the pot and mix well.
2. Seal the pot, choose MANUAL mode, and cook at HIGH pressure for 8 minutes.
3. Release the pressure naturally and let sit for 5 minutes or until the sauce has thickened.
4. Serve and enjoy.

Nutrition:
Calories: 218
Fat: 5 mg
Carbs: 54 g

242. Apple Couscous Pudding
Preparation Time: 10 minutes
Cooking Time: 25 minutes
Servings: 4
Ingredients:

- ½ cup couscous
- 1 and ½ cups milk
- ¼ cup apple, cored and chopped
- 3 tablespoons stevia
- ½ teaspoon rose water
- 1 tablespoon orange zest, grated

Directions:

1. Heat up a pan with the milk over medium heat,
2. add the couscous and the rest of the ingredients, whisk, simmer for 25 minutes, divide into bowls and serve.

Nutrition:

Calories 150 Fat 4.5

Fiber 5.5 Carbs 7.5

Protein 4

243. Ricotta Ramekins

Preparation Time: 10 minutes

Cooking Time: 1 hour

Servings: 4

Ingredients:

- 6 eggs, whisked
- 1 and ½ pounds ricotta cheese, soft
- ½ pound stevia
- 1 teaspoon vanilla extract
- ½ teaspoon baking powder
- Cooking spray

Directions:

1. In a bowl, mix the eggs with the ricotta and the other ingredients except the cooking spray and whisk well.
2. Grease 4 ramekins with the cooking spray, pour the ricotta cream in each and bake at 360 degrees F for 1 hour.
3. Serve cold.

Nutrition:

Calories 180 Fat 5.3

Fiber 5.4

Carbs 11.5

Protein 4

244. Papaya Cream

Preparation Time: 10 minutes

Cooking Time: 0 minutes

Servings: 2

Ingredients:

- 1 cup papaya, peeled and chopped
- 1 cup heavy cream
- 1 tablespoon stevia
- ½ teaspoon vanilla extract

Directions:

1. In a blender, combine the cream with the papaya and the other ingredients, pulse well, divide into cups and serve cold.

Nutrition:

Calories 182

Fat 3.1

Fiber 2.3

Carbs 3.5

Protein 2

245. Almonds and Oats Pudding

Preparation Time: 10 minutes

Cooking Time: 15 minutes

Servings: 4

Ingredients:

- 1 tablespoon lemon juice
- Zest of 1 lime
- 1 and ½ cups almond milk
- 1 teaspoon almond extract
- ½ cup oats
- 2 tablespoons stevia
- ½ cup silver almonds, chopped

Directions:

1. In a pan, combine the almond milk with the lime zest and the other ingredients, whisk, bring to a simmer

and cook over medium heat for 15 minutes.

2. Divide the mix into bowls and serve cold.

Nutrition:

Calories 174

Fat 12.1

Fiber 3.2

Carbs 3.9

Protein 4.8

246. Strawberry Sorbet

Preparation Time: 15 minutes

Cooking Time: 10 minutes

Servings: 6

Ingredients:

- 1 cup strawberries, chopped
- 1 tablespoon of liquid honey
- 2 tablespoons water
- 1 tablespoon lemon juice

Directions:

1. Preheat the water and liquid honey until you get homogenous liquid.
2. Blend the strawberries until smooth and combine them with honey liquid and lemon juice.
3. Transfer the strawberry mixture in the ice cream maker and churn it for 20 minutes or until the sorbet is thick.
4. Scoop the cooked sorbet in the ice cream cups.

Nutrition:

Calories 30,

Fat 0.4 g,

Fiber 1.4 g,

Carbs 14.9 g,

Protein 0.9 g

247. Vanilla Apple Pie

Preparation Time: 15 minutes

Cooking Time: 50 minutes

Servings: 8

Ingredients:

- 3 apples, sliced
- ½ teaspoon ground cinnamon
- 1 teaspoon vanilla extract
- 1 tablespoon Erythritol
- 7 oz yeast roll dough
- 1 egg, beaten

Directions:

1. Roll up the dough and cut it on 2 parts.
2. Line the springform pan with baking paper.
3. Place the first dough part in the springform pan.
4. Then arrange the apples over the dough and sprinkle it with Erythritol, vanilla extract, and ground cinnamon.
5. Then cover the apples with remaining dough and secure the edges of the pie with the help of the fork.
6. Make the small cuts in the surface of the pie.
7. Brush the pie with beaten egg and bake it for 50 minutes at 375F.
8. Cool the cooked pie well and then remove from the springform pan.
9. Cut it on the servings.

Nutrition:

Calories 140,

Fat 3.4 g,

Fiber 3.4 g,

Carbs 23.9 g,

Protein 2.9 g

248. Cinnamon Pears

Preparation Time: 2 hours

Cooking Time: 0 minutes

Servings: 6

Ingredients:

- 2 pears
- 1 teaspoon ground cinnamon
- 1 tablespoon Erythritol
- 1 teaspoon liquid stevia
- 4 teaspoons butter

Directions:

1. Cut the pears on the halves.
2. Then scoop the seeds from the pears with the help of the scooper.
3. In the shallow bowl mix up together Erythritol and ground cinnamon.
4. Sprinkle every pear half with cinnamon mixture and drizzle with liquid stevia.
5. Then add butter and wrap in the foil.
6. Bake the pears for 25 minutes at 365F.
7. Then remove the pears from the foil and transfer in the serving plates.

Nutrition:

Calories 96,

Fat 4.4 g,

Fiber 1.4 g,

Carbs 3.9 g,

Protein 0.9 g

249. Ginger Ice Cream

Preparation Time: 15 minutes

Cooking Time: 10 minutes

Servings: 6

Ingredients:

- 1 mango, peeled
- 1 cup Greek yogurt
- 1 tablespoon Erythritol
- ¼ cup milk
- 1 teaspoon vanilla extract
- ¼ teaspoon ground ginger

Directions:

1. Blend the mango until you get puree and combine it with Erythritol, milk, vanilla extract, and ground ginger.
2. Then mix up together Greek yogurt and mango puree mixture. Transfer it in the plastic vessel.
3. Freeze the ice cream for 35 minutes.

Nutrition:

Calories 90,

Fat 1.4 g,

Fiber 1.4 g,

Carbs 21.9 g,

Protein 4.9 g

250. Cherry Compote

Preparation Time: 2 hours

Cooking Time: 0 minutes

Servings: 6

Ingredients:

- 2 peaches, pitted, halved
- 1 cup cherries, pitted
- ½ cup grape juice
- ½ cup strawberries
- 1 tablespoon liquid honey
- 1 teaspoon vanilla extract
- 1 teaspoon ground cinnamon

Directions:

1. Pour grape juice in the saucepan.
2. Add vanilla extract and ground cinnamon. Bring the liquid to boil.
3. After this, put peaches, cherries, and strawberries in the hot grape juice and bring to boil.

4. Remove the mixture from heat, add liquid honey, and close the lid.
5. Let the compote rest for 20 minutes.
6. Carefully mix up the compote and transfer in the serving plate.

Nutrition:
Calories 80,
Fat 0.4 g,
Fiber 2.4 g,
Carbs 19.9 g,
Protein 0.9 g

Conclusion

Optavia is a weight management program that has been approved by the FDA. It is an independent initiative taken by the American Medical Association (AMA). It is a scientifically researched and proven diet program, which has been tested and found to be 100% successful . Some great benefits of Optavia over some other diet programs are:

The Optavia diet applies to healthy people of all ages and only requires that they stick to it; no medical assistance or monitoring is required.

A person can lose up to 3 pounds in the initial week of the program and continue to lose weight at a steady pace. If these 3 lbs aren't lost within 1 week, it is advisable to consult a physician .

The Optavia diet plan is Low in protein and Low in fat. and has been found to protect a person from obesity. Optavia diet does not require major lifestyle changes.

The Optavia diet is a series of three plans, two of which concentrate on weight reduction and better at managing weight. The program's foods are lower in calories and carbs and higher in protein to promote weight reduction. Each strategy demands that you consume at least half of your food in the form of Optavia pre-packaged food. Since the menu calls for eating carbs, protein, and healthy fat to be eaten, it is a reasonably healthy diet for healthy food. As far as weight reduction goes, experts agree that Optavia can benefit because its diet is low in calories, for the positive. Still, it's unlikely to change your eating habits significantly. You're likely to regain weight once you quit your diet.

Hence optavia diet has proven to be extremely helpful in controlling and maintaining weight. Still, when optavia lean & green food merges with air frying, it can make this diet much easier for people to follow. Air frying food cuts the cooking time in half and makes the food more nutritious.

You can get many benefits if you follow optavia lean & green air frying recipes along with targeted weight reduction.

The Optavia Weight Loss Plan promotes weight loss through low calorie prepackaged meals; Homemade food with easy carbohydrates and personalized coaching.The Optavia diet advances weight reduction using low calorie prepackaged foods, low carb natively constructed suppers, and customized instructing.

However, the diet is costly, repetitive, and doesn't accommodate all nutritional wishes. what's extra, Extended calorie limit may also result in nutrient deficiencies and different potential health issues.

Be that as it may, the eating routine is costly, monotonous, and doesn't suit every dietary need. Additionally, expanded calorie limitation may bring about supplement insufficiencies and other potential health concerns.

Simultaneously, as this system promotes quick-time period weight and Fat's loss, similarly research is wanted to assess whether it encourages the everlasting way of life adjustments needed for long-time period achievement.

I hope you have learned something

In a nutshell, the Optavia Diet is meant to be followed for short term, and is mainly designed to help people lose weight.

Made in the USA
Middletown, DE
11 March 2021